Nonmetropolitan Industrial Growth and Community Change

Nonmetropolitan Industrial Growth and Community Change

Edited by
Gene F. Summers
University of Wisconsin

Arne Selvik
The Institute of Industrial
Economics

Lexington Books
D.C. Heath and Company
Lexington, Massachusetts
Toronto

Library of Congress Cataloging in Publication Data

Main entry under title:

Nonmetropolitan industrial growth and community change.

Papers presented at a seminar held in conjunction with the annual meeting of the Rural Sociological Society, Aug. 30–Sept. 3, 1978 in San Francisco.
Includes index.
1. Regional planning—Congresses. 2. Industries, Location of—Congresses. 3. Sociology, Rural—Congresses. I. Summers, Gene F., 1936–
II. Selvik, Arne. III. Rural Sociological Society.
HT391.N57   338.6'042   78-22652
ISBN 0-669-02820-7

Copyright © 1979 by D.C. Heath and Company

Published simultaneously in Canada

Printed in the United States of America

International Standard Book Number: 0-669-2820-7

Library of Congress Catalog Card Number: 78-22652

Contents

Preface

The growing concern with unbalanced regional development and the political attention paid to this problem through regional development policies can be understood as part of a general concern about social distributional problems. Most technologically advanced societies have gradually realized that a free enterprise economic system creates complex socioeconomic imbalances.

This realization is reflected in national systems of personal taxation, which vary in their equalization measures and redistributional effects from society to society. Such systems are mainly designed to reduce income differentials between social classes and are basically nonspatial. As appendixes to these systems, a range of income transfer programs assist low-income groups.

Regional development policies, on the other hand, are designed to reduce the spatial differences in income and employment opportunities, which in most countries are as serious as the social or class differences. These policies do not usually tax or subsidize individuals directly according to the location of their residence but are supposed to benefit rural residents through stimulating private and public economic activity in depressed areas.

Within the industrially advanced nations, industry has been migrating from established urban-industrial centers into the nonmetropolitan hinterland since the mid-1950s. In recent years, the rate of migration has been increasing. Most nations now encourage this geographic redistribution of basic economic activities. But regardless of the existence of national programs devised to encourage this migratory process, it is almost certain to continue. In most industrial nations, market forces appear to create a natural force toward the relocation of at least some types of industrial activity. It seems to us that the potential impact of this process on nations can hardly be overstated, for it is a process of societal realignment with a scope and magnitude rivaling the emergence of industry in the last century and the mechanization of agriculture in this century.

Efforts to provide rational guidance to the dispersion of basic economic activity and of population away from large metropolitan centers to regional focuses of potential growth are subsumed under the concept of regional economic development, growth-center strategies being common models. Economic implications of the growth-center strategies have been given considerable attention. To a lesser extent, demographic and population dynamics intrinsic to economic development based on industrial migration also have received attention from social scientists. But the social structural and sociocultural elements, which most surely are involved in the process, have been ignored generally.

Based on the assumption that any effective strategy to achieve more balanced growth through nonmetropolitan development must rest heavily upon the expansion of employment opportunities in nonmetropolitan regions, most interventionist efforts have focused on expanding the export base of rural communities. Historically the export base of these communities has been extractive industries (agriculture, mining, forestry, fishing), which have undergone changes that have resulted in declining employment opportunities. For many years there appeared to be little hope of creating employment opportunities that might replace the losses. However, since World War II, conditions have shifted and have made possible the decentralization of manufacturing and other secondary industries. Therefore the interventionist strategy of bringing jobs to people is logically feasible. Indeed decentralization of industrial activity is a common characteristic of technologically advanced nations throughout the world.

Many factors are involved in producing nonmetropolitan industrial growth. They are not well understood, but the universality of the phenomenon challenges the adequacy of earlier industrial location theories purporting to have captured the necessary and sufficient conditions in the political economies of nation–states since the process is occurring under a variety of political and economic arrangements. Thus, for example, an explanation lodged in the operation of a capitalist, free–market economy will not be persuasive in the case of Poland, nor will one built on the premise of a managed economy account for the U.S. experience. It appears to us that conditions necessary for the decentralization of industry, such as an adequate local labor supply, transportation, communication, and separability of phases of production, are satisfied in most technologically advanced nations. The conditions needed to motivate central planners, public officials, and industrial managers to initiate the movement are also present even though these conditions of sufficiency probably vary among nations according to structural attributes of the political economy. Whatever the explanations, there is no denying the fact of nonmetropolitan industrial growth.

Experience gained from our several years of research into the social, economic, demographic, and political impacts of new industry on nonmetropolitan communities in the United States and Norway convinces us that multinational comparative analyses are essential to a fuller understanding of the redistributive process. Research must focus on how the character of rural areas and small towns is affected by industrial growth. Among the many specific questions needing attention are the following:

Will the expansion of industry into nonmetropolitan communities hasten their transformation into metropolitan centers with manifestations of existing metropolitan ills, or will new industry enhance the social conditions of the host community?

Within the host community that benefits from the new industry, are there categories of persons who do not benefit?

What is the effect of new industry on the structure of political power and the decision-making processes within the host community?

How is the local autonomy of the host community affected by new industry? Do vertical linkages increase the number of social problems that are in the community but not of the community?

Is industrial development necessarily followed (or accompanied) by increased urbanization?

What are the sources of population growth (or stabilization) that accompany industrial development?

How are the industrial and occupational structures of the host community affected by the introduction of new industry?

How does new industry affect the fiscal burden of local government? Are the public sector net gains positive or negative?

These questions illustrate the range of issues needing clarification in order to create an adequate knowledge base for a more rational guidance of the process of nonmetropolitan industrial growth.

Regional development policies, with industrial location as the primary policy instrument, are supposed to benefit sparsely settled and marginal regions by stimulating economic activity in these communities. Our research in the United States and Norway, however, has produced equivocal evidence, which motivated us to search for comparable studies of community consequences of nonmetropolitan industrial growth from other nations. Through this effort, we became aware of colleagues in other nations who were struggling with many of the same concerns. For reasons of language barriers and disciplinary boundaries, these colleagues often were unaware of their common interests and research activities. Consequently we initiated an effort to convene a seminar devoted to exploring some of these issues of mutual interest on the premise that such an exchange would be helpful to our individual efforts and to the progress of cross-national research in an important intellectual and public policy domain.

Permission was granted by the Rural Sociological Society (U.S.A.) to hold the seminar in conjunction with its annual meetings, which were held in San Francisco from August 30 to September 3, 1978. The following chapters are the seminar presentations with appropriate revisions for publication.

The chapters are organized into four parts. Part I provides an overview of contemporary research emphases in Poland, Great Britain, Scandinavia, the United States, and Continental Western Europe.

In Poland industrialization has progressed almost as rapidly as it has in Japan since World War II. Initial nonmetropolitan efforts were concentrated on building the bases for future industrialization: energy and raw materials. More recent nonmetropolitan locations are designed to absorb surplus labor in rural areas. This dimension gives the Polish research the distinct character of analyzing the effects of rapid, large-scale industrialization in rural communities. Bivand's presentation examines the institutional framework for research, styles of analysis, and some important issues of concern underlying them. He describes research methods and presents a typological sketch of results. Finally he discusses the role of models, theories, and hypotheses in these studies and in the development of the field.

Great Britain has had a long and fairly successful history of regional policy in encouraging manufacturing development in nonmetropolitan areas. There has been very little assessment of the effects of the various policies, however, but in recent years academics from various disciplines have begun to examine these effects. The chapter by MacKay, Sadler, and Sewel covers the main current research emphases—in particular, the effects of politics in terms of employment creation, increases in income, and reductions in unemployment and emigration; the role of rural development agencies; the role of new towns and communities in nonmetropolitan growth; the response of local authorities to economic change; center–periphery models; and the relationships between local residents and inmigrants. A major stimulus to nonmetropolitan industrial growth in Britain has come from the discovery of oil and gas in the North Sea, and the chapter pays particular attention to the current work of social scientists in this area. Finally, the authors attempt to place recent case studies of particular development and communities in the context of the broader research emphasis.

Industrialization in the Scandinavian countries has been based upon their natural resources in metals, minerals, forests, fishing, agriculture, and—as a source of energy—waterfalls. The location of these resources, which reflect the geographical characteristics of the countries, may explain the relatively scattered location pattern formed by the manufacturing industries. Today this pattern is highly vulnerable to structural changes resulting from technological change and new market conditions. Regional and local effects of these changes have been a main policy concern since the late 1950s. Under the present economic situation these problems are receiving more attention than ever. Various social sciences have contributed to the understanding of this process of change. Paul Olav Berg emphasizes some of the research approaches employed in the Scandinavian countries to analyze changes in industrial structure and industrial location.

A number of theoretical and empirical studies have contributed to a more thorough understanding of contemporary industrial development. Until recently, analysis took place within the framework of a general industrial expansion, but now prospects seem different. The major question now is which industrial and regional policies should be designed to meet new problems raised by the industrial concentration that seems likely in years to come. Present research within the social sciences is an important contributor to a better understanding of problems ahead.

Despite the absence of national programs designed to promote decentralization (these are underway in other countries, especially in Europe), the United States appears to be experiencing an areally extensive transformation of its industrial landscape. A growing awareness of the magnitude and character of a process reversing a decades-long trend toward spatial agglomeration has provoked a surge of research activity in all social science disciplines. H.L. Seyler surveys both the dimensions of empirical work—examining social, economic, and political impacts on nonmetropolitan areas—and the theoretical formulations being recast because earlier models do not yield satisfactory insights about the nature of the process or the implications for affected communities.

The national problems of industrial development in nonmetropolitan areas are very different among the Western European countries and depend upon their historic evaluation. Generally, however, as noted by Istel and Robert, nonmetropolitan regions after World War II were characterized by a very low degree of industrialization and by obsolete agricultural production, particularly in Southern Europe. The modernization of agricultural production, strongly promoted and advocated by the European Commission, rapidly led to unemployment in rural regions, and millions of agricultural workers and operators of small farms had to find other employment. The solution to this unemployment problem, the need to curb down migration flows to metropolitan regions, the expansion of which could not easily be accommodated, and the generally recognized objective of providing equivalent living conditions in the various regions led to policies of industrial promotion of rural regions in all European countries. The postwar history of nonmetropolitan regions in Western Europe has been characterized by attempts both to rationalize and modernize agriculture and to promote industrial development. The rapid expansion of industrial production following World War II offered possibilities of industrialization in nonindustrialized, nonmetropolitan areas. In some countries—for instance, West Germany—the location of industries in rural areas succeeded; however, it usually took the form of new branches of larger enterprises, which are very unstable and the most threatened by economic crises.

These enterprises rarely provide employment opportunities for highly skilled people. Their management remains in the metropolitan centers, so that this type of industrialization is not accompanied by the relocation of decision-making functions. In some regions, the industrialization process was far less successful, so that out-migration flows continued and the population decreased, sometimes below critical thresholds to maintain economic activity and the necessary facilities in such regions.

Various countries have set up programs of both sectoral and regional nature to promote the creation of industry. In the absence of scientific research that could have provided valuable information on the effects and consequences of infrastructural investments and incentives, decisions were made mainly on the basis of political criteria. Because of the scarcity of this type of research during the 1950s and the 1960s, more recent efforts have been characterized by important attempts to investigate the conditions of regional economic promotion. Another important area of research concerns the regional impacts of the expansion of corporate firms. This type of study is of a less quantitative nature and attempts to trace back the regional effects of large-scale restructuring of the private economy. The special problems, research types, and issues are exemplified for some selected countries (West Germany, France, Italy, and the Netherlands) by Wolfgang Istel and Jacques Robert.

Part II is devoted to a discussion of the nonmetropolitan industrial growth phenomenon by Robert T. Averitt, Jerald Hage, and Glen Pulver. Together they offer some explanations for this migration process and draw some implications for local communities.

In *The Dual Economy* (1968) Averitt outlined the structure of the American industrial economy. He began by distinguishing between center and periphery firms. Center firms are large in economic size. They tend toward vertical integration, geographic dispersion, product diversification, and managerial decentralization. Periphery firms are smaller, less well integrated, geographically confined, relatively specialized, and commonly dominated by one person or a family. Business dualism is related to the technical anatomy of an industrial economy. To explore this anatomy, Averitt divided manufacturing into three production categories: unit and small batch, large batch and mass, and process production. Center firms tend to specialize in mass- and process-production techniques. Finally, using eight loosely related criteria, he defined a set of key manufacturing industries. With small exception, key industries are dominated by center firms. Thus *The Dual Economy* outlines a hierarchy of business firms, of production techniques, and of industries. In chapter 6 to this book, Averitt relates *The Dual Economy* themes to the product cycle, wherein a product progresses through the stages of innovation, to rapid growth, and on to standardization. Structural shifts in manufacturing generate new, rapidly expanding sectors, and new growth sectors are locating in growing regions within the United States. The evolution of economic structure through time is related to the economics of geographic space.

In chapter 7 Hage argues that the implications of the new postindustrial society for the small community (under fifty thousand) have not been evaluated. The shift from industrial to postindustrial society in North America and Western Europe means a change in the direction of continual concentration of the population in ever–larger urban areas and a move away from the process of suburbanization. He maintains that the causes of this movement need to be explored. The nature of the small community in the future will change; it will be less dependent upon agriculture or manufacturing and more on services, which will be a growing sector. He suggests a typology and makes a number of planning recommendations to facilitate and harmonize this process of deurbanization and service development so as to maintain regional balance.

The future potential role of the service sector in nonmetropolitan community development is also one of several alternatives in Pulver's comprehensive strategy of community economic development. For many years, developers have placed almost total reliance on increased productivity in agriculture, greater exploitation of natural resources, and the addition of new manufacturing industries as strategies for community economic development in nonmetropolitan areas. The study of secondary data from the International Labor Office and the United States Bureau of Labor Statistics indicates that the rate of job growth in goods–producing industries is declining rapidly in highly developed countries. In contrast, employment in the service sector is increasing. As a consequence, alternative strategies for economic growth must be found in postindustrial economies.

Pulver's theoretical analysis of all options for economic development indicates that the current concentration on expanding goods–producing industries is unnecessarily narrow. Improving the efficiency of existing firms, attracting basic employers from the nonmanufacturing sector, encouraging business formation, capturing more of the existing income, and increasing aids received from broader governmental levels are all viable community economic development alternatives. A comprehensive policy that considers all options may allow nonmetropolitan areas to participate fully in future economic growth.

The three chapters in Part III draw attention to critical dimensions of community change produced by the in-migration of industry and the associated modification of the community economic base. The first of these deals with the changing dynamics of power. Newby and associates examine the underlying premises of the pluralist, Marxist, and nondecision-making views of power. Although they suggest that each has something to offer, they propose a new conceptual device for assessing community power relations: contextual interest. The argument and the utility of the concept is illustrated with reference to their recent study of local politics in a rural area of eastern England.

In chapter 10, Gudmund Hernes and Arne Selvik argue that most of the literature on corporatism focuses on the national level in spite of trends in several countries toward the development of corporatist structures at the local level. Drawing heavily on Norwegian experience, they argue that this growth has come about partly as a result of changing market conditions, often expressed politically in coalitions of business executives, trade unionists, and local officials. But in part, it is also due to new legislation aimed at regulating economic activity and putting more discretionary power at the local (district and municipal) level, providing an incentive for institutional innovations to affect the use of the new authority. The response has been both an offensive to strengthen the local branches of industry associations, so that they can more effectively cope with the new challenges and opportunities, and the establishment of new public positions, such as industrial consultants and advisory boards with functional representation. Several important actual and potential consequences range from the growth of neomercantilist policies to increased community competition for industrial establishments. Further analysis is needed to map differences between countries and to be able to identify the processes that cause variations in local adaptations.

Improving the conditions of life in rural regions is one of the foremost justifications of interventionists who recommend nonmetropolitan industrial growth as a policy instrument. Using data from three-hundred nonmetropolitan counties, Paul Eberts reports that in the more rural northeast United States, growth in income, manufacturing, and population size from 1950 to 1970 was correlated positively with most quality-of-life indicators. But this growth also has negative correlations with certain other important variables, some of which, in turn, correlate negatively with quality-of-life indicators. Assessing the effects of growth on quality-of-life indicators, therefore, requires a consideration of both direct and indirect effects.

Part IV is a working set of chapters. Where boundaries of disciplines, nations, and language interrupt easy communication of theoretical discussions and research results, they become formidable with respect to data acquisition and comparability. All too often individual researchers set out to collect new and frequently extremely costly data without full knowledge of existing data that might fulfill their needs. Indeed our observations indicate that researchers often do not know where to search for community-level data outside their own nation and sometimes even at home. Recognizing this handicapping trait of social sciences, we asked Stein Rokkan and Terje Sande to describe European data archives and Jerome Clubb and Michael Traugott to provide a similar overview of U.S. archives. All four have been in the forefront of international efforts to create data archives for use by social scientists.

Rokkan and Sande indicate that in most Western European countries today, at least one archival institution maintains and updates machine-readable data sets on territorial units. Their chapter offers brief presentations of these institutions, as well as of the recently established umbrella organization, IF–DO. The major part of the chapter is devoted to a survey of the relevant data holdings in each country. They describe the files in terms of variables, time spans, and units of aggregation. They draw heavily on the descriptions presented in the *European Political Data Newsletter.* They conclude by assessing the current situation and developments now under discussion.

The chapter by Clubb and Traugott is concerned with contemporary and historical data resources for the study of nonmetropolitan communities in the United States and Canada. The resources of major national social science data archives, governmental agencies, and research centers are considered, as are data files held by individual scholars, and problems of access and use are discussed. They emphasize data for counties and other equivalent or smaller subnational units and, where relevant, refer to collections of sample survey data. The authors stress computer–readable data resources but also mention important categories of noncomputer–readable data.

As social scientists awaken to the task of assessing the effects of industrial growth in recent years, they are also being asked to make projections concerning future impacts. Concerns for the ecological well–being of our countryside and cities forced public officials in many nations to act, and often the result of their action has been the creation of legislation requiring developers to inform a public overseer agency of the probable impact of planned developments. Assessment requirements were developed because of a concern for the physical, plant, and animal elements of the ecosystem impact and quickly were extended to encompass social and economic components. Social scientists were unprepared for this demand but are now beginning to meet the challenge.

One of the most sophisticated assessment models developed in the United States to date, which has a near–isomorphic relation between theory, empirical data, and computing algorithims, was developed by Steve Murdock and Larry Leistritz and is described in chapter 14. They present a computerized model for projecting the effects of large–scale energy projects on the economic and social systems of the community nearby. The model currently provides baseline and single– or multiple–project impact projections for a fifteen–county area in western North Dakota. Outputs are available at the regional, county, and municipal levels and include such variables as employment by type, population by age and sex, school enrollments by age, housing requirements by type, and public–sector costs and revenues by type. (Personal income and dollar volume of business activity are available at the regional level).

The model was developed in response to needs expressed by public officials at the local, state, and federal levels and by private citizens and development firms for projections of the economic and social effects of lignite coal development. Applications to data have included impact evaluation for coal mines, coal-fired electric generating plants, and coal gasification plants. The effects of altering the location and construction schedule of individual projects and the effects of various public–policy measures (such as alternative taxation formulas) have been evaluated. The model could have wide application in projecting the impacts of new energy facilities and other industrial projects.

Discussions of nonmetropolitan economic growth and its effects on communities inevitably are explanations and interpretations of change, logically they cannot be otherwise. Yet many research efforts are cast in cross–sectional or synchronic molds. Change is omitted since time is eliminated from the analytic model. In chapter 15, E.M. Beck and Gene Summers outline conceptual and theoretical implications of employing different functional models of social change. In particular, they explore the ramifications of additive, multiplicative, and mixed models (models containing both additive and multiplicative terms). These models are explained in terms of standardized functional forms to be utilized in studies of change at the community level.

While planning the seminar, we hoped that the presentations would help communication across disciplinary and national boundaries and contribute to our collective and individual efforts to deal as scientists with an important and challenging intellectual and public policy phenomenon. By the end of the seminar, we were thrilled by an awareness that the excellence of our colleagues' contributions had fulfilled and surpassed our hopes. We are especially pleased to have the opportunity of sharing their presentations with the many colleagues who could not join us in San Francisco.

November, 1978

Gene Summers
Arne Selvik

Acknowledgments

The conception of the San Francisco seminar and much of the organization effort occurred while Professor Summers was a Fulbright Senior Research Fellow to Norway. We therefore want to acknowledge our gratitude to the Fulbright program for its support. While in Bergen, Norway, colleagues in the University of Bergen and the Institute of Industrial Economics were most supportive of our joint venture. Indeed the institute provided resources that were essential in organizing the seminar, and we want to acknowledge our awareness of the power of such support. But applauding an institute is too impersonal to satisfy our feelings for the persons who made the decisions and took the necessary actions: Svein Dåvøy, Turid Hilland Hansen, and Kellis Akselsen. To them we offer a personal expression of appreciation.

As editors of a collection of papers written by colleagues, we obviously owe the creative effort to them. We believe that the combined efforts have achieved our initial objective of furthering the intellectual and scientific pursuit of a clear cross-national and interdisciplinary understanding of nonmetropolitan growth trends.

The cosponsorship of the San Francisco seminar by the Rural Sociological Society was essential in legitimating an international gathering of scholars. Therefore we want to thank the Program Committee of the society. Fred Buttel, committee chairman, was helpful far beyond the call of duty and we are pleased for the opportunity to thank him.

Acknowledgments invariably end with recognition of the staff who does the work of typing, proofreading, copyediting, and the other skilled crafts and trades involved in producing a book. But few have done so much in so short a time as is true of our staff. We owe a special sense of gratitude to Caroline McCarley and Carol Snarey of Lexington Books and Nancy Trager, our manuscript typist.

Part I
Contemporary Research
Emphases

1

Contemporary Research Emphases in Poland

Roger Bivand

The rapid tempo of the growth in Poland's investments in the recent past,[1] linked with the initial postwar state of the country's industry,[2] make it clear that industrial growth is a phenomenon of great importance. Much of the recent investment has taken place in metropolitan areas (figure 1-1), as it has in other countries, but in a substantial number of cases, nonmetropolitan locations have been chosen. It is useful to distinguish between the renewal of equipment and the establishment of new plants in new locations, since investment has swung from one to the other and back again during the postwar period. Getting industry back into production after World War II was accomplished generally without major nonmetropolitan investment. In the late 1950s and early 1960s, such investments were made in a number of places in large plants, which were to form the basis for further economic growth.[3] Since 1970, industrial growth has changed character, with stress being put on a qualitative shift in terms of appropriately qualified personnel and the replacement of worn-out machinery by efficient and flexible high-technology production lines. This change has been accompanied by a move from accounting in terms of meeting physical output targets to the use of financial criteria in somewhat more independent enterprises.

The role of the state in investment and industrial growth in Poland is by no means limited to the period after nationalization in 1946. Included among the chief achievements of the interwar period are the building of the port at Gdynia and the planning of the Central Industrial Area in very backward regions belonging to the former czarist Russian and Austrian partitions.[4] (Unfortunately no long-term studies have been undertaken on community development in these areas, partly because of the total break caused by the war and postwar migration.) The factors influencing these investments were historical—establishing a Polish port on the Baltic—and strategic—establishing a modern engineering industry capable of arming against aggression. The factors underlying the postwar location policies contrast in their image of the needs of the country. Polish statehood is now emphasized in meeting the needs of the people, a goal treated as reachable through industrialization and planned, socialist industrialization.

I should like to express my appreciation to Professor Zbyszko Chojnicki and Dr. Wieslaw Maik for their observations on the subject of this chapter. I also wish to thank Panstwowe Wydawnictwo Naukowe, the authors, and the editors of *Geographica Polonica* for permission to reproduce figures 1-1 and 1-3, and the author and editors of *Biuletyn KPZK* for figure 1-2.

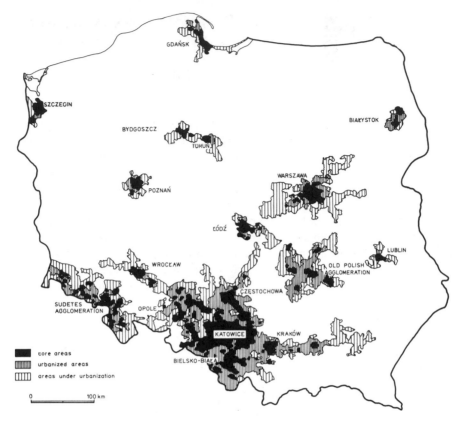

Figure 1-1. Recent Industrial Investments

The approach adopted in the first postwar decades was to concentrate on building up the bases for industrial expansion, especially in terms of energy and raw materials. Systematic geological surveying at this stage revealed a number of resources that were linked into the overall plans. It is in areas where investment took place in the 1956–1970 phase of Poland's industrial development that one has to look for the most carefully studied cases of nonmetropolitan industrial location: in energy, the lignite mines of Konin and Turoszów and the oil refinery at Płock; in metals, the copper mines and smelters in the Legnica–Głogów area and the aluminum smelter at Konin; and in chemicals, the sulphur mines and processing plant at Tarnobrzeg, fertilizer plant at Puławy and Włocławek, and downstream petrochemical processing at Płock (see figure 1–2).[5] Except for Puławy, Płock, and Włocławek, these are raw material locations, but even in these three cases the availability of water from the Vistula was of great importance. More recent location decisions, such as the Huta Katowice steel plant

Figure 1-2. Metropolitan Areas of Poland

in the Upper Silesian agglomeration[6] and the new oil refinery on the coast at Gdańsk, seem to have broken this pattern.[6] One of the reasons given to support nonmetropolitan location has been the surplus labor in rural areas that could be enlisted in industrial production. Thus recent research has examined the effects of rapid, large-scale industrialization on rural communities.

The Institutional Framework

In order to assess the achievements of those researching current problems, it is useful to understand the extent of resources available to them. In addition, the way in which academic journals in Poland operate bears directly on the visibility of the profile of research in progress. In addition to research undertaken by university employees, the situation in Poland is deeply influenced by the Academy of Sciences. The committees of the academy coordinate funds coming from the state budget and other sources, delegating the execution of particular tasks to groups of researchers in universities or to its own research institutes and departments. It is fairly normal for Ph.D. candidates to receive parts of these projects to work on; the same applies to postdoctoral work, the results of which are published. Journals and monograph series are published by universities, by scholarly associations, and by committees of the Academy of Sciences. University professors are not pressured to publish regularly, but that is not the case for research workers in the academy. In a number of cases, the availability of funds and the pressure to publish results in an excessive number of publications, reporting results that are of little interest or importance.

In the area of interest at hand, a number of units of the Academy of Sciences have been active. The chief ones are the Department of Rural Sociology, which publishes *Roczniki Socjologii Wsi;* the institute of Geography and Spatial Planning, which publishes *Przegląd Geograficzny, Geographia Polonica* (primarily in English), and a monograph series; the Committee for Space Economy and Regional Planning, which publishes *Biuletyn* and a monograph series; and the Committee for Research on Regions under Industrialization, which publishes *Zeszyty* and a monograph series. In addition, other work has been printed in a wide range of journals and in book form.

The approaches that these organizing bodies have adopted regarding funding research and publishing results have greatly influenced the way in which research has been and is conducted. Consequently the current research emphases are very much a function of the weightings placed on different methods and topics. In addition, the relative influence of the different bodies has not always been proportional to their potential contribution. Had rural sociology, geography, or spatial planning had a greater voice in the organization of past studies, it seems likely that other methodologies, especially modeling and theorizing ones, would have been more dominant.

Styles of Research and Issues of Concern

As Olędzki has pointed out, the actual confrontation of the social sciences with the possibility of applying their findings to the newly developing industrial areas could provide data for a study in the sociology of research activity.[7] This would, however, extend far beyond the range of the present survey. Instead I have chosen one major research sponsor from among those active in the field in order to concentrate on the major issues involved.

Consequently I will touch on the work of geographers, spatial planners, and rural sociologists only where it impinges directly on the work of this one body, the Committee for Research on Regions under Industrialization (KBRU). (In passing, it is worth noting a few of the most important positions published by the agencies not dealt with here. In geography and spatial planning, a collection edited by Secomski provides a good outline of the theoretical positions held by Polish scholars.[8] This may be supplemented by a number of more recent articles and synthesizing monographs.[9] In rural sociology, two volumes of papers edited by Turowski and Szwengrub are of importance.[10] And the contributions by Galeski, Dobrowolska, Turowski, and Jałowiecki are of direct relevance to studies of nonmetropolitan industrial growth and community change.[11])

The KBRU was set up to counter the one-sided approach of industrial planners locating plants in nonmetropolitan places who had paid attention only to reserves of natural resources, production technology, and the availability of labor. Ignar believed that the implementation of an appropriate industrial policy should be conditional on knowledge of the region before plans are made, the forecasting of its development during investment, and the accurate evaluation of the total future effects of industrialization.[12]

The mandate of the KBRU was to monitor six areas undergoing industrialization: Płock, Puławy, Tanobrzeg, Konin, Lubin, and Bełchatow (the last is only now being developed). The overriding aim of the studies was to provide information for the authorities so that further investment and planning decisions could be made. Secondarily it was hoped that the study of socioeconomic change during intensive industrialization would provide data that could be used to isolate the essence of the development of a socialist society in Poland. It is possible to equate these statements with the instrumental basis of this approach, summarized by Ignar as "practical utility for the socioeconomic changes taking place under the influence of industrialization."[13] The methodological basis of this approach is not simply descriptive since it not infrequently includes elements of diagnosis, and comparison with most often unstated norms. The theoretical basis of the KBRU approach is very difficult to unravel. It is quite clear that certain common precepts underlie the research undertaken, but what they are, and what they are derived from, is much less clear. Of course, it has this problem in common with much empirical research undertaken in the social sciences.[14]

Methods and Data

The methods used in these studies may be described as generally conservative. Most of the papers in the KBRU Publications are hinged around a group of tables of frequencies by various categories. Frequently changes between a base year and the date when the work was carried out are the subject of study, with an implicit assumption that some features of the altered values are due to the growth of industry. This focus may partly reflect the building block approach to these studies, with different students receiving segments to work on, which are then tied together by a coordinator.[15] Most often, the studies are weakly dog-legged and concentrate on one topic in one region. Studies on the same topic in other regions and on other topics in the same region are referred to only in notes.[16] Occasional studies on the same topic across regions have been conducted (most notably on retail trade by Dietl), and more recently this kind of comparative work is increasing in frequency.[17] Dietl and Lewy argue that such comparison is hindered by the ways in which official statistics are collected, justifying the use of sample survey techniques.[18]

Because of the methods used, research projects become bound very quickly by the availability of information. Census data are available for the period to 1975 within the former administrative divisions of *powiats,* as are industrial and agricultural census results. Yearly population, employment, and production information were also available by *powiat*, but because the extent of influence of a given plant seldom extended to more than a few *powiats,* this information did not differentiate the impact precisely. For matters like migration and journeys to work, large changes could take place in patterns without being reflected in official statistics because boundaries were not being crossed. In 1975, the first tier of local administration, the *voivodeship,* was radically reformed. The number of units was increased from seventeen to forty-nine and included new *voivodeships* based on most of the centers undergoing nonmetropolitan industrial growth: Konin, Włocławek, Płock, Tarnobrzeg, and Legnica. The *powiat* tier ceased to exist and was replaced by the much smaller *gmina.* This new division will strengthen the statistical surveys within the new *voivodeships,* but the *gmina* are so small that quite a few categories reported for *powiats* are now not produced for *gmina*.

Many students find that the categories used for the offical data (for part-time farmers, for example) are far from satisfactory. For this reason, they often resort to survey work, which they may carry out either by using lists of employees as sampling frames or simply by extracting data about employees from employment record cards. In general, employers in these areas are accustomed to scholars' using their files and, given approval from the correct agencies, do their best to assist. Consequently mapping journeys to work may be carried out in this way, as may samples concerning the effects of employment in industry on farming where the employee is head of a farm household or samples concerning living conditions.[19]

Other institutions are also prepared to reveal useful information—for instance, savings bank deposits and retail turnover—but it is difficult to knit all the data together into the same time periods. The result is that interpretation is hindered, often ruling out the use of more sophisticated approaches. In some cases, statistical analysis, extending to correlation and multiple regression, has been used. Multivariate methods have been applied to *powiat-* and *gmina-*level data sets, serving to extract the leading features of the spatial pattern of industrialization's impact.[20] Graph methods have been used in a number of cases,[21] and more elaborate and theoretically based models, like the intervening opportunities model, in a very few.[22]

At the Coal Face

At the beginning of the 1970s, it appeared that the previous ten years' work was about to be pulled into shape and some general conclusions drawn from completed studies.[23] At that stage, six regions were under study by seven divisions of the KBRU: Płock, Puławy, Tarnobrzeg, Legnica–Lubin–Głogów, Konin, and Turoszów. The themes covered by the divisions were: population and employment; social organizations, education, and culture; agrarian structure and agricultural production; living conditions; rural community changes; urban community changes; and settlement system changes.[24] Each of these main themes was generally divided into subsections, and the progress of work was monitored at the level of these subsections for each region. Frenkel gives the subsections used in the first division, together with the number of works completed to 1970; these are shown in table 1–1.[25] These divisions are still used today.[26] Table 1–2 shows subsec-

Table 1–1
Research Themes and Completed Reports to 1970 of the Population and Employment Division, Committee for Research on Regions under Industrialization, Polish Academy of Sciences

Theme	No.
1. Occupational activity and general labor force balance	46
2. Migration	34
3. Formation and structure of personnel of new establishments	32
4. Education, upgrading personnel and skilled manpower balance	22
5. Social division of labor, labor relations in rual areas	18
6. Changes and structure of employment in center and hinterland	13
7. Worker mobility	2
8. Principles, instruments and institutions in employment policy	1
9. Multi–theme works	10
10. Others	12
total	190

Table 1-2
Completed Reports to 1970 of the Living Conditions Division of the Committee for Research on Regions under Industrialization by Theme and Location of the Study

Theme	Konin	Legnica Glogow	Plock	Pulawy	Tarno-brzeg	Turo szow	Others	General	Total
1. Methods of study	—	—	3	—	—	—	—	6	9
2. Multi-theme	1	4	13	4	1	1	—	—	24
3. Incomes, expenditure	11	6	7	4	9	4	3	2	46
4. Housing	2	1	10	3	2	1	—	—	19
5. Durable consumer goods	2	—	2	1	1	—	—	—	6
6. Retail trade and services	3	1	2	1	—	1	—	—	8
7. Diet	1	—	2	4	2	—	—	—	9
8. Health	—	—	1	4	—	—	—	—	5
9. Recreation	2	1	—	—	1	1	—	—	5
10. Social participation	1	—	3	—	—	—	1	—	5
11. Forecasting	—	2	3	—	1	—	—	—	6
Total	23	15	46	21	17	8	4	8	142

tions adopted by the fourth division, broken down further by the areas in which they were carried out.

Reports of results have been published for two areas: Plock[27] and the Legnica-Lubin-Glogów region.[28] These are edited collections of divisional and subsection studies, with little synthesis across category boundaries. In the latter volume, a number of interesting aspects are covered; they have been amplified in a recent general collection of papers, which in part duplicates already reported work.[29]

The topics that have been worked up for the whole country are migration[30] and journey to work.[31] The range of population and employment topics has been examined for Wloclawek in Mortimer-Szymczak et al.,[32] and work-force turnover and the sociology of the new enterprises in the Konin area formed the basis for Lączkowski's monograph.[33] Agrarian structure and agricultural production have been treated in two studies: one by Lachert and Dembowska on Płock[34] and one by Michna on both Puławy and Płock.[35] Educational research has been undertaken by Galant[36] in the Konin area and by Kwiecińzski and Winclawski in villages near Płock.[37] An overall survey of changes in living conditions was made by Adamczyk[38] for Płock, of rural infrastructure by Kuciński[39] for Plock, and for retail trade in a selection of areas by Dietl.[40]

Changes in rural communities have been widely surveyed, but there is a considerable division between approaches typified by Gałęski,[41] which are not simply descriptive-diagnostic, and those produced by the KBRU. An example of a study from outside the KBRU environment is Turowski's work on Milejów.[42] Another is Jałowiecki's study of Polkowice in the Legnica-Głogów area.[43] Reports from within the KBRU tradition include Gałaj on Płock[44] and Pochwicki[45] on Konin. Urban community changes have received very little attention; there is one study on small towns near Konin by Zechowski[46] and a general survey by Węgleński.[47]

Perhaps the major redeeming aspect of the research is the strength and independence of studies of settlement system changes and regional planning. The reason seems to be that researchers from outside the KBRU environment became involved in these topics and used certain theoretical constructs and modeling approaches. An early work on Konin and associated centers is by Domański.[48] Research on changes in the Tarnobrzeg region is reported by Dobrowolska and Zioło.[49] A seminal work, which has led to the further development of an overall location, is Musiał's doctoral dissertation.[50] His sketched causal diagram for Turoszów (figure 1-3) has been developed for the Legnica-Głogów area and for Konin. Zagożdżon has published a series of articles illustrating the development of his concept of settlement network change,[51] and Zipser has made use of simulation methods in relation to the Legnica-Głogów area.[52] Mahl, Stelmachowski and Panko, and B. Winiarski and F. Winiarska have tackled the organiza-

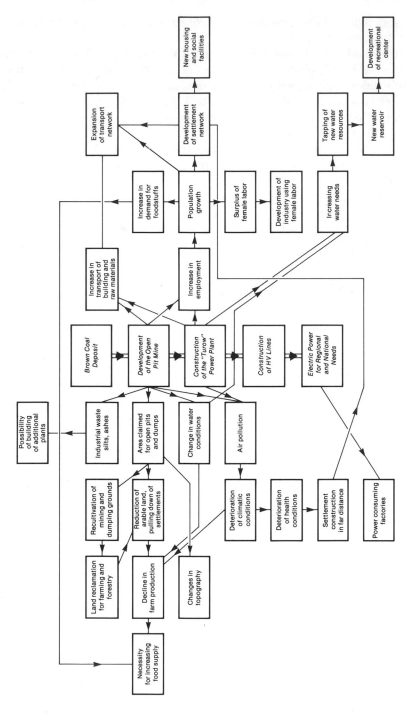

Source: Adapted from M. Musiał.

Figure 1-3. Causal Diagram of Settlement System Change.

tion problem of planning in a nonmetropolitan area of rapid growth, again based on the Legnica-Głowów area.[53] Finally Bagdziński has surveyed settlement system change in the Włocławek area,[54] and Zajchowska et al. in the Konin area.[55] Another interesting study of the Konin area is reported by Wojtasiewicz, who has continued working on related problems.[56]

This by no means exhaustive listing of finished projects only skims the surface of the empirical results produced for the regions studied by the KBRU and, of course, a number of studies have been undertaken on other cases of nonmetropolitan industrial location.

Models, Theories, and Research Prospects

In an article written over a decade ago, Gałęski provided a commentary that has endured.[57] He wrote that the results of empirical research are very rarely used as statements in general studies. Additionally, convictions or feelings expressed during such general studies are not normally accepted in empirical research as starting points, assumptions, or hypotheses, which is not surprising since these statements are usually formulated in a way not conducive to their direct use in questionnaires or table headings. The nonmetropolitan industrial growth field in Poland seems to have witnessed a methodological conflict, a passive one in which the KBRU has been struggling with its empirical indigestion and slowly succumbing to it. Rural sociologists, geographers, and spatial planners have been trying to introduce explanatory, causal approaches, but they have not been greatly successful. The most recent papers suggest the introduction of theoretical elements, perhaps rather dated, in the form of growth pole theory and, of more interest, the territorial production complex.[58] A major weakness of such work to date has been the lack of an economic perspective, which would increase explanatory power. Both the causal sketches and the multivariate statistical analyses have been lacking in their ability to generalize and, especially, to make useful predictions of future community changes brought about by industrial growth. One hopes that the more theoretical, model-based approaches will come to the fore now that the descriptive approach has ground to a halt under the weight of its own output. It seems probable that this methodological question may resolve itself in time under the influence of changes taking place in the social sciences. Until then, it is necessary to conclude that although the many empirical studies of nonmetropolitan industrial growth and community change in Poland are valuable source material for generalization about the processes involved, they do not provide a coherent picture of the impact of large industrial plants upon rural areas.

Notes

I have used two abbreviations here: KPZK, Komitet Prezestrzennego Zagospodarowania Kraju (Committee for Space Economy and Regional Planning), and ZBRU, Zeszyty Badań Rejonów Uprzemysławianych.

1. Investments in fixed prices where 1960   100, had reached 482 in Japan and 476 in Poland by 1975 according to *Rocznik Statystyczny,* 1977, p. 468.

2. In industry 35 percent of buildings, 45 percent of equipment, and 52 percent of power plants were destroyed during the war. B. Winiarski, *Polityka Rgionalna* (Warsaw: PWE, 1976), p. 111.

3. S. Zadawzki, *Polska-Przestrzeń-Społeczeństwo* (Warsaw: PWE, 1973), pp. 272–280.

4. S. Zawadzki, "Centralny okręg przemysłowy," *Przegląd Geograficzny* 35 (1963): 47–60.

5. These observations are based on the works of T. Lijewski, "Tendencies in the Location of New Industrial Plants in Poland in the Years 1945–1970," *Geographia Polonica* 33, no. 2 (1976): 157–170, and K. Dziewoński and B. Malisz, "Przeksztatcenia przestrzenno-gospodarczej struktury Kraju," *Studia KPZK* 62 (1978): 28–35.

6. Interview with Zbigniew Szałajda, managing director of Huta Katowice, Polityka 29, July 22, 1978. He stressed the importance of a skilled labor force and the industrial traditions of Upper Silesia.

7. M. Olędzki, "Z problematyki kształtowania rozwoju społeczno-ekonomicznego rejonów uprzemysławianych," *ZBRU* 66 (1977): 220–229.

8. K. Secomski, ed., *Spatial Planning and Policy: Theoretical Foundations* (Warsaw: PWN, 1974).

9. In particular, see: K. Dziewoński, "Research for Physical Planning in Poland, 1944–1974," *Geographia Polonica* 32 (1975): 5–22; B. Malisz, "Research Work as an Input in the Construction of the National Plan," *Geographia Polonica* 32 (1975): pp. 113–132, and *Problematyka Przestrzennego Zagospodarowania Kraju* (Warsaw: PWN, 1977); A. Kukliński, "Regiony silne i słabe w polityce społeczno-ekonomicznej, *Region Białostocki* 5 (1977): 55–68; B. Winiarski, "Retrospektywna ocena polityki aktywizacji regionów zaniedbanych w Polsce," *Region Białostocki* 5 (1977): 160–170; S. Zawadzki, "Przyspieszenie rozwoju obszarów słabiej rozwiniętych jako problem planowania perspektywicznego," *Region Białostocki* 5 (1977): 9–18; and Dziewoński and Malisz, "Przeksztatcenia Przestrzenno-gospodarczej struktury Kraju."

10. J. Turowski and L.M. Szwengrub, eds., *Rural Social Change in Poland* (Wrocław: Ossolineum, 1976), and *Rural Socio-Cultural Change in Poland* (Wrocław: Ossolineum, 1977).

11. B. Gałęski, "Types of Industrialization," in J. Turowski and L.M. Szwengrub, eds., *Rural Social Change in Poland* (Wrocław: Ossolineum,

1976), pp. 11–32; M. Dobrowoslska, "The Impact of Industrialization on the Transfromation of the Rural Settlement Structures and Social and Occupational Structures in Southern Poland," in Turowski and Szwengrub, *Rural Social Change,* pp. 109–139; J. Turowski, "Changes in the Rural Community," in Turowski and Szwengrub, *Rural Socio-Cultural Change,* pp. 9–26; B. Jałowiecki, "Transformations in Rural Areas Under Industrialization," in Turowski and Szwengrub, *Rural Socio-Cultural Change,* pp. 101–112.

12. S. Ignar, "Badania naukowe procesów industiralizacji w Polsce Ludowej," *ZBRU* 59 (1974): 5–35.

13. Ibid.

14. D. Gałaj, "Problems of Research in Poland's Regions Under Industrialization," in J. Szczepański, ed., *Empirical Sociology in Poland* (Warsaw: PWN, 1966), pp. 53–78.

15. The following statement typifies the style of work: "The research discussed was collective. . . . Its results have been described in a number of articles, communiques, scientific papers, three major dissertations, and fifteen Master's theses." In H. Mortimer-Szymczak et al., *Problemy Demografii i Zatrudnienia w Rejonie Włocławskim* (Warsaw: KBRU/ PWN, 1978).

16. As a recent example see ibid., p. 11n.

17. J. Dietl, *Handel i Rynek w Rejonach Uprzemysławianych* (Warsaw: KiW, 1970).

18. J. Dietl and B. Lewy, "Przydatność masowej statystyki regionalnej do badań warunków rynk oraz obsługi handlowej ludności w rejonach uprzemysławianych," *ZBRU* 49 (1971) : 9–67.

19. See, for example, I Adamczyk, *Warunki Buty w Płockim Rejonie Intensywnej Industrializacji* (Warsaw: KBRU/PWN, 1974).

20. For examples, see H. Rogacki, *Uprzemysłowienie jako Czynnik Urbanizacji* (Poznań: Wydawnictwo Naukowe UAM, 1976), and J. Parysek, "The Application of Principal Components Analysis to the Study of Socio-Economic Spatial Structure and Its Changes," *Queastiones Geographicae* 4 (1977): 131–148.

21. R. Domański, *Syntetyczna Charackterystyka Obszaru na Przykładzie Okręgu Przemysłowego Konin-Łęczyca-Inowrocław* (Warsaw: PWN, 1970).

22. T. Zipser, "Model konkurencji szans w badaniu i optymalizacji rejonu uprzemysławianego," in S. Golachowski and A. Zagożdżon, eds., *Dolynośląski Okręg Miedziowy, 1960–70* (Warsaw: KBRU/PWN, 1974), pp. 271–288.

23. The proceedings of a conference at Tarnobrzeg in 1969 were subsequently published in Polish—E. Jagiełło-Łysiowa et al., eds., *Rejoni Uprzemysławiane: Problematyka i Badania* (Warsaw: KBRU/PWN, 1971).—English—*Regions Under Industrialization: Problems and Research*

(Warsaw:KBRU/PWN, 1971)—and French. In the Zeszyty series, number 46 (1971) was dedicated to a discussion of a set of proposals for topic-by-topic syntheses from the different regions.

24. D. Gałłaj, "Bydania społecno-ekonomiczne w a regionach uprzemysławianych," in Jagiełło-Łysiowa et al., *Rejony Uprzemysławiane*, pp. 27–48.

25. I. Frenkel, "Próba systematyzacji i ocena dotychczasowych kierunków badań Zatrudnienia w rejonach uprzemysławianych," *ZBBU* 47 (1971): 5–26.

26. Mortimer-Szymaczak et al., *Problemy Demografii*, pp. 9–10.

27. D. Gałaj, ed., *Rozwój Społeczno-gospodarczy Rejonu Uprzemysławianego na Przykładzie Rejony Płocka* (Warsaw: KBRU/PWN, 1973).

28. Golachowski and Zagożdżon, *Dolonśaski Okręg Miedziowy*.

29. A. Stelmachowski, ed., *Kształtowanie Rozwoju Społeczno-Ekonomicznego Rejonów Uprzemysławianych* (Warsaw: KBRU/PWN, 1975). A previous such collection is Jagiełło-Łysiowa et al., *Rejony Uprzemysławiane*.

30. I. Fierla, *Migracje Ludności w Polsce a Uprzemysłowienie* (Warsaw: KBRU/PWN, 1976).

31. J. Cegielski, *Problemy Dojazdów do Pracy: Próba Syntezy* (Warsaw: PWN, 1977). Two other publications by Dziewoński and associates treat some of the same subjects in a more rounded way: K. Dziewoński, "Changes in the processes of industrialization and urbanization," *Geographia Polonica,* 33 (1976): 39–58, and K. Dziewoński et al., "Rozmieszcenie i migracje ludności a system osadniczy Polski Ludowej," *Prace Geograficzne,* 117 (Wrocław-Warsaw: Ossolineum, 1977).

32. Mortimer-Szymczak et al., *Problemy Demografii.*

33. P. Łączkowski, *Warunki Stabilizowania Się Załóg Pracowniczych w Rejonie Upszemysławianym* (Warsaw: KBRU/PWN, 1977).

34. Z. Lachert and Z. Dembowska, *Urbanizacja a Rolnictwo: Powiat Płocki 1960-1965* (Warsaw: KBRU/PWN, 1973).

35. K. Michna, *Rolnictwo a Uprzemysłowienie* (Warsaw: KBRU/ PWN, 1971).

36. W. Galant, "Zmiany stosunku rodziny wiejskiej do szkoły Związane z Procesem Uprzemysłowienie się Rejonu Konińśkiego," *Reczniki Socjologii Wsi* 2 (1964): 167–173.

37. Z. Kwieciński, *Funkcjonowanie Szkoły Wiejskiej w Rejonie uprzemysławianym* (Warsaw: KBRU/PWN, 1973), and W. Wincławski, *Przemiany Środowiska Wychowawczego Wsi w Rejonie Uprzemysławianym* (Warsaw: PWN, 1973).

38. Adamczyk, *Warunki Bytu w Płockim.*

39. K. Kuciński, *Przestrzenne Zróżnicowanie Infrastruktury Wsi a Uprzemysłowienie* (Warsaw: KBRU/PWN, 1977).

40. Dietl, *Handel i Rynek.*

41. B. Gałęski, *Basic Concepts of Rural Sociology* (Manchester: Manchester University Press, 1972).

42. J. Turowski, "Przemiany wsi pod wpływem zakładu przemysłowego: studium rejonu Milejowa," *Studia KPZK* 8 (1964).

43. B. Jałowiecki, *Polkowice: Przemiany Społeczności Lokalnej pod Wpływem Uprzemysłowienia* (Wrocław: Ossolineum, 1967).

44. D. Gałaj, *Chłopi-Robotnicy Wsi Płockiej* (Warsaw: PWPiL, (1964).

45. M. Pochwicki, *Przeobrażenia Społeczności Rolniczej* (Warsaw: KBRU/PWN, 1975).

46. Z.A. Żechowski, *Przemiany Małych Miast w Procesie Uprzemysłowienia* (Warsaw: PWN, 1973).

47. J. Węgleński, *Społeczne Problemy Małych Miast* (Wrocław: Ossolineum, 1974).

48. Domański, *Syntetyczna Characterystyka.*

49. M. Dobrowolska, "Dynamika struktur osadniczych i ich układów przestrzennych," *Folia Geographica* 3 (1970): 5-34, "The Growth Pole Concept and the Socio-economic Development of Regions undergoing Industrialization," *Gegraphia Polonica* 33 (1976): 83-102, and *Impact of Industrialization;* and Z. Zioło, "Development Tendencies of a New Industrial Region as Exemplified by the Tarnobrzeg Industrial Regions," *Folia Geographica* 9 (1976): 111-113.

50. M. Musiał, "Zmiany Geograficzne i Gospodarcze Powstałe w Wyniku Realizacji Wielkich Inwestycji na Przykładzie Regionu Turoszowa" (Ph. d. diss., University of Wrocław, 1971).

51. A. Zagożdżon, "Problems of Development of a Settlement Network in a Region Under Industrialization," *Geographia Polonica* 27 (1973): 159-174, "Rozwój sieci osadniczej w LGOM-ie," in Galochawski and Zagożdżon, *Dolonoński Ogręg Miedziawy* pp. 201-238, "Przekształcanie sieci osadniczej w rejonach uprzemysławianych Polski," *Biuletyn KPZK* 89 (1976): 95-131, and "Rejon uprzemysławiany na przykładzie Legnico-Głogowskiego Okrżgu Miedziowego," *Biuletyn KPZK* 95 (1977): 207-232.

52. Zipser, "Model konkurencji."

53. J. Mahl, "Planning Problems of a New Industrial Region. A Case Study of the Legnica-Głogów Copper District," *Studia KPZK* 17 (1967): 101-112; A. Stelmachowski and W. Pańsko, "Struktura prawno-organizacyjna a model zarządzania rejonem uprzemysławianym," in Golachowski and Zagożdżon, *Dolonślaski Okreg Miedziowy* pp. 289-313; and B. Winiarski and F. Winiarska "Problematyka sterowania Lompleksowym rozwojem rejonu uprzemysławianego," in ibid., pp. 239-260.

54. S.L. Bagdziński, *Przemiany Struktury Przestrzennej i Funkcjonalnej Układu Osadniczego na Przykładzie Rejionu Włocławka* (Warsaw: KBRU/PWN, 1975).

55. S. Zajchowska et al., "Rola uprzamysławianego rejonu koniń-

skiego W strukturze społeczno-gospodarczej byłego województwa poznańskiego," *ZBRU* 65 (1976): 7-77.

56. L. Wojtasiewicz, "Konin Industrial Region in the Economic and Social Development of Poland," in A. Kukliński, ed., *Growth Poles and Growth Centers in Regional Planning* (The Hague: Mouton, 1972), pp. 221-230.

57. B. Gałęski, "Typy uprzemysłowienia," *Studia Socjologiczne* 27 (1967): 7-25, and reprinted as "Types of Industrialization," in Turowski and Szwengrub, *Rural Social Change,* pp. 11-32.

58. See also L. Murray, "Socioeconomic Development and Industrial Location in Poland: The Merging of Growth Pole and Growth Center Theories in a Socialist Economy," *Antipode* 62 (1974): 125-141, for a survey of the status of growth-pole theory in Poland.

2 Contemporary Research Emphases in Great Britain

G.A. Mackay, Peter G. Sadler, and John B. Sewel

Britain has a long history of regional policy, presumably because of its long history of regional problems, dating from the Industrial Revolution. If we use the old definition of problem regions—congested areas, declining industrial areas, and declining agricultural areas—British regional policy has concentrated heavily on the declining industrial areas. For policy purposes, however, little distinction has been made between the different types of problem areas, and in geographical terms, the assisted areas (those benefiting from regional policy assistance) cover more than half the country. There are some gradations in levels of assistance; the highest is available only in special development areas, which are all urban areas with declining heavy industries (such as coal mining, steel, and shipbuilding).

The only notable exception to this national regional policy was the establishment in 1965 of the Highlands and Islands Development Board, a special body set up to alleviate the economic and social problems of the Highlands and islands of Scotland, the most northerly and sparsely populated part of the country. It could be argued that the region has peculiar problems, but its unique treatment actually stems from longstanding historical and political reasons. The board has been decreed a success by the civil servants and politicians involved—although many other people would disagree with that view—and a similar, though smaller, body has recently been set up for the rural parts of Wales—the Development Board for Rural Wales (DBRW).

During modern history, Britain has been primarily an industrial country, and political power in terms of votes has been concentrated in the industrial areas, which have almost always been found in the urban rather than the rural parts of the country. Equally important, the British political system, at least as far as the constitution is concerned, is not designed to give any weighting to factors other than population as represented by voting power (unlike, for example, the American system where the House of Representatives is elected on a population basis and the Senate on a geographical basis or the Norwegian system in which rural votes are given a different weighting from those in urban areas). Consequently the only way in which rural areas with their weak political power can influence political decisions is when as a minority they threaten the fortunes of one of the major parties by the marginal effects of shifts in voting patterns.

Interest has been focused on many of the rural areas in recent years because of several changes that have posed threats to the main political parties; the most notable of these is the rise of nationalism in Wales and Scotland. The western and northern periphery of Britain, which contains the most sparsely populated areas of the kingdom, is often called the Celtic fringe. The development of political nationalism with the wooing of voters toward the nationalist parties has posed a new problem particularly for the Labour party, which without Scottish and Welsh support would never have been able to have formed a government.

Second, the movement toward national planning introduced in 1965, which enjoyed a brief history in British politics, saw the rural areas as sources for improvement in Britain's growth performance; it regarded them not as reservoirs of labor but as recipients of part of a growing population, which would relieve the congestion in the growing urban areas. National planning as then envisaged was never adopted as policy, and the concept of regionalism that it embodied died with it. Also recent amended forecasts of the size of the population by the year 2000 indicate a stable and perhaps declining population, whereas the assumptions of 1965 were that the population would be expanding right up to that period. Consequently the idea that a way to spread the population is the spread industry is being rethought.

Third, Britain's membership in the European Economic Community (EEC) has required a different attitude toward rural areas in accordance with the aims of the treaty of Rome, which requires that policy be directed toward eradicating income differences between the richer and the poorer regions of the community. Many policies must be examined against criteria that will reflect this policy.

Notwithstanding the last point, preoccupation in Britain has been largely with regional employment rather than regional income levels. Employment figures are published monthly and are politically more emotive than are levels of income. Thus the designation of special areas, for which extra assistance is available, has always been on the basis of unemployment. Indeed not long ago when nationalist movements were particularly strong, the central government issued a report on the comparative flows of income and expenditure between the central government and Wales and Scotland "proving" that the flow was greater outward than inward in each case. It therefore claimed that the center was supporting the periphery, but it did not consider that much of this support was rendered necessary by the lack of local development and the consequently low local income in peripheral regions.

Regional Policy

Government attitude toward regional development since the early 1960s, with its emphasis on employment levels, has encouraged research into the development of tests of efficiency. This research has been almost exclusively economic in nature; sociologists and those in other disciplines have been relegated to the role of critics of the results of policy. There has been little, if any, concerted attempt to provide a normative planning framework that would unite the social and economic research necessary for the development of policies that would regard regional development in its wider context. Consequently tests of efficiency based upon economic criteria alone are lopsided, particularly when applied to the rural peripheral areas of the United Kingdom, where the problems that so often arise are not only economic but social and cultural also. Even more unfortunately, these tests of efficiency are usually applied ex ante in the sense that economic effects may be assessed in ceteris paribus conditions, but due to the nature of general economic change, it is often impossible to isolate the effects of a single policy or a single aspect of that policy from effects resulting from other forces.

Moore and Rhodes have produced a number of estimates of the contribution toward national employment and output.[1] Their approach is to estimate the levels of activity without regional policy and attribute the difference between actual and hypothesized levels to the various policies. More recently, they have used the same approach to look at effects in individual areas, such as Scotland, and there is no reason why this method could not be used for the regions that make up Scotland, including the rural areas. The smaller the geographical area, the poorer the statistical data become, however, and this is one of the main reasons why so little regional work has been done in Britain. At subnational level, the only regular and accurate official statistics are for unemployment, and most researchers have to rely on their own collection of data.

Disaggregated work of a different type has been undertaken by Ross MacKay on individual policy instruments, such as the regional employment premium, which was a labor subsidy used for a few years in the assisted areas.[2] MacKay's results conflict with the conclusions of Moore and Rhodes—for example, regarding the usefulness of the regional employment premium—and it is clear that further empirical research is needed in this area before agreement is reached.

Industrial Mobility and Location Studies

At the microlevel, the most notable feature of recent research has been the resurgence of interest by geographers in industrial location studies of both a theoretical and practical nature. Little of this interest has been concerned exclusively with rural areas, but it has some relevance. The main concerns of recent work have been with the organizational structures of the firms involved, particularly foreign, multinational, and multiplant firms. It has frequently been argued that a lack of consideration of organizational structures and behavior has been a big gap in earlier work, and the emergence of multiplant and multinational firms necessitates a reworking of the old theories. If looked at from an objective point of view, however, it is probably fair to say that these justifications remain to be proved because much of the work has come up with very few new ideas or policy recommendations. It is a pity that more economists have not participated in this debate because many of the issues discussed at length could be solved by a knowledge of simple microeconomic theory, particularly related to oligopolistic industries. The distinctive feature of most of the industries currently under examination is not that they are denoted by multinational or multiplant firms but that they are oligopolistic.

By way of summary, Wood has identified what he calls "three new principles of modern industrial geography":

1. Locational change and choice in manufacturing arise from the investment strategies of different types of firms;
2. Relationships and interdependencies between individual plants reflect operational ties both within and between industrial firms or other organizations. Linkages in geopgraphical space, both of materials and information, are therefore manifestations of ownership and commercial exchange patterns;
3. Regional economies are increasingly open and interdependent.[3]

These principles have led those involved, mainly geographers, to pay much more attention to the environment in which the firms and plants operate and to discuss the ways in which environmental factors can vary. It is usually argued that these factors (such as the local labor market, availability of materials, and public and private infrastructure) vary significantly from region to region, that local and regional influences are usually most important for smaller firms, and that for larger firms, the national and international influences are of greater importance.

A common theme has been that industrial mobility has increased in recent years, which means that more firms have been moving from urban areas to other locations. The proof of this shift is still incomplete, but it is probably true that there has been a marked move from city center to suburban locations. Any significant movement to rural areas, in net terms, has yet to be demonstrated conclusively, however.

There appears to have been an opposing trend in the service sector, however, with office and other service employment being increasingly concentrated in urban centers. It is becoming very common for the nonproductive parts of establishment (among them, research and development, administration, and distribution) to be separated from the manufacturing plant and to be located in larger centers such as London, Glasgow, and

Edinburgh. Obviously this dichotomy has long-term implications with the shift away from employment in the manufacturing and primary sectors, and there have been a few recent studies of the location of office employment, notably that by Goddard.[4]

In an extensive study of industrial mobility, Hamilton has claimed that "smaller, lighter, labor-intensive activities were moving out of traditional urban areas by establishing branches or by relocating to areas where they could obtain labor without serious competition from other employers and control by unions. . . . Other important explanations are local government policies such as rural industrialization, low land rents, the growth of frozen-foods and related packaging industries, and the increasing local significance to small or medium-sized firms to access to residential amenities."[5] Generally, though, too little empirical work has been done to date for these conclusions to be widely accepted, but they do point to interesting avenues for future work.

Another related aspect that has been of great interest to a range of social scientists in recent years has been the relationship between ownership and industrial movement (the latter includes aspects such as plant closures and employment changes). Because policy is concentrated on industrial mobility rather than growth in indigenous activities, much of the increase in local employment and economic activity has been attributed to firms moving in from other parts of Britain or from abroad. Little concern was expressed at the time about this influx of nonlocally controlled activities, but during the course of the industrial recession in Britain since the early 1970s, many firms have closed down or reduced their level of operations. Research has shown that the propensity to close down has been much higher in nonlocal than in local firms. A consequence has been a noticeable resurgence in interest in the possibilities of indigenous growth.[6] The main proponents of this approach have been the new regional authorities set up in Britain a few years ago when the local government system was reorganized. These authorities are larger than their predecessors and now have a planning staff to enable them to undertake research in their own right. Not surprisingly, they have paid much more attention to local possibilities. As an example of practical implementation, the Highlands and Islands Development Board introduced in 1978 a scheme for setting up community cooperatives in their area, following closely along the lines of similar (presumably successful) experiments in Ireland.

Local Economic Impact Studies

Early work at the local and regional level concentrated on the use of the regional multiplier. Other writers in this vein, however, quickly realized the inadequacy of the regional demand multiplier as a measure of policy and even more so as a guide to policy. They realized that regional effects could differ among regions, and more importantly, one industry or one activity could have different effects from another industry, as well as different effects according to the region in which it was encouraged. Appeals were being made for much more disaggregated information to assess the effect of different policies and different industries or activities, and attempts were already being made to undertake some form of regional accounting in Britain. Work continued toward improving regional input-output techniques as a means of policy formulation and testing and rejecting the effective demand approach embodied in the expenditure multiplier. This work would explain the short-circuiting of the export base multiplier, which had come into favor elsewhere. The aim, of course, was to attempt to assess the impact of activity on the local areas by the industrial and other linkages, which could vary immensely, as opposed to the impact of the demand on the consumer on local output, which would in general be much more stable in its proportionality. It was quickly obvious too that the smaller the area being studied, the greater the variations in the former would probably be.

The development of input-output studies since that date in the United Kingdom has taken two main directions. The first is toward their descriptive uses for the larger regions, notably the development of a new set of social accounts for Wales and input-output tables for Scotland. The developments on this plane do not concern us, however; the others, which have been developed on the local level, are our concern. Six small-area input-output tables are available so far; each has been prepared with somewhat different objectives in view. The first was a study of the small town of St. Andrews in Fife, Scotland, by Blake and McDowall in 1967, then the Anglesey study by Sadler et al. in 1973, closely followed by the Peterborough study by Morrison and the study of the Invergordon area by Mackay. The Gwynedd study by Sadler et al. and the study of the Shetland economy by McNicoll are the others.[7] All but the Peterborough study were of very rural areas, and agriculture made up a much greater proportion of total activity in each of these.

The St. Andrews study was a comparison of the effects of tourism and a traditional university on a small county town and its surrounding district. The Anglesey study was designed to provide a test of the hypothesis that under certain circumstances income multipliers could be negative, to test the effect on a rural economy of the implantation of a large aluminum smelter in the area, and to provide information for planning purposes for the local authority. The Peterborough study was designed to provide a framework for forward planning, and the Invergordon study proposed to examine the local impact of a new aluminum smelter. The Gwynedd study hoped to provide information on the economy of a new county that was to be established by the amalgamation of three in North Wales, one of which was

Anglesey, and the Shetland study was completed as a base study against which changes caused by the development of the large oil terminal would be measured. The largest area in terms of population was Gwynedd (219,000 in 1971); the smallest were the Shetland Islands, with a population of just under 18,000, and St. Andrews, with a population of only 10,500.

Recently researchers have begun to use these studies in various ways to draw conclusions on other aspects of social and economic change. Even considering their limitations of input–output analysis, they appear to be the most useful tool available for extension into other directions—for example, the addition of a labor dimension in which the input of various categories of labor for each classification of industry is being developed and the consequences of various forms of labor demand for migration are being studied. It is likely that a new generation of input–output studies devoted to labor and environmental questions as a tool for socioeconomic research as opposed to economic research only may not be far off.

The biggest stimulus to research on rural industrial growth in recent years has been the discovery of oil and gas in the North Sea, in particular off the east coast of Scotland.[8] In our view, the most interesting research underway concerns the impact of the oil and gas developments on the north of Scotland. The oil developments are of great importance to the national economy because of their contribution to government revenue and to the balance of payments, and they have attracted a great deal of attention. The onshore developments are concentrated in a few locations in Scotland, where there have been substantial increases in local industrial output, investment, and employment. By an accident of geography, most of these developments are in the more rural and sparsely populated areas. Thus islands such as Orkney and Shetland have probably received more attention over the last five years from central government than they have in the preceding fifty, and much more thought has been given to their problems than to future development.

For many years, economists at Aberdeen University have undertaken research into the economic development of the north of Scotland, and it was natural when the oil developments occurred for a number of oil-related studies to be started. In Aberdeen, therefore, we had the great advantage of having comprehensive pre-oil data and individuals with extensive knowledge of the areas involved. This earlier work made the analysis of the impact of oil developments much easier and better. Unfortunately very few sociologists had had previous interests in the north of Scotland, so prestudies and poststudies are virtually impossible.

On the economic side, early work concentrated on simply monitoring developments. Recently we have turned our attention to the analysis of the nature of the impacts. All of the local authorities concerned and the central government agencies welcomed the advent of the oil industry because of the jobs it brought. Virtually all of the areas had high rates of unemployment and emigration. It would probably be true to say that the majority of local people were of the same view, although there was opposition in a number of areas.

As a generalization, the North Sea discoveries have been of net economic benefit at the national level. This would also be true at the Scottish level, largely because of the forty thousand jobs created, but at the local level the balance of economic benefits and costs is less clear. Thus our current work is concentrating on the evaluation of industrial developments from the point of view of the local community.

For most communities the benefit side is fairly obvious and quantifiable: increases in employment, wage rates, and incomes, reductions in unemployment and emigration, and improvements in infrastructure and social services. Most of the local economic impact studies mentioned earlier have covered these aspects in great detail, but they have rarely looked at the costs side, which includes the loss of labor by local industries, increased competition for housing and other services, the extent to which the more skilled and highly paid jobs are filled by incomers rather than by locals, and the small contribution made to the solution of the employment problems of the more marginal groups (the unemployed, the disabled, and, to a lesser extent, the female labor force). We are currently investigating these aspects in order to obtain some view of the real net benefit or cost to the communities involved.

In Shetland, for example, the economy was traditionally dominated by the crofting, fishing, fish-processing, and knitwear industries. The local labor force was about seven thousand. The main oil-related activity is the construction of the landfall oil terminal, which requires a peak construction labor force of over four thousand and a permanent operating force of around six hundred. In addition there are supply bases, a helicopter base, and a few smaller activities, bringing the peak labor force to over five thousand, or 70 percent of the original local labor pool. Apart from social problems, there are great worries that some of the traditional firms or industries will be forced out of business through labor policies and increased competition for other inputs and services. The main concern is with the post-oil phase. Will the local economy revert to its pre-oil state? Are local firms able or willing to take back people who had left them for oil-related employment? If not, what has happened and will happen to local industries and the local labor force? Have the employment and migration experiences and expectations of individuals changed markedly?

Sociological Research

British sociologists in the past have tended not to be particularly interested in the social implications of nonmetropolitan industrial growth. The British tradition of community studies has concentrated either on small rural villages, where the attempt has been to describe as fully as possible the social structure of the village, or of urban and especially inner-city areas with its discovery of urban villages. Where community-based studies have been linked with economic change, the focus has not been on examining the relationship between industrial growth and community change but on looking at the effects of industrial decline on communities. Perhaps this direction has been the product of the general economic problem facing Britain in the post-World War II period: the decline of its staple nine-teenth-century industries. The urban direction of action- and policy-oriented research has been further emphasized by government-backed programs, such as the community development projects, which when not based in urban areas concentrated on declining industrial rural communities.

In the context of economic decline, the coal industry during the 1960s was the subject of a series of studies. Although they are not directly related to economic growth, they supply some interesting starting-off points and indicate the sort of topics that could be studied in relation to economic growth and community change. The relevance of the coal industry here is its nonmetropolitan nature. Indeed the traditional coal-mining areas of Britain have been the nonmetropolitan areas of south Wales, Scotland, and the north of England. Within these areas, coal mining often developed within one-industry villages and small towns. The best-known community study of the coal industry *Coal Is Our Life,* concentrated on how the relationships and social system of the colliery carried over into the social system of the community.[9] Indeed Dennis et al. looked at the distribution and interrelationships of class, status, and power in the industry and the community. The period of decline in the mid- and late 1960s led to a different kind of study that instead emphasized the response of individuals and communities to economic decline. Taylor studied miners in the Durham coalfield who had the possibility of making use of an internal National Coal Board transfer scheme to the more prosperous coalfields of the English Midlands. Instead of just establishing the numbers who went, he examined the different types of migrant and nonmigrant groups who emerged during the process of decline.[10] A study by Sewel in south Wales looked at the migration and job expectations of miners who were faced with the possibility of redundancy and studied the political response of the community if decline in the coal industry continued.[11]

A traditional British community study that perhaps comes closest to examining nonmetropolitan growth is one of Banbury by Stacey.[12] Although there must be some doubt as to whether Banbury is nonmetropolitan, the major theme of the study was the impact that the coming of an aluminum works had on the social relationships of a medium-sized town. From this study came the important social division of cosmopolitans and locals—a distinction between those whose orientation and frame of reference was the wider metropolitan society and those for whom it was the local community.

North Sea Oil and Related Effects

There is little doubt that the more recent interest of British sociologists in nonmetropolitan industrial growth has received its main impetus from the discovery of North Sea oil and the effect that oil–related activities is likely to have on small communities in northern Scotland. Before the coming of oil, there was only one Scottish study that could come under the heading of nonmetropolitan industrial growth and community change. Varwell, who studied the social impact of the Invergordon aluminum smelter, emphasized the relationships established by incomers with the local community and the social and political response of local organizations to the problems of change.[13]

The coming of oil created a tremendous research opportunity, and it was possible to identify a number of promising topics for research. Robert Moore indicates that this opportunity was very largely missed and places a great deal of responsibility for this lack on the body responsible for promoting research—the Social Science Research Council.[14]

By the early 1970s, it was clear that in a number of sparsely populated areas within northern Scotland, large–scale, on–shore, oil–related activities were likely to take place, among them, the building of oil or gas terminals and the fabrication of steel and concrete production platforms. An examination of the regional and local press at the time revealed that in many of the affected localities, debates ensued between the proponents and opponents of development. Claims were made about how development would affect the local way of life. In many of the areas, developers, transnational corporations, speculators, landowners, local authorities, central government, and local interest groups were involved and played a part in determining the final shape of what took place, where it took place, and by whom. In none of the areas has this initial, yet critical, phase in the history of oil–related activity been studied as it took place. To some extent Moore has recreated the events and the actions of those early years in Peterhead, but his work is based on reconstructing events rather than on studying them as they took place.

Once on–shore activities got underway, it was clear that large numbers of itinerant workers would be recruited and employed in areas that had previously been sparsely populated and had small local labor markets. In these areas, local labor could be expected to be attracted into the oil–related sector and move out of other more traditional sectors of the economy. New managerial groups could be expected to move to the area, and trade unions were likely to become established. It is reasonable to hypothesize that these changes would be likely to lead to changes in employment and migration expectations and behavior, changes in work relationships and relationships among workers and between workers, trade unions, and management, and that the existing structures of class status and authority in the localities would also be subject to change. There has been no comprehensive study of these local changes and processes; indeed no study based on the systematic interviewing of those employed in oil-related activity has been published. The Department of Sociology at the University of Aberdeen has been conducting a series of studies on oil-related work forces designed to look at the effect of labor migration on industrial and community relations in the North of Scotland. Grieco is examining return migrants in the context of oil-related development, as is Prattis on the Isle of Lewis.[15] On the basis of some preliminary fieldwork, Birks and Sewel have attempted to identify different population groups generated by oil development and differentiated according to their attitudes and expectations toward oil-related employment and local residents.[16]

The research topic that has received most coverage in the local press in oil-affected areas is that of change in the local way of life. It is sometimes difficult to identify what this term encompasses, but among other indicators of change that have been cited are increases in crime, prostitution, drunkenness, industrial conflict, greed, and greater materialism. Mageean has written about change in the social stratification of Shetland in response to oil-related development.[17] Following his study of the Invergordon smelter, Varwell has now begun a study of how the way of life in different communities has been affected by oil activity.[18] Cohen rightly points out the limited nature of much oil-related research activity and emphasizes the lack of intensive, long-term, ethnographic fieldwork that has been undertaken, an approach that he claims is uniquely suited to the description of cultural processes.[19]

Some of the limited research emphasis has resulted from the difficulties faced by local and central government, and here is the area of the social impact study that stands in direct antithesis to the kind of ethnographic work advocated by Cohen. Even if the ephemeral impact studies are ignored, work derived from the interests of government is limited to problems of infrastructure provision and planning difficulties. Thus Grigor has written a detailed account of the responses of local authorities to the housing demands made by large-scale construction and fabrication activity in East Ross.[20] The Institute for the Study of Sparsely Populated Areas carried out work that identified different planning strategies used by local authorities in responding to the discovery of the North Sea oil. Hunt has drawn attention to how local authorities may accept a definition of oil-related activity that support the authorities' own desired definition of development rather than one that accurately describes the nature of the activities taking place.[21]

At a more abstract and theoretical level, the relationship between oil and social change has been studied in the context of the continuing debate about the relationship between the Highlands and islands and British capitalism. Although more recent work draws from Hechter's *Internal Colonialism* the main contribution to the debate and the starting-off point of much that has since been written is the work of Ian Carter.[22] Carter took the traditional dual-economy model of the relationship between the Highlands and the British economy, which was explicit in the work of Gillanders and implicit in the policies of development agencies such as the Highlands and Islands Development Board, and demonstrated its inadequacy.[23] Such a model sees the Highland economy as being insulated and separated from the British economy. Consequently development is made possible by opening up this traditional and backward economy to the modernizing effects of the market economy and capitalism. Carter demonstrated that throughout different historical phases, the Highland economy had been very much part of and integrated with the British economy and that the histories of the black cattle trade, the kelp industry, and sheep farming were determined by forces operating within the British economy. The Highlands was an area of primary resources and primary production, the exploitation of which led to little reinvestment in the Highlands. What investment there was usually was not under local control. The dominant model that has emerged from the debate is that of the center and the periphery, together with the application of the concept of dependency. Following Carter's pre-oil work, this theme has been taken up by Moore, Mewett, Prattis, and Hunt, who have applied it in developing an understanding of how oil-related activity can be expected to contribute to the development of peripheral Scotland.[24] Not surprisingly, the application of the model to oil activity has emphasized the very limited development gains that can be expected from oil in terms of promoting and sustaining economic growth.

The usual type of sociological debate as to whether research has been too empirical without sufficient emphasis on theory or whether model building has gone ahead without establishing a sufficiently strong empirical base is particularly sterile in the context of research carried out on social change in northern Scotland. Cohen's point remains true: little long-term ethnographic work has been promoted, and it is doubtful whether the story of oil and northern Scotland can ever be told. The lack of research, despite the establishment of the SSRC North Sea Oil Panel, is all the more depressing considering the advantages that could have been obtained at relatively little cost if the decision had been taken in the early 1970s to finance long-term community-based studies in two or three of the localities that could have been identified as major centers of oil activity. If that had been done, British sociology would have stood a better chance of making a contribution to the topic of nonmetropolitan industrial growth and community change.

Notes

1. B.C. Moore and J. Rhodes, "Regional Policy and the Scottish Economy," *Scottish Journal of Political Economy* 21 (1974): 215–235.

2. Ross R. MacKay, "The Impact of the Regional Employment Premium," in A. Whiting, ed., *The Economics of Industrial Subsidies* (London: Her Majesty's Stationery Office, 1976).

3. P.A. Wood, "Industrial Organization, Location and Planning," *Regional Studies* 12 (1978): 143–152.

4. J.B. Goddard, *Office Location in Urban and Regional Development* (London: Oxford University Press, 1975).

5. F.E.I. Hamilton, "Aspects of Industrial Mobility in the British Economy," *Regional Studies* 12 (1978): 156

6. J.R. Firn, "Indigenous Growth and Regional Development," in W.F. Lever, ed., *West Central Scotland: Appraisal of Economic Options* (Glasgow: University of Glasgow, 1973).

7. C. Blake and S. McDowall, "A Local Input-Output Table," *Scottish Journal of Political Economy* 14 (1967): 227–242; Peter G. Sadler et al., *Regional Income Multipliers* (Cardiff: University of Wales Press, 1973); W.I. Morrison, "The Development of an Urban Interindustry Model," *Environment and Planning* 5 (1973): 369–383; G.A. MacKay, *The Economic Impact of the Invergordon Aluminium Smelter* (Inverness: Highlands and Islands Development Board, 1978); Sadler et al., *Regional Income Multipliers.* I.H. McNicoll, *The Shetland Economy* (Glasgow: Fraser of Allander Institute, 1976).

8. D.I. MacKay and G.A. MacKay, *The Political Economy of North Sea Oil* (London: Martin Robertson, 1975), and G.A. MacKay et al., *The Economic Impact of North Sea Oil on Scotland* (London: Her Majesty's Stationery Office, 1978).

9. N. Dennis, F. Henriques, and C. Slaughter, *Coal Is Our Life* (London: Eyre and Spottiswoode, 1957).

10. R.C. Taylor, "The Implications of Migration from the Durham Coalfield" (Ph.D. diss., University of Durham, 1966).

11. John Sewel, *Colliery Closure and Social Change* (Cardiff: University of Wales Press, 1975).

12. Margaret Stacey, *Tradition and Change* (London: Oxford University Press, 1960).

13. A. Varwell, "A Study of Industrial Settlements in a Sparsely Populated Area" (Ph.D. diss., Aberdeen University, 1977).

14. Robert Moore, "Northern Notes Towards a Sociology of Oil," in

Proceedings of the British Sociological Association, Scottish Branch Conference, Oil and Scottish Society (forthcoming).

15. M. Grieco's work is expected to be published in 1979; J.I. Prattis, *Economic Structures in the Highlands and Islands of Scotland* (Glasgow: Fraser of Allander Institute, 1977).

16. J.S. Birks and John Sewel, "A Typology of Oil-stimulated Population Movement in Northern Scotland," *Town Planning Review* (in press).

17. D. Mageean, "Oil and Development in Shetland," in John Sewel, ed., *Proceedings of the Fourth International Seminar on Marginal Regions* (Aberdeen: University of Aberdeen, Institute for the Study of Sparsely Populated Areas, 1978).

18. Varwell, "Study of Industrial Settlements."

19. A.P. Cohen, "Oil and the Cultural Account: Reflections on a Shetland Community," in British Sociological Association, *Oil and Scottish Society.*

20. I. Grigor, "Local Authority Accommodation to Oil in Easter Ross," in British Sociological Association, *Oil and Scottish Society.*

21. D. Hunt, "Oil Myths and Reality," in British Sociological Association, *Oil and Scottish Society.*

22. M. Hechter, *Internal Colonialism* (London: Routledge Kegan Paul, 1975); Ian Carter, "Economic Models and the Recent History of the Highlands," *Scottish Studies* 15 (1971): 99–120, and "The Highlands of Scotland as an Underdeveloped Region" in E. de Kadt and G. Williams, ed., *Sociology and Development* (London: Tavistock, 1974).

23. F. Gillanders, "The Economic Life of Gaelic Scotland Today," in D.C. Thomson and I. Grimble, eds., *The Future of the Highlands* (London: Routledge Kegan Paul, 1968).

24. British Sociological Association, *Oil and Scottish Society* (forthcoming) and Prattis, *Economic Structures in the Highlands and Islands of Scotland.*

3

Contemporary Research Emphases in Scandinavia

Paul Olav Berg

Because few Scandinavian city regions correspond to metropolitan areas in size, the problems of nonmetropolitan economic growth and community change per definition apply to virtually all parts of the Scandinavian (Nordic) countries. Referred to as regional problems, they have increasingly been attracting attention both in public debate and as a matter of government concern.

Regional Problems

In a historical perspective, economic development in the Nordic countries has been based on natural resources.[1] The location of these resources—agricultural land, forests, fishing grounds, mineral deposits, and waterfalls—formed the threshold for an existence and has resulted in a pattern of small settlements and towns scattered over wide areas. Dependence on one resource or type of economic activity in particular sites makes them vulnerable to structural changes in the economy.

Even if the distribution of resources and other geographical characteristics cause regional problems on a similar scale in the three Nordic countries (Finland, Norway, and Sweden), there are differences, which should be noted. Rationalization and the corresponding reduction of the employment base in agriculture and forestry took place earlier and has been carried further in Sweden and Denmark than in Norway and Finland. Structural change through industrialization and urbanization has taken place within a relatively short span of time in Finland, gaining momentum after the nation got its independence in 1917. This rapid transformation has caused regional structural problems that are among the most severe in the North, as reflected by the heavy migration from the northern and eastern parts of the country and also by the out-migration—particularly to Sweden—that gained momentum during the 1960s. Economic activity and settlement based upon the traditional occupational combination of agriculture and forestry in Finland and Sweden has proved more vulnerable to structural change in the economy than settlement based upon the combination of agriculture and fishing in Norway. Common to the three countries is the vulnerability caused by lack of alternative economic activity in areas where settlement is dependent upon one type of resource. These problems are aggravated by long distances and—in the case of Norway—by difficult topographical conditions.[2]

The problems are not of recent origin, although they have been accentuated by the rapid postwar economic development. They are partly of a general nature and will be found in any country that undergoes an economic development accompanied by structural changes in the economy. But they are also of a more specific nature and reflect geographical characteristics of the Nordic states. The problems arise from regional disparities in levels of income, in employment opportunities, and in the provision of services and other welfare components. What is new is the way that they are conceived. Reflecting the political ambitions of the welfare state, these problems are thought best resolved through various forms of government action. Based on generally accepted policy goals, such action has been considered necessary in all Nordic countries.

Regional Policies

In a mixed economy where approximately half the volume of total economic activity is managed by the public sector, governments have substantial possibilities to influence living conditions, as well as the location of economic activity, throughout the country. Such an influence—more or less with built-in regional policy goals—to a certain extent has been exerted through general and sectoral policy measures as part of the general economic and social policy. Even if the strength of these efforts has differed somewhat among the Nordic countries, planners and decision makers agree that these have not been sufficient. More specific policy measures are necessary in order to prevent regional problems from attaining untolerable levels.

Specific regional policy measures fall mainly in two categories: (1) attempts at affecting the location of economic activity, mainly manufacturing industry, through financial inducements and administrative regulations, and (2) attempts at better coordination of general sectoral policy measures within a regional policy framework.

Influencing the location of economic activity has taken place mainly through financial incentives such as investment grants, investment loans, and guarantees for loans, given at favorable terms. Tax concessions, transportation subsidies, manpower training grants, and wage subsidies have also been used. Industrial estates (parks) have been built in advance for rent or sale. For example, in order to achieve a more balanced regional development, Sweden is decentralizing more than ten thousand government jobs from Stockholm to other regions. And to control its regional growth pattern better, Norway has passed legislation making the establishment or expansion of firms above a certain size subject to government approval.[3]

Better coordination of general and sectoral policy measures has been attempted through the provision of comprehensive planning at the regional level, particularly on the county administrative level. There also have been attempts to integrate regional policy goals into national policy and planning in various fields of government activity.

Evaluating Regional Policy

Attempts to coordinate general and sectoral policy measures within a regional policy framework have had only limited success. Comprehensive regional planning at the county level can hardly be effective when most policy measures are controlled by national political and administrative bodies that are relatively independent in their decision making and planning. None of the Nordic countries have achieved an effective coordination, which is the responsibility of the national government. The extent to which the present process of delegating from national to regional and to local government will contribute to regional policy goals is still an open question. However, some important results have been attained in terms of integrating regional policy goals into national policy and planning for communications, education, health and social care, subsidies for primary industries, and transfers to local governments.

The financial incentives and administrative regulations of the regional policy proper were in most cases introduced during the period of strong economic growth of the late 1960s and the early 1970s. It is generally believed that these measures have effectively promoted consolidation of economic activity and employment growth in development areas. It has, however, been questioned whether this policy has encouraged the right kind of employment, considering the long-term prospects of growth in the different branches of industry, as well as the qualitative aspects of the new jobs from the point of view of individuals and local communities.

A few attempts at evaluating results achieved by regional policy have been made recently, although they are difficult to separate and meaure. This fact may be attributed to lack of statistical information on actual results as well as lack of theoretical tools for follow-up studies. The latter raises the question of the role of the social sciences in this field. To what extent have government policies been influenced by research? What characteristics may be attributed to this influence?

The Role of Research

Any link between research and government policies is at least an indirect one. The decision process shaping government policies rests on a general level of knowledge to which research in a broad sense will have contributed substantially. In some cases, research focusing on certain problems has stimulated the introduction of particular policy measures. Generally, however, the direct influence from research is but one of several factors incorporated into decision making. The attention of social sciences to a particular policy field often may lag several years behind the introduction of the policy programs in question. With some exception for Sweden, this certainly has been the case in the field of regional policies in the Nordic countries.

Traditionally research takes place at universities and in other educational bodies at the university level. In the Nordic countries, these are on the whole owned and financed by the national governments; nevertheless the governments do not have much influence on the direction of the research. In most cases topics for research will be decided on by the researcher or student, who will choose an activity that can be sponsored and also meet with professional acceptance and recognition. For many reasons, such recognition is not always given to research in fields where new knowledge is scant.

Such factors together with the limited capacity for research may explain why the main expansion in research activity over the last thirty years has taken place in specialized research institutes rather than in universities. These are financed by industry and other privately owned bodies, by government-sponsored research boards, and, recently, directly by government ministries. In these institutes, which have no teaching obligations, research is a full-time activity. The project orientation indicates an emphasis on applied research. Differing from the universities, their sponsors will exert an influence on the direction of the research and on priorities.

Research within social sciences has generally lagged behind government policy programs in this field. This also applies to the research institutes, which are mainly organized along disciplinary or sector lines. Social research constitutes a relatively small part of total research activity. Also, sponsors of research often represent disciplinary or sector interests. These factors may explain why multidisciplinary research aiming at comprehensive studies related to local or regional levels of society has been given relatively low priority.

To some extent this general picture has been modified during the last few years because both researchers and sponsors have felt a responsibility to focus attention on development trends and problems that have been neglected.

An increased influence on the direction of research on the part of government bodies, however, leaves open the question on which principles such an influence should be based. What kind of research policy will best support the general policy goals in this field?

Research Emphases

Various social sciences specialize in certain aspects of society. Together they form a picture of reality that is more representative than one reflected by a single discipline. An individual student or researcher will have to choose a few disciplines for specialization and will consequently acquire a narrower picture of reality as an expert. The relative position gained by the various social sciences may differ from one country to the other. There are interesting differences between countries in this respect.

As a basis for a general understanding of regional economic development, economics is, of course, of fundamental importance. Among the social sciences, economics traditionally has a strong position, particularly in Norway, where economists have made important contributions to the development of the conceptual framework for national accounts and to macroeconomic planning at the national level.[4] However, there has been little interest in regional economics. With the exception of a school within Swedish economics, which has focused on the theory of international and interregional trade, the same may be said of economists in the other Scandinavian countries. Nevertheless economic models and analytical tools (multiplier, cost–benefit models and, to some extent, input–output models) have been widely used in regional analyses.[5] A recent Swedish evaluation of the effects of regional development measures between 1965 and 1975, based upon an analog model, compared actual employment changes with projected normal development trends.[6]

Traditionally sociologists and political scientists also have shown little interest in regional aspects of their disciplines. In recent years this tendency has changed, and several interesting contributions have been made. Core-periphery aspects of regional development have been receiving attention. Recent studies of the power structure of the Norwegian society have illuminated processes influencing regional development.[7]

Within social anthropology, a school influenced by populism has focused on development processes in small communities in peripheral areas. This research has contributed to a better understanding of an important aspect of Norwegian regional problems.[8]

Regional studies have a central position in geography. Whereas earlier studies often had a predominantly descriptive character, there has been an increasing interest within the discipline for analyzing processes behind regional development. Particularly in Sweden, geography has been a leading discipline within regional research.[9] Generally studies of the use of natural resources, migration, settlement, and location of economic activity have formed important parts of geographical analysis in all Nordic countries. Recent development within location theory has diminished the traditional weight on the transportation cost factor and emphasized information and organizational factors.[10]

Research activity referring to regional problems and policies has increased substantially since the mid-1960s in both universities and in research institutes, although no doubt there are still many areas where intensified research could contribute to a valuable widening of the knowledge base on which policy programs rest. This point of view reflects the prevailing favorable attitude toward research. A realistic appraisal of research, however, should also include a clear understanding of restrictions inherent in the role of research. As a contribution to such a discussion, some points of view put forward recently by the Swedish geographer Gunnar Törnqvist are noteworthy.[11]

Törnqvist questions the possibilites scientists have today to explain or to understand societal changes that take place or to tackle current problems in society. Several circumstances may have contributed to a situation where such possibilities are fewer than before. Society has very quickly become complicated to a degree that might be characterized as unnatural. At the same time an increasingly higher degree of specialization within the social sciences has made it more difficult to see or comprehend the total picture. Advances within the social sciences have not kept pace with society. Probably the use of mathematics, computers, and too strong a belief in the possibilities of generalization have given many researchers and planners a false feeling of security and too strong a belief in the possibilities of attributing coherence and order in a society that is built upon an advanced specialization and division of labor.

Törnqvist believes that both geographers and economists have been too tied to the perspectives of classical location theory. Much research has focused on conditions for location and possibilities for expansion for various types of economic activity in various regional units. But subjects like these belong to a phase of expansion that in many respects culminated in the 1960s in the Nordic societies. The necessary production capacity has already been established. Within certain regions and sectors, there is already surplus capacity. Employment within manufacturing and handling of goods has stagnated. An increase in one region or sector is countered by a corresponding decrease in another. In the postindustrial society, few new plants are built; the ones that are replace others. Within companies, administration grows more slowly than before. Only the public sector experiences genuine expansion. On this basis Törnqvist has sketched three lines along which a reorientation of research in regional problems should take place.

First, it seems essential to raise questions related to risks of change and possibilities of adaptation. Too little research has been devoted to questions of how firms and households can adapt to drastic changes in their surroundings. Examples of such changes may be foreign competition of hitherto unknown strength, lack of energy, or lack of raw materials.

Second, regional research has concentrated on physical realism. Studies have concentrated on tangible phenomena that could be measured easily. Interest has been concentrated mainly on external possibilities and constraints for government, firms, and households. In current research in Swedish geography, there is a trend toward a more person-centered and humanistic view of life. For instance, how do decision makers and members of households conceive of their own situation? How much information on possibilities and constraints influence decisions and actions?

Third, there is a serious need to coordinate the scattered attempts that have been made in the field of regional research. Many researchers know how difficult it is to achieve integrated results through cooperation among specialists. The task of assembling and integrating knowledge from different disciplines is greater than it has ever been.

Research Policy

The role of government as sponsor of research and consumer of its results raises several questions of both practical and fundamental significance. By what arrangements should government bodies direct research? How should priorities be decided? And how can planners and policy makers use the research?

The policy in this field has differed among the Nordic countries. In Denmark and Finland, research activity has been concentrated mainly in the universities, and in Norway separate research institutes have played an increasing role for many years. In recent years funds have been put at the disposal of government ministries, which sponsor projects in research institutes, including regional research, even if activity in this field has been relatively low until now.

At an early stage Sweden developed a special way of organizing regional research. With the introduction of its first regional development program in 1965, a group of experts (*Expertgruppen för regional utrednings-verksamhet—ERU*) was appointed by the Swedish government. They were senior representatives of various social sciences and high officials from government ministries. The objectives were to initiate and to stimulate

research that could improve the factual framework for the recently introduced regional policy and thus supply the government with a better base for
formulating and reevaluating regional policy.

The ERU has initiated a large number of studies, which have been
carried out partly within universities and partly by working groups. A
number also have been made by ERU's own staff, which includes researchers from various disciplines. One is ERU's most recent study, an evaluation
of the effects of regional policy measures used between 1965 and 1975.[12]

Research reports, together with ERU's own summaries and recommendations, were published in 1970 and 1974, and a third round will be
published in 1979.[13] These reports have been used by the government
directly as a basis for formulating regional policy goals and programs.
Recently a decision has been made to decentralize ERU's activity by establishing groups of researchers and experts based on the six university regions
in Sweden.

Related to ERU, a Nordic working group on regional policy research
was established in 1967 (*Nordisk arbeidsgruppe før regionalpolitisk forskning*—NordFEFO). This group has members representing government
ministries responsible for regional policies in the various Nordic countries.
It has served as a center for the exchange of information and experiences
gained. Five project groups with researchers from participating countries
have been established, covering the following themes:

1. Environmental preferences and living conditions for households.
2. Conflicting objectives in regional policy.
3. Alternative patterns for settlement structures.
4. Analysis of effects of regional policy measures.
5. Administrative conditions for regional planning.[14]

Reports from the various groups will be published during 1979 in the
NordREFO publication series.

One study initiated by the project group focuses on conditions for
firms' utilization of regional development measures and various characteristics of firms of that category.[15] Effects from such measures on Sweden's
northern-most region are also analyzed. Another study is based on a general
model of a firm.[16] Within this model results from various financial inducements upon the firm's financial results and its development over a span of
years is analyzed. Moreover, results of various types of policy measures
used in different regions within the Nordic countries have been analyzed.

The research activity initiated by ERU in Sweden has been a stimulus to
regional research in the other Nordic countries. ERU's data-processing
techniques were developed within geography at an early stage. Statistical
data were integrated in a finely masked grid system covering the whole

country. This has been a valuable tool for the processing of analytical maps and for analyzing spatial patterns. In other disciplines, a valuable development of methods has taken place, improving the foundations for regional analysis. Altogether this research activity has aroused interest in regional problems, influenced government policies, and improved the foundations for studies and professional training in the field of planning and public administration.

As Törnqvist, who has been an influential contributor to research initiated by ERU, points out there is need for considerably more research before the social sciences can supply the answers needed. Scarce resources should thus be allocated to fields where research and a better knowledge base are most in need. Thus research policy is a matter of fundamental importance.

The examples given here represent solutions at an early stage, and they need improvement. The double role as sponsor and consumer of research may put government bodies in a position of strength if they can be supplied with an expertise necessary to live up to their responsibilities. The relative strength among the social sciences in a country may decide priorities within research policies. But it will be necessary to balance priorities so that the interests of less–privileged groups will be paid regard. There is certainly a strong argument for pluralism and for a research policy in favor of weaker societal groups. Moreover a proper balance should be made between work on applied and basic research. The future role of research will depend on the answers to problems like these, which are found within the framework of research policy, in the years to come.

Notes

1. Hans W. Ahlman, ed., *Norden i Kart og Tekst. Norsk, Svensk og Dansk Utgave. Svenska Sällskapet för Antropologi och Geografi* (Stockholm, 1976).

2. Paul Olav Berg, "Regional Development Problems in Norway," in Maurice Broady, ed., *Marginal Regions: Essays on Social Planning* (London: Bedford Square Press, 1973), and Hallstein Myklebost, "Befolkning og Bosetting," in Just Gjessing, ed., *Norges Geografi* (Oslo: Universitetsförlaget, 1976).

3. For more detailed information on policy measures, see OECD, *Regional Problems and Policies in the OECD Countries* (Paris: OECD, 1976), vols. 1–2, and *Regional Policies: The Current Outlook* (Paris: OECD, 1977).

4. Leif Johansen, *Lectures on Macroeconomic Planning* (Amsterdam: North–Holland, 1977).

5. Monica Aase, *Regional Økonomi og Regional Planlegging: En Bibliografi* (Bergen: Norges Handelshøyskole, Biblioteket, 1974); Håkon Gundersen og Arne Selvik, *Industri i Distrikts-Norge: En Annotert Bibliografi* (Bergen: Universitetet i Bergen, Sosiologisk Institutt, 1975).

6. Lennart Olsson, Ch. 2-7 in SOU (1978:47) *Att Främja Regional Utveckling: En Utvärdering av det Regionalpolitiska Stödet till Industrien.* [Promotion of Regional Development. A Report by the Expert Group of Regional Studies (ERU), Ministry of Industry.] (Stockholm, 1978).

7. Gudmund Hernes, ed., *Forhandlingsøkonomi og Blandingsadministrasjon* (Oslo: Universitetsforlaget, 1978); Johan P. Olsen, ed., *Politisk Organisering* (Oslo: Universitetsforlaget, 1978).

8. Ottar Brox, *Hva Skjer i Nord-Norge?* (Oslo: Pax Forlag, 1966), and *Avfolkning og Lokalsamfunnsutvikling i Nord-Norge* (Bergen; 1971).

9. Allan R. Pred, *Urbanization, Domestic Planning Problems and Swedish Geographic Research,* vol. 5: *Progress in Geography* (London: 1973).

10. Gunnar Törnqvist, *Contact Systems and Regional Development,* Lund Studies in Geography, series B, Human Geography, no. 35 (Lund: 1970).

11. Gunnar Törnqvist, *Om Fragment och Sammanhang i Regional Forskning,* in Expertgruppen för Regional Utredningsverksamhet, *Att Forma Regional Framtid: 13 Forskares syn på Regionala Problem* (Stockholm: Publica, 1978).

12. SOU (1978:46, 47) *Att Främja Regional Utveckling: En Utvärdering av det Regionalpolitiska Stödet till Industrien* (Stockholm, 1978).

13. These include *Balanserad Regional Utveckling,* SOU (1970:3); *Urbaniseringen i Sverige,* SOU (1970:14); *Regionalekonomisk Utveckling,* SOU (1970:15) *Orter i Regional Samverkan,* SOU (1974:1); *Ortsbundna Levnadsvillkor,* SOU (1974:2); *Produktionskostnader och Regionala Produktionssystem,* (1974:3); and *Regionala Prognoser i Planeringens Tjänst,* (1974:4).

14. NordREFO (1978:1), *Information on Regional Policy and Regional Policy Research in Nordic Countries,* Nordic Commission on Regional Policy Research (Stockholm; 1978).

15. Carl Fredrikson och Leif Lindmark, *Företagen och Regionalpolitiken,* Bilaga 4 till Slutrapport från NordREFO's forskningsprosjekt Analys av Regionalpolitiska Medels Effekter (Stockholm: NordREFO, 1978).

16. Carl Fredriksson och Leif Lindmark, *Regionalpolitiskt Stöd i Norden—En Effektstudie Utifrån Företagets Perspektiv,* Bilaga 7 till Slutrapport fran NordREFO's forskningsprosjekt Analys av Regionalpolitiska Medels Effekter (Stockholm: NordREFO, 1978).

4

Contemporary Research Emphases in the United States

H. L. Seyler

Contemporary research emphases focusing on nonmetropolitan industrial growth and community change reflect a nexus of disciplinary and inter-disciplinary activity identified by a community of interests. An incomplete list includes the labors of demographers, economists, geographers, political scientists, and sociologists. One must also recognize the endeavors of various interdisciplinary groups, such as the Community Development Society, regional scientists, regional planners, and those involved with research on social indicators. At the same time that this commonality of interests presents an unusually exciting body of diverse work, the growing flood of published material issuing from active participation, and the semantical problems of integrating contrasting (and internally conflicting) disciplinary paradigms, should cause any intrepid synthesizer to be decid-edly cautious.

A judicious and defensible strategy to follow under these circumstances would be to narrow the scope of inquiry. I will restrict my overview of research endeavors to that of the role of industry as a community change-inducing element as being synonymous with manufacturing growth. By community change, I refer to economic growth and development, the latter construed in the broadest sense of improvement in general well-being. I define contemporary as the last ten years. I will overlook work devoted to effecting industrial growth. Rather than attempt a summary of research activity by discipline, I will focus on themes provoking scholarly attention that elude easy disciplinary labeling.

I will address three facets of the topic at hand. To provide a context, I will describe research inventorying contemporary changes in the American industrial landscape; provide a survey of efforts to analyze and to deepen our awareness of the impacts of industrialization on nonmetropolitan areas; and conclude with an attempt to relate the first two parts to implications they hold for future public policy initiatives.

The Role of Industrial Activity as a Community Change–Inducing Element

Addressing the role of industrial growth as a community change-inducing element for nonmetropolitan areas, especially in the United States, can be defended on at least four counts. Industrial activity is heavily emphasized in the literature devoted to nonmetropolitan development, and deservedly, because its importance relative to other economic sectors is enlarging in many nonmetropolitan areas. The United States is amid an areally extensive redistribution of industry where nonmetropolitan areas are registering impressive absolute gains and dramatically increasing their share of the nation's total industrial activity. Finally, for a host of reasons, manufacturing is an economic activity favorably disposed toward nonmetropolitan areas.[1]

A focus on industrial activity does not deny the potential for change induced by the primary or tertiary sectors. Increased agricultural productivity through land and/or capital intensification is an important element in community change, and one that warrants more research than it is getting today. Additional resource harvesting in mining, forestry, and fishing deserve attention as well, though these activities are significantly restricted by locational conditions favoring or limiting their exploitation in a given technological environment.[2]

Although the complex of activities comprising the public and private services sector are often identified as potentially change inducing, for most metropolitan areas services are more likely to be following rather than leading activities. Growth (or decline) of private activity in this sector—personal and business services and trade—generally responds to change in other sectors. Most nonmetropolitan areas with smaller communities in more sparsely settled portions of the landscape do not satisfy entry-level thresholds or local amenities to support firms that have large and sometimes noncontiguous market areas. Those nonmetropolitan areas with local natural amenities may be able to exploit recreation or tourism.[3] However, there appears to be a divergence between growth and developmental effects where this occurs. Hansen, for example, found that serious costs obtain for many residents in communities where growth is based on resort activities.[4]

Certain restrictions must also be noted in the public sector. Placing or expanding governmental facilities in nonmetropolitan communities is certainly a method to induce growth and change. Political realities intrude here, however. Places that already have state or federal installations use their political influence to retain or enlarge them. Larger, especially metropolitan, communities invariably have more political influence than nonmetropolitan areas do and usually obtain regional governmental offices. Three other factors also intervene. First, there are just so many new military bases, regional offices, research labs, and similar installations that can be established. Second, many facilities are logically placed in locations most accessible to clients in their service areas, meaning in or near large population and activity concentrations. A third factor involves the functional efficiency of and local service base needed by governmental facilities. A high frequency of personnel interaction and the broad array of linked private–sector services often reinforce locational concentration. Without an effective state and federal policy of facility dispersal, the public sector seems to hold a limited potential as a change–inducing element. And even where it can be realized, the developmental impacts may not be positive, as evidenced by an appraisal of a water resources project in Oregon where public service requirements during several years of construction activity and the dramatically reduced demand after construction left the residents with huge public indebtedness.[5]

Thus the tertiary sector as a leading or forcing growth and development element seems to be absolutely and locationally constrained.[6] Moreover, of those places that successfully grow and develop as a result of leading tertiary activities, many are flirting with, and will achieve, metropolitan status, bringing us full circle back to industry as an appropriate focus of efforts to understand its role as a change–inducing activity.

Industrial Dispersal and Community Change

An obvious type of nonmetropolitan community change is vested in increasing magnitudes of industry, whether measured in terms of employment, wages, and salaries earned or aggregate income attributable to manufacturing. Current data emerging from federal reporting agencies provide unequivocable evidence that a fundamental restructing of the American industrial landscape is underway. Building upon earlier indications of a dispersal of industry on a regional level through the 1950s, contemporary researchers are just beginning to survey the character and locational redistribution of manufacturing to nonmetropolitan areas.[7] A trend toward these areas during the 1960s has now been documented.[8] Haren has demonstrated that participating industries, quite diversified by type, were electing location, relocation, or expansion in less–urbanized areas at rates and levels that were higher in nonmetropolitan than metropolitan areas.[9] His predictions of continued expansion of this sort in the 1970s have subsequently been confirmed.[10] The locationally pervasive dispersal of industry encompasses every region of the country, though the amount and rate of change varies. Without question, there is a genuine spatial restructuring where growth in less–urbanized areas nonadjacent to metropolitan concentrations is greater than that attributable to exurban or metropolitan spillover growth.[11] For nonmetropolitan areas as a whole, employment gains as a result of this process are substantial. Manufacturing is the growth sector for much of the nometropolitan landscape, and one recent projection suggests that it will continue to be so in the future.[12]

Thus far the inventory efforts provoked by a growing awareness of the scope and areal extent of this dramatic transformation are fragmentary. Researchers are asking how much of what is going where and why it is occurring.[13] We can thus anticipate a cascade of studies more completely detailing both the composition of dispersing industry and its locational disposition across the nonmetropolitan landscape. Moreover, we can expect an expanding empirical ledger as analysts attempt to gauge the impact on communities that host dispersing industries. Even if the current shift slows or abates altogether, the relative immobility of plant and equipment suggests a future industrial landscape significantly different from that obtaining but two or three decades ago.

That this locationally extensive economic transformation is occurring in the absence of any national program to promote decentralization, so representative of other advanced industrial countries, intensifies curiosity. In addition, it is almost inextricable interrelated with a general redistribution of population now taking place in the United States.[14] After decades of migration outflows and marked population decreases in many cases, nonmetropolitan areas are enjoying a resurgence of growth that includes both sharply reduced out-migration and increased inflows of migrants.[15] Many metropolitan areas, particularly the older and larger ones, are now recording net outflows and absolute population losses.[16] The redirection of migration is producing remarkable gains in nonmetropolitan counties that are not adjacent to metropolitan concentrations.[17] Predictably, the association between population shifts and industrial dispersal has attracted the attention of researchers.[18] Although much detail is yet to be provided, industrial growth seems to be both the cause and consequence of the dramatic shifts in population growth.

Area development analysts are striving to understand why the process of nonmetropolitan industrialization is occurring and accelerating, particularly without benefit of a consistently supportive national policy. Researchers are asking what has changed the calculus that had for decades favored the agglomeration of manufacturing. Attention has been directed to the interplay of the "filtering-down process";[19] changing forms of industrial organization;[20] redefinition of the nature of agglomeration economies;[21] the effects of areal and regional wage differentials;[22] the effects of varying strengths of unionization;[23] improvements in the transportation system and incidence of footloose industries;[24] the growing sophistication of community development bodies;[25] and firms' responses to perceived attractions of nonmetropolitan areas as contrasted with disutilities of larger metropolitan areas.[26]

Of these research clusters, the phenomenon of filtering down has been accepted as a principal feature of the accelerated pace of nonmetropolitan industrialization. Drawing on a characterization originating with Thompson, area development analysts have concluded that nonmetropolitan areas are competing effectively for an enlarged share of mature, labor-intensive industry as it disperses from metropolitan areas through relocation and branch plants.[27] Although most researchers agree that nonmetropolitan areas are hosting more mature, often slowly growing, or nationally declining industries, there are indications that some of this dispersal involves higher-technology, higher-wage manufacturing.[28] Thus the nature of industrial composition effects remains somewhat cloudy. Certainly the evolving empirical data suggest markedly differing industrial profiles, so one must be cautious in discussions of nonmetropolitan areas as though they were a homogeneous population.

What appears to be another promising research avenue is just now being probed. The very fact that the United States is experiencing a general industrial dispersal to nonmetropolitan areas challenges previously held understandings of the role of agglomeration advantage. Former advantages of direct backward and forward interindustry linkages, and the indirect benefits often described as urbanization economies, seem to have been diluted over the last quarter-century.[29] Related to the filtering-down phenomenon and the apparent need to rethink agglomeration benefits is a revealed trend in industrial organization that is supportive of dispersal. Researchers are finding that large, multiplant firms can continue to realize the economies and amenity advantages of metropolitan areas by concentrating management functions and redistributing production to nonmetropolitan areas.[30] From this developing perspective, recent locational reallocation of manufacturing can be viewed as a response to an altered organizational and informational milieu that forces a reappraisal of the relative cumulative advantage for industrial growth of all areas.

The role of perceived disutilities of larger metropolitan areas as it does or does not favor nonmetropolitan industrialization is a murky, but actively visited, research avenue.[31] Far more scholarly effort has been devoted to the perceptions of individuals and groups that constitute either parts of an industrial work force or elements of a supporting service base than to the supposed affect on decision makers.[32] Although elements of the population express a preference for less heavily urbanized areas, those living in these areas produce highly variable evaluations of residential qualities.[33] Just how these general preferences of the population, or constituent groups, affect industrial location decisions is unclear.

Community Impacts of Industrialization
in Nonmetropolitan Areas

Research emphasizing community changes associated with nonmetropolitan industrialization has a clearer record. However, these endeavors have focused upon a relatively narrow field within the spectrum of potential impacts. Although the word *development* appears frequently in the titles and text of contemporary studies, attention seems to be upon growth, or changes in aggregates, rather than developmental changes. If we take development to mean compositional or structural changes in economic profile and related transformations that affect the well-being of individuals and groups, more recent research has focused largely upon two themes: income and labor force changes. Smith's list of dimensions of well-being reinforces this point.[34] Of the seven dimensions, or macrocharacteristics, that differentiate well-being, only two have received significant attention: income, wealth, and employment, and some assessment of educational changes. Appraisals of change in the living (built) environment, health, social order (or disintegration), social belonging, or recreation and leisure as they relate to nonmetropolitan industrialization have been neglected by researchers.[35]

Industrialization and Growth

Assessments of change in community aggregates have occupied researchers in a variety of forms. The prevailing view emerging from this line of inquiry is one of *measured reserve.* There is a growing awareness that industrial growth will produce less positive impacts than some, particularly advocates of industrialization, would expect.[36] It is now obvious that growth models developed in a metropolitan or large regional context do not transfer well to nonmetropolitan settings. Employment or income multipliers and inter-sectoral linkages are significantly different in the less-diverse economies characteristic of nonmetropolitan communities.[37] Generally the smaller and more open a nonmetropolitan economy is, the less appropriate are attempts to obtain a multiplier. Opportunities for round-by-round multiplicative effects are wanting in these settings. Clearly research efforts suggest a need for a family of models that would be applicable to classes of nonmetro-politan communities distinguished by size range, economic profile, location relative to other larger (especially metropolitan) places, and the pattern of population distribution in their vicinity.[38]

Researchers seem to agree that the openness of nonmetropolitan econ-omies and the difficulty of adequately bounding the area of impact help produce highly variable findings.[39] Different patterns of consumption by community households (geographically and by market basket), varying amounts of inputs purchased locally by resident firms, and commuting by workers into a community from surprisingly long distances result in large and variable leakages in nonmetropolitan areas. The net effect of the leak-ages is often substantial, reducing the growth of population, employment, aggregate income, and governmental revenues compared to that which would be observed in a metropolitan setting.[40]

Attempts to judge growth impacts do seem to be temporal. Earlier research efforts tend to be more positive in their appraisals of costs and benefits.[41] Later analysts, those who fall into the contemporary category, are much more reserved, possibly because they are attempting to be more comprehensive.[42] The messages appearing in more recent publications are not comparable. Case studies cover different periods, regional settings, and communities of varying size and economic structure. Conflicting findings are an inevitable feature of such a situation.

Industrial Growth and Developmental Impacts

Research attempting to gauge developmental impacts of nonmetropolitan industrial growth fall into two roughly defined classes. One involves efforts to assess income change for households and groups in communities experiencing varying amounts of industrial expansion. The second category includes a more diverse range of studies examining labor force impacts in terms of unemployment, underemployment, labor force participation rates, and qualitative improvements in the work force.

Just as aggregate or community growth impacts from nonmetropolitan industrialization are constrained, researchers are determining, on balance, that developmental gains are limited as well. Case studies of income effects have found no significant differences in income gains for household heads in an area experiencing industrial growth and another control area;[43] insignificant changes in median, low, or high household incomes with changes in industrial employment;[44] and negative repercussions for elderly persons in industrializing areas.[45] Some evidence from one case study indicates that industrial growth in areas with high unemployment might reduce the share of households below a specified poverty level.[46] Because of differences in research design and study settings, it is extremely difficult to render a judgment about the state of art in this arena. Researchers do seem to be providing evidence of something less than striking developmental gains at the household level as industrial growth occurs.

Change in labor force characteristics associated with industrial expansion have been found to be both positive and negative. Nonmetropolitan industrial gains seem to produce an increase in younger and better educated household heads and some elevation in occupational status.[47] More women enter the labor force.[48] Findings with respect to other facets are not so positive. Unemployment does not contract as one might anticipate. The reason seems to be a direct consequence of in-migration and commuting. Industrial growth is accompanied by substantial in-migration, including the return of former residents of nonmetropolitan communities.[49] Being younger with more education and/or training , and often better skilled, these in-migrants tend to compete more effectively for industrial jobs than do longer-term, especially poorer, residents.[50] Commuters from locations outside a community hosting industrial growth share characteristics of in-migrants. The net effects of migration and commuting yield few jobs for the most disadvantaged, including members of minority groups.[51] At best, there is a selective upgrading of the labor force, with restricted benefits for those in greatest distress. Clearly there is a need for more research to resolve what distributed benefits generally obtain for segments of the population in communities hosting industrial expansion.

*Growth and Developmental Aspects of
Community Change*

Indirectly, at least, researchers are raising the question of whether growth produces developmental change. Here the question involves the issue of attaining some critical mass. Expansion of the industrial sector by producing added jobs not offset by losses elsewhere will expand some aggregates, even allowing for commuting and other leakages. While multiplier effects may be minimal, local sales and governmental revenues can rise, possibly yielding improvements in both private- and public-sector benefits. In the former, increased sales could satisfy entry-level thresholds for additional personal services and trade establishments. The resulting enlarged array of shopping alternatives could be viewed directly as a developmental benefit and indirectly if quality of service and price competition were to develop. Any decrease in the time, cost, and inconvenience experienced by residents who can substitute local purchases of goods or services that previously required a nonlocal trip would yield gains. Unfortunately this aspect has not been adequately researched with respect to nonmetropolitan areas recording industrial growth.[52]

Researchers are beginning to examine public sector impacts from industrial growth.[53] In particular they are looking at whether industrial expansion produce improved public services. Summers and associates found that an increase in the number of manufacturing plants seemed to be unrelated to improvement in the public sector and concluded, "There is very little relief from fiscal burdens on the public sector attributable to net gains in manufacturing."[54] As revenues increase, there are corresponding increases in demands for public services. Even if there are no per-capita gains, benefits that might emerge from attainment of some critical mass through an enlarged array of public services is an issue yet to be researched.

Neglected Aspects of Research

A thread running throughout the dialogue on industrialization and community change, sometimes subtly, links contemporary dispersal patterns to elevated levels of well–being. Referencing national polls or preferences elicited from a more restricted population, some members of the area development fraternity would argue that industrialization, by restraining potential migrants and attracting in–migrants, permits a larger number of Americans to realize a preferred living environment.[55] In this line of reasoning, qualities of well–being that are difficult to define and analyze would compensate for the less than dramatic developmental gains reported by researchers. Thus well–being is improved when people are allowed to reside in bucolic landscapes, which they say they prefer. But insufficient attention is given to a distinction between perceived, highly subjective, evaluations of what people feel and more objectively defined measures of well–being. A recent study of a sample of nonmetropolitan areas found that subjective assessment by residents did not coincide with widely accepted, objectively determined index of well–being.[56]

Certainly the literature devoted to industrial growth and community change is seriously deficient without a more comprehensive appraisal of other components of well–being. Far more effort is justified in the analysis of components identified by Smith if we are to resolve the question of intangible benefits realized from residence in less–urbanized areas.[57]

Policy Implications of Industrial Growth and Community Change

One might reasonably expect those participating in the inventory and appraisal segments of research on nonmetropolitan industrialization to venture into policy quarters. Some have, but a reluctance to stray in normative avenues seems to divert most. When one enters the policy environment, a disjointedness is observed between the unfolding empirical record, appraisals of the functionally and locationally fragmented American policies and programs, and advocates of nonmetropolitan industrialization.[58] On the one hand we are aware of the remarkable industrialization currently favoring nonmetropolitan areas. Assessments of resulting positive impacts are generally reserved, both in terms of growth and developmental gains. At the same time, evaluations of the effectiveness of recent developmental initiatives at the federal level are almost uniformly negative.[59] Even those who argue that programs were conceptually attractive conclude that there have been operational breakdowns.[60] Yet contemporary programs continue to emphasize the industrial development encouraged by many.[61] For example, a major provision of the still operative Rural Development Act of 1972 commissioned the Farmers Home Administration to assist in the financing of industrialization in communities up to fifty thousand population, with special emphasis being placed on communities of less than twenty-five thousand.[62] The much criticized programs of the Economic Development Administration continue to support industrialization first in communities of highest unemployment by legislative necessity.[63] And despite the commitment to areas that by definition have not been effective competitors for economic expansion, many areas are bypassed by industrial dispersal, particularly heavily black nonmetropolitan areas in the South.[64]

Clearly there is a responsibility for those researching contemporary issues of industrial growth and community change to become involved in the dialogue and, ultimately, in the design of policies and programs. Students of nonmetropolitan development could contribute to a reasoned discussion of probable costs and benefits of alternative pathways to achieve a more desirable form of national growth and development. Our colleagues in other industrialized countries are well ahead of us in this respect.[65] We need to move the discussion of the benefits and costs of trade-offs between social and economic efficiency and regional equity out of the abstract, linking it to the case studies we labor so mightily over. And in turn, we need to frame case studies in the larger context of the national space economy as it unfolds under what appears to be a reordered set of locational forces that now are inducing industrial dispersal and that will induce change in nonmetropolitan communities.

Notes

1. See R.E. Lonsdale and H.L. Seyler, eds., *Nonmetro-Industrialization* (New York: Wiley-Halstead, forthcoming), chaps. 1-6. The authors have sketched the nature of an unfolding transformation of the American industrial landscape.

2. The role of the primary sector in a regional context is outlined in Harvey S. Perloff et al., *Regions, Resources, and Economic Growth* (Baltimore: Johns Hopkins University Press, 1960).

3. See Robert A. Harper, Theodore H. Schumudde, and Frank H. Thomas, "Recreation Based Economic Development and the Growth Point Concept," *Economic Geography* 42 (1966): 95-101.

4. Niles M. Hansen, *The Future of Nonmetropolitan America* (Lexington, Mass.: D.C. Heath, 1973), pp. 120-123, 161.

5. C.L. Smith, T.C. Hagg, and M.J. Reagan, "Economic Development: Panacea or Perplexity for Rural Areas," *Rural Sociology* 36 (1971): 173-186.

6. The highly locationally variable affects of transfer payments should be acknowledged. An inflow of funds to households in nonmetropolitan areas from government or investment returns from the private sector obviously can enlarge the tertiary sector by way of enlarged local consumption. However, this is largely beyond the control of local policy makers. While such inflows should be factored into local development plans, attempts to manipulate them as developmental catalysts seem infeasable.

7. For a historical perspective, see Benjamin Chinitz and Raymond Vernon, "Changing Forces in Industrial Location," *Harvard Business Review* 38 (1960): 126–136; Wilbur Zelinsky, "Has American Industry Been Decentralizing? The Evidence for the 1939–1954 Period," *Economic Geography* 38 (1962): 251–269; and Daniel Creamer, *Manufacturing Employment by Type of Location* (New York: National Industrial Conference Board, 1969).

8. Claude C. Haren, "Rural Industrial Growth in the 1960's," *American Journal of Agricultural Economics* 52 (1970): 412–436, and "Industrial Production and Distribution," in L.R. Whiting, ed., *Rural Industrialization: Problems and Potentials* (Ames: Iowa State University Press, 1974), pp. 3–26.

9. Haren, "Rural Industrial Growth."

10. Claude C. Haren and Ronald Holling, "Industrial Development in Nonmetropolitan America: A Locational Perspective," in Lonsdale and Seyler, *Nonmetro-Industrialization,* chap. 2.

11. Ibid.

12. See U.S. Department of Commerce, Regional Economic Analysis Division, *OBERS Projections, Economic Activity in the U.S.,* vol. 6: *Non-SMSA Portions of Bea Economic Areas* (Washington, D.C.: U.S. Government Printing Office, 1974).

13. For a well cross–indexed listing of sources, see SRDC Functional Network, *A Bibliography: Industrialization of Rural Areas* (Mississippi State, Miss.: Southern Rural Development Center, 1978).

14. See Brian J.L. Berry, "The Counterurbanization Process: How General?" in Niles M. Hansen, ed., *Human Settlement Systems* (Cambridge, Mass.: Ballinger, 1978), pp. 25–49; Calvin L Beale, *The Revival of Population Growth in Nonmetropolitan America,* Economic Research Service, Report No. 605 (U.S. Department of Agriculture, 1975); and George Sterlieb and James W. Hughes, *Current Population Trends in the United States* (New Brunswick, N.J.: Center for Urban Policy Research, 1978).

15. Peter A. Morrison, "The Current Demographic Context of National Growth and Development," in L.S. Bourne and J.W. Simmons, eds., *Systems of Critics: Readings on Structure, Growth, and Policy* (New York: Oxford University Press, 1978), 473–479.

16. Sterlieb and Hughes, *Current Population Trends,* 69–70.

17. Morrison, "Current Demographic Context; p. 478; for evidence that this is indeed a truly extensive process affecting all parts of the country, see Berry, "Counterurbanization Process," pp. 34–41.

18. For a recent assessment, see Glenn V. Fuguitt and Tim Heaton, "Nonmetropolitan Industrial Growth and Net Migration Change," and John A. Kuehn, "Nonmetropolitan Industrialization and Migration: An Overview with Special Emphasis on the Ozarks Region," in Lonsdale and Seyler, *Nonmetro-Industrialization,* chaps. 8 and 9. respectively.

19. See R.A. Erickson, "The Filtering-Down Process: Industrial Location in a Nonmetropolitan Area," *Professional Geographer* 28 (1976): 254–260; R.A. Erickson, "Nonmetropolitan Industrial Expansion: Emerging Implications for Regional Development," *Review of Regional Studies* 6 (1977): 35–48; and R.A. Erickson and T.R. Leinback, "Characteristics of Branch Plants Attracted to Nonmetropolitan Areas," in Lonsdale and Seyler, *Nonmetro-Industrialization,* chap. 4.

20. See G. Krumme, "Notes on Locational Adjustment Patterns in Industrial Location," *Geografiska Annaler* 51B (1969): 15–19; D.J. North, "The Process of Locational Change in Different Manufacturing Organizations," in F.E.I. Hamilton, ed., *Spatial Perspectives on Industrial Organization and Decision-Making* (London: Wiley, 1974), pp. 213–244; and G.B. Norcliffe, "A Theory of Manufacturing Places," in Lyndhurst Collins and David Walker, eds., *Locational Dynamics of Manufacturing Activity* (New York: Wiley, 1975), pp. 19–57, esp. pp. 32–37.

21. See, in this book, Robert T. Averitt, "Implications of the Dual Economy for Community Economic Change"; John N.H. Britton, "Environmental Adaptation of Industrial Plants: Service Linkages, Locational Environment and Organization," in Hamilton, *Spatial Perspectives,* pp. 363–390; and Allan R. Pred, "Industry, Information and City-System Interdependencies," in ibid., pp. 105–139.

22. See R.E. Lonsdale, "Background and Issues," and R.E. Lonsdale and Steven R. Kale, "Factors Encouraging and Discouraging Plant Location in Nonmetropolitan Areas," in Lonsdale and Seyler, *Nonmetro-Industrialization,* chaps. 1 and 3, respectively.

23. Lonsdale and Kale, "Factors," pp. 4–6; and R.E. Lonsdale, "Rural Labor as an Attraction for Industry," *American Industrial Development Journal* 4 (1969): pp. 11–17. See also Steven R. Kale, "Labor Supplies for Rural Manufacturing Plants" (Ph.D. diss., University of Nebraska, 1978).

24. See Niles M. Hansen, "Factors Determining the Location of Industrial Activity," in Whiting, *Rural Industrialization,* pp. 24–45, and Howard G. Roepke, "Industrial Possibilities for Nonmetropolitan Areas," *American Industrial Development Council Journal* 8 (1973): 27–45.

25. See Lonsdale and Kale, "Factors"; James Williams, Andrew

Sofranko, and Brenda Root, "Change Agents and Industrial Development in Small Towns," *Journal of the Community Development Society* 8 (1977): 19–29; and Hansen, *Future,* pp. 74–75.

26. Lonsdale and Kale, "Factors," pp. 10–13; Thomas R. Doering and John C. Kinworthy, "The Community Satisfactions on Nonmetropolitan Manufacturers," in Lonsdale and Seyler, *Nonmetro-Industrialization,* chap. 5; Robert Foster, "Economic and Quality of Life Factors in Industrial Location Decisions," *Social Indicators Research* 4 (1977): 247–265; and R.E. Lonsdale, J.C. Kinworthy, and T. Doering, *Attitudes of Manufacturers in Small Cities and Towns of Nebraska* (Lincoln: Nebraska Department of Economic Development, 1976).

27. Wilbur R. Thompson, "The Economic Base of Urban Problems," in N.W. Chamberlain, ed., *Contemporary Economic Issues* (Hernewood: Richard D. Irwin, 1969), pp. 1–47; Hansen, *Future.* See also note 19.

28. Thomas E. Till, "Industrialization and Poverty in Southern Non-metropolitan Labor Markets," *Growth and Change* 5 (1974): 18–24. Also see Haren, "Rural Industrial Growth."

29. See note 21.

30. Norcliffe, "Theory of Manufacturing Places," pp. 34–37. Also see footnote 20.

31. Niles M. Hansen, "Where Is a Big City Too Big," in *The Challenge of Urban Growth* (Lexington, Mass.: Lexington Books, D.C. Heath, 1975), pp. 49–62; C.T. Haworth and D.W. Rasmussen, "Determinants of Metropolitan Costs of Living Variations," *Southern Economic Journal* 40 (1973): 183–192; and Doering and Kinworthy, "Community Satisfactions."

32. See James J. Zuiches and Glenn V. Fuguitt, "Public Attitudes on Population Distribution Policies," *Growth and Change* 7 (1976): 28–33; Clinton J. Jesser, "Community Satisfaction Patterns of Professionals in Rural Areas," *Rural Sociology* 32 (1967): 56–59; Ronald L. Johnson and Edward Knop, "Rural-Urban Differentials in Community Satisfaction," *Rural Sociology* 35 (1970): 548–554; and Dean J. Rojek, Frank Clemente, and Gene F. Summers, "Community Satisfaction: A Study of Contentment with Local Services," *Rural Sociology* 40 (1975): 177–192.

33. For a summary overview, see Doering and Kinworthy, "Community Satisfactions."

34. D.M. Smith, *The Geography of Social Well-being in the United States* (New York: McGraw-Hill, 1973), pp. 69–72.

35. Ibid., p. 70.

36. A recent, comprehensive effort to assess a broad range of impacts is found in Gene F. Summers et al., *Industrial Invasion of Nonmetropolitan America* (New York: Praeger, 1976). For an overview of economic activity change, see Ron E. Shaffer, "The General Economic Impact of Industrial

Growth on the Private Sector of Nonmetropolitan Communities," in Lonsdale and Seyler, *Nonmetro-Industrialization,* chap. 7. See also Luther Tweeten and George L. Brinkman, "Industrialization," in *Micropolitan Development: Theory and Practice of Greater-Rural Economic Development* (Ames: Iowa State University Press, 1976), pp. 226–255.

37. See Steven J. Weiss and Edwin G. Gooding, "Estimation of Differential Employment Multiplier in a Small Regional Economy," *Land Economics* 44 (1968): 235–44; Rodney A. Erickson, "The Regional Impact of Growth Firms: The Case of Boeing, 1963–1968," *Economic Geography* 50 (1974): 127–136; and M.H. Atkins and T.W. Buck, "Industrial Structure and Regional Economic Growth," *Review of Regional Studies* 5 (1975): 12–18.

38. See Daniel W. Bromley, "An Alternative to Input–Output Models: A Methodological Hypothesis," *Land Economics* 48 (1972): 125–133.

39. Impacts of industrial growth, both positive and negative, reach beyond the host community. For a discussion of boundary problems, see John T. Scott, Jr., *Profile Change When Industry Moves into a Rural Area,* Working Paper RID 73.7 (Madison: Center of Applied Sociology, University of Wisconsin, 1973).

40. See Frank Clemente and Gene F. Summers, *Rural Industrial Development and Commuting Patterns,* Working Paper RID 73.15 (Madison: Center of Applied Sociology, University of Wisconsin, 1973); Charles B. Garrison, "Industrial Growth in the Tennessee Valley Region 1959 to 1968," *American Journal of Agricultural Economics* 56 (1974): 50–60; and Shaffer, "General Economic Impact."

41. For example, see R.B. Andrews et al., *Effects of Industrialization on Six Small Wisconsing Cities* (Madison: Bureau of Business Reserach, University of Wisconsin, 1963), and Fred D. Lindsey, *What Industrial Jobs Mean to a Community* (Washington, D.C.: Chamber of Commerce of the United States, 1962).

42. See Summers et al., *Industrial Invasion;* Ron E. Shaffer, "Rural Industrialization: Local Income Analysis," *Southern Journal of Economic Analysis* 6 (1974): 97–102; and Gene F. Summers, "Nonmetro Industrial Growth: Warts and All," statement presented to the U.S. Senate Committee on Agriculture and Forestry, September 1975.

43. E.M. Beck, Louis Dotson, and Gene F. Summers, "Effects of Industrial Devlopment on Heads of Households," *Growth and Change* 4 (1973): 16–19.

44. H.L. Seyler, "Industrialization and Household Income Levels in Nonmetropolitan Areas," in Lonsdale and Seyler, *Nonmetro-Industrialization,* chap. 10.

45. Frank Clemente and Gene F. Summers, *Large Industry in Small Towns: Who Benefits,* Working Paper RID 73.9 (Madison: Center of Applied Sociology, University of Wisconsin, 1973), and "Industrial Devel-

opment and the Elderly: A Longitudinal Analysis," *Journal of Gerontology* 28 (1973): 479–483.

46. Till, "Industrialization and Poverty"; Also see Jerry West and Roselee Maier, "Income Distribution Consequences of Rural Industrialization" (paper presented to the annual meeting of the American Agricultural Economics Association, 1975), and Shaffer, "Rural Industrialization."

47. E.M. Beck, Gene F. Summers, and Louis Dotson, "Effects of Industrial Development on Heads of Housing," *Growth and Change* 4 (1973): 16–21.

48. William H. Miernyk, "Local Labor Market Effects of New Plant Locations," in J.F. Kain and J.R. Meyer, eds., *Essays in Regional Economics* (Cambridge: Harvard University Press, 1971) pp. 171–172; Kale, "Labor Supplies," p. 181; and David L. Rogers, William Goudy, and Richard O. Richards, "Impacts of Industrialization on Employment and Occupational Structures," *Journal of the Community Development Society* 7 (1976): pp. 54–55.

49. Kuehn, "Nonmetropolitan Industrialization."

50. Ibid.; also see L.D. Bender, B.L. Green, and R.R. Campbell, "Trickle–Down and Leakage on the War on Poverty," *Growth and Change* 2 (1971): 34–41.

51. See Summers, "Nonmetro Industrial Growth."

52. For an example, see Lindsey, *What Industrial Jobs Mean.*

53. Gene F. Summers, E.M. Beck, and C. Matthew Snipp, "Coping with Industrialization," in Lonsdale and Seyler, *Nonmetro–Industrialization,* chap. 11. Also see Charles B. Garrison, "New Industry in Small Towns: The Impact on Local Government," *National Tax Journal* 24 (1971): 493–500.

54. Summers, Beck, and Snipp, "Coping with Industrialization."

55. For a summary of residential preferences, see Zuiches and Fuguitt, "Public Attitudes."

56. Patricia A. Lambert, "Comparisons of Social Well–being Components and Perceived Quality of Life Indicators in Rural Kansas Counties" (Master's thesis, Kansas State University, 1977).

57. Smith, *Geography of Social Well–being.* For a work that addresses a broader array of costs and benefits, see Frank Clemente, *What Industry Really Means to A Small Town* (University Park: Extension Form Economics, Pennsylvania State University, 1975).

58. For a historical review of American community development policy, see Curtis H. Martin and Robert A. Leone, *Local Economic Development: The Federal Connection* (Lexington, Mass.: Lexington Books, D.C. Heath, 1977).

59. For a critique of the EDA growth center strategy, see Economic Development Administration, *Program Evaluation: The EDA Growth Center Strategy* (Washington, D.C.: Department of Commerce, 1972), and

Niles M. Hansen, *Rural Poverty and the Urban Crisis* (Bloomington: Indiana University Press, 1960), pp. 3–4, 152–159. See also Center for Political Research, *Federal Activities Affecting Location of Economic Development* (Washington, D.C.: U.S. Department of Commerce, 1970), and Peter A. Morrison et al., *Review of Federal Programs to Alleviate Rural Deprivation,* Report R = 1651 = CF (Santa Monica: Rand Corporation, 1974).

60. Sar A. Levitan and Joyce K. Zickler, *Too Little But Not Too Late* (Lexington, Mass.: Lexington Books, D.C. Heath, 1976).

61. See E.O. Heady, foreword to L.R. Whiting, ed., *Communities Left Behind: Alternatives for Development* (Ames: Iowa State University Press, 1974).

62. See James G. Maddox, *Towards a Rural Development Policy* (Washington, D.C.: National Planning Association, 1973).

63. See Hansen, *Rural Poverty,* and Center for Political Research, *Federal Activities.*

64. Thomas Till, Allen Thompson, and Ray F. Marshal,, *Stages of Industrial Development and Poverty Impact in Nonmetropolitan Labor Markets of the South* (Austin: Center for the Study of Human Resources, University of Texas, 1975).

65. See James L. Sundquist, *Dispersing Population: What America Can Learn from Europe* (Washington, D.C.: Brookings Institution, 1975).

5 Contemporary Research Emphases in Western Europe

Wolfgang Istel and
Jacques Robert

There are many differences among the nine countries of Western Europe regarding natural factors, population density and distribution, level of industrialization and welfare, the objectives of regional economic development, and instruments to implement them (Bockelmann et al., 1973; Hellberg et al., 1977). In each country, research emphases are mainly directed toward specific problems. Therefore, we shall first describe the general spatial development that has taken place in Europe in the postwar period and then provide examples of research about nonmetropolitan regions for selected countries.

Spatial Development Since 1945

All European countries have a free market structure; industrialists are free to decide upon the location of their enterprises. The external economies comprising localization and urbanization economies are the most important considerations prevailing in the location of new industries, the removal of plants, and the location of branches. The operation of such externalities largely explains the postwar concentration of enterprises in the traditional industrial regions and large towns. The enormous expansion of the industrial sector induced immigration from the rural zones because the increased demand for labor often exceeded the supply, and the wage level of industrial work was higher than that in agriculture. After World War II, mechanization in the agricultural sector was minimal or nonexistent. Simultaneously with the rapid expansion of industrial production, agriculture became increasingly mechanized. Both production and, later, productivity increased significantly. Less manpower was needed in agriculture, which in turn reinforced emigration from rural to metropolitan areas, and disparities between metropolitan and nonmetropolitan regions increased continuously.

In a short time, the advantages of metropolitan location of industrial expansion were significantly reduced by the weight of urban growth. Various factors, then, influenced new directions in the location of industry. At first, it was recognized that agglomeration economies were advantageous for management functions but much less so for certain productive functions. Second, the expansion of industrial firms in metropolitan areas became difficult because of the scarcity and high cost of industiral land. Third, wage levels were much lower in rural regions, inducing the expansion of the industrial sector in some rural regions, mostly in the form of branch plants. Despite these new trends, however, the most backward regions did not benefit significantly from industrialization, and regional disparities remained great.

One of the major objectives agreed upon by national governments was to provide equivalent living conditions in the various regions. Thus policies for correcting regional imbalances were elaborated in nearly all Western European countries. Although the objectives underlying these policies were rather similar, the peculiarities of national programs required rather different instruments and measures for their implementation.

West Germany

The progressive concentration of population and activities in metropolitan areas of West Germany after World War II led researchers in social and regional science to focus primarily on economic, physical, and social problems of metropolitan and urban areas. A main direction of research concerned the definition, delimitation, and functional analysis of metropolitan areas. The differentiation between metropolitan and nonmetropolitan areas was attempted using criteria of homogeneity, especially socioeconomic indicators.

Research focusing on nonmetropolitan regions was secondary in terms of the attention it received. In such studies, the supply of infrastructure and public facilities was the dominant concern. Following the initial works of Christaller (1933) and Lösch (1962), investigations were conducted focusing on inventories of existing central facilities, centrality thresholds, and central hierarchies.

Development strategies advocated by the Länder were originally directed toward dispersal and decentralization. The inefficiencies of measures undertaken to implement this strategy led to a reconsideration and adoption of an alternative approach, which was to promote a higher degree of concentration in central places and growth centers with a minimum population of about fifty thousand inhabitants in the center and its hinterland on average. However, the absolute minimum for promotion was as low as five thousand inhabitants in some of the Länder (Heidtmann et al., 1974, 1976). This means that incentives and subsidies are still distributed according to a dispersed pattern, the so-called watering-can principle (*Giesskannenprinzip*).

In 1965 the institutionalization of the concentration principle in general, especially for the development of rural zones, occurred with the passage of a federal law on regional planning. Previously the choice of centers to be promoted had been guided by central place theory, and therefore the level of supply of public facilities prevailed, but now the choice was to be made mainly through consideration of regional labor markets (Klemmer and Kraemer, 1975).

Research efforts were concerned primarily with the issue of which criteria should be used for the delimitations of regional labor markets, such as minimum threshold of the amount of nonagrarian employment and share of commuters. Further research was devoted to the delimitation of problem and assisted areas and was concerned mainly with the theoretical validity of such delimination criteria as manpower reserves, regional income differences, and infrastructural facilities. Most recently research efforts have moved progressively toward concepts integrating those of regional labor market and spatial functional differentiation and in which criteria of accessibility to the center have a key position (Marx, 1975). As an alternative, the concept of large-scale priority areas for particular functions, mainly of ecological character (for instance, as ecological compensation areas), was created.

Current research is attempting to harmonize these two concepts by integrating that of priority areas in a small-scaled manner within that of spatial functional differentiation. The economic and demographic decline that West Germany is currently experiencing surely will generate new directions in research. New distribution patterns must be developed in the context of increasing scarcity of resources and reduced development potentialities (Fester, 1976).

France

Postwar research emphases in France correspond to the various steps undertaken to reduce regional imbalances. In the mid-1960s the promotion of the so-called equilibrium metropolises, designed to act as countermagnets to the Paris metropolitan area began. This policy was inspired by the works of Perroux (1961) on growth-pole theory. In line with that school, a number of applied investigations were undertaken to examine the prospective spread effects of the promoted growth poles in the peripheral regions and potential benefits of regional economic integration (Boudeville, 1968). The policy of the promotion of equilibrium metropolises significantly affected nonmetropolitan areas. Indeed part of the rural emigration benefited these metropolises instead of contributing to the further congestion of Paris (Durand, 1972).

But the objective of reducing rural emigration was not achieved by this policy (Coyand, 1973; Prud'homme, 1974). At the end of the 1960s, it became obvious that the promotion of medium-sized towns in rural areas was also necessary to stabilize the population there. This concern induced a new trend of research that focused on medium-sized towns as potential attraction centers of rural emigration. Promotion occurred mainly in the field of public facilities. However, incentives granted to industry were still distributed on a dispersed basis within assisted areas.

The 1975 census revealed, however, that in some rural areas emigration was so great that population had already dropped below the minimum threshold necessary to maintain organized rural communities and social life. It was therefore decided to investigate the conditions of maintaining a minimum amount of population in the threatened rural areas. Clearly this objective could not be achieved through the promotion of agriculture alone so emphasis was placed on promoting artisan activities. Because the demand for traditional regional products has been increasing, particularly within the urban populations, the promotion of artisanship appeared suitable to stabilize rural population and even to revitalize rural communities, although high growth rates are not expected.

The recent promotion of rural areas has been inspired by research concerning the social evolution and the decline of rural communities. These emphases appear to result both from the fear of a progressing desertification in rural and mountainous areas and from the follow-up of the ecological movement, which advocated the promotion of a new way of life much in line with that existing in rural regions (Pascolon, 1978).

Benelux Countries

The Benelux countries have a very high population density; in the Netherlands, it is higher than four hundred inhabitants per square kilometer. Thus most rural zones are situated within the area of influence of large towns. Only the north of the Netherlands and southeast Belgium can be considered nonmetropolitan areas. In such a context, it is not surprising that most research efforts were devoted to problems of urban settlements. In the Netherlands, research efforts led to the definition of a national strategy of urbanization, which is currently being implemented.

Rural zones in the Benelux countries generally perform two functions: agricultural production and, because of the proximity of large towns, recreation. The influence of urban life in rural zones is higher in the Benelux countries than in larger European countries. Research undertaken about rural zones generally considers them as complementary to urban spaces.

Recently greater attention has been paid to the role of rural settlements in the definition of the national strategy of physical development in the Netherlands (Rijksplanologische Dienst, 1977). Relatively few research efforts have been devoted to the development problems of rural zones. That research is mainly of economic character and generally pays little attention to the consequences of industrialization for community change. Research efforts are being developed in Belgium to create a specific development strategy for the rural province of Belgian Luxembourg, allowing an increase of welfare and avoiding environmental problems resulting from industrialization.

Italy

Italy is certainly the most contrasted of the European countries from the viewpoint of regional imbalances. Industrialization is mainly concentrated in the north. The south, called *Mezzogiorno*, is an extremely backward area, characterized by a dominant share of the precapitalistic labor-intensive primary industry and a low degree of division of labor. Initial backwardness and poverty, accentuated by a rapidly growing population and the decline of agriculture as a source of employment, has led to massive emigration. Without it, the problem of poverty would presumably be more severe, but the emigration also represents a drain of the more active age groups. Because of the prevailing agriculture, the settlement structure is not strongly marked by a hierarchy of centers. Villages and small towns equipped with a scanty and unimportant provision of infrastructure facilities and deficient educational institutions have few opportunities for industrial growth.

Since the initiation of a positive regional policy aimed at promoting the economic growth of the *Mezzogiorno*, there has been progress in industrialization and growth in income levels (Hayward, 1975). To some extent new industrial growth has been offset in southern Italy by the decline of some established industries facing increased competition from the north. Recent industrial development in the south of Italy has been accompanied by the decline of industries that are predominantly of precapitalistic character.

Just as in France, the theoretical concepts underlying industrialization strategies in Italy were those of the growth poles. The policy of growth pole development had only a limited success in south Italy because the spread effects and the economic integration with existing structures were very low. That strategy did not benefit the most remote and backward rural areas. Consequently an alternative policy of promoting small industrial enterprises in the backward areas has been advocated recently (Annesi, 1973). Apart from the very few large towns that new industries were established in, many smaller towns were not able to jump over the threshold of self–sustaining growth. However, this problem did not correspond to growth–pole theory.

Summary

Thus, most research emphases of the postwar period in Europe were related to problems of urbanization and urban settlements. The progressing concentration of industrialization in and around metropolitan areas brought with them similar problems and therefore similar research topics in the various countries. Research about nonmetropolitan regions mainly concerned problems of the development of settlements, demographic evolution, and economic progress. The development problems of rural areas were very different from country to country, which explains some dissimilarities in research priorities (Emanual, 1973).

Different methodological approaches led to different theories for the development of the settlement structure and to different principles of regional policies, especially for the industrialization of rural zones. In northern European countries (for instance, West Germany, the Netherlands, Denmark, Austria, and Switzerland) central place theory and the principle of concentrated public facilities inducing growth prevail. In southern countries (France and Italy), the theory of growth poles has led to a different concept of regional policy (EFTA, 1971; OECD, 1974).

Western European Comparisons

The industrialization of nonmetropolitan regions, which has never been very intensive in Western Europe except in some particular areas (for instance, coastal regions and areas situated along main rivers), has produced important social changes in the communities.

The far–reaching changes in the employment and settlement structure of many problem regions inevitably require substantial and sometimes painful adjustment by individuals to a new situation. A change of jobs may mean that workers, many of them no longer young, have to face a major change in their work habits. The discipline and routine of factory work may prove irritating after work on the land, where the length of working day and the nature of the daily tasks vary according to the seasons. The less arduous work of the factory may result in a substantial change of values. Workers may have to acquire new skills and may face considerably longer journeys to work than they have been accustomed to in the past. Moreover, when people have to leave communities to which they feel strong ties of family, custom, or language and to establish new relationships in unfamiliar surroundings, the changes can be painful.

Although the heaviest impact of declining employment may be over, any further decline may take many small communities, which are not near larger towns, below the threshold of activity necessary for continued existence. The ability of such small centers to attract new employment is very limited. Their labor reserves are too small for the majority of firms seeking a new location, and they lack those services demanded by industry and workers alike. The growing size of firms, such as multinational corporations, and plants and the growing importance of urban services in personal expenditure patterns mean that the smaller centers, unless they are reasonably accessible to a larger center, are likely to remain unattractive both to industry and people. To some extent, their future will depend upon the settlement pattern within the region where they are situated and the role they play in the hierarchy of centers.

Some research has been addressed to the advantages and disadvantages of the passive regional renewal development model, which is a policy promoting out-migration from depressed and underdeveloped areas into other regions, especially into small centers. This practice tends to produce subregional areas that have a population density corresponding to the regional carrying capacity and residual areas of agriculture and forestry and offer only basic infrastructure facilities. Adoption of this model on a reduced scale in subregional areas is intended to prevent large-scale passive regional renewal characterized by depopulation of larger areas.

Community changes take place not only in the center where industrial enterprises locate but also in the communities within the commuting zone. The communities where the commuters reside are particularly confronted with a new way of life and behavior, and the noncommuting population is affected by it as well. The residents of these communities increase their mobility not only for the journey to work but also for other basic functions, such as recreation, education, goods supply, and services. This evolution induces an enlargement of the living space of the rural population, the so-called process of scale-enlargement (*Prozeb der Mass-stabsvergrosserung*).

Industrialization is not the only factor of community change in nonmetropolitan regions, and perhaps not the most important one. The expansion of second homes, summer cottages, weekend recreation, and tourism exert a strong influence. Moreover, telecommunication suggests permanently new behavioral and consumption patterns, which also induce community changes in rural areas. For the residents of rural communities, there is a growing temptation to imitate urban life-styles.

References

Amnesi, M. *Nuove Tendenze dell' Intervento Publico nel Mezzogiorno.* Foma, 1973.

Bockelmann, D.; Hemberger, H.; and Hübener, A. *Raumordnung in den Mitgliedstaaten der Europäischen Gemeinschaften, in Österreich und in der Schweiz.* Schriftenreihe "Raumordnung" des Bundesminsters für Raumordnung, Bauwesen and Städtebau, 06.014. Bonn, 1977.

Boudeville, J. R. *L'espace et les Poles de Croissance.* Paris, 1968.

Christaller, W. *Die zentralen Orte in Suddendeutschland.* Jena: 1933.

Coyand, L. M. *L'urbanisation des Campagnes.* Paris: Centre de Recherche d'Ursbanisme, 1973.

Durand, P. *Industrie et régions.* Paris: Documentation Française, 1972.

EFTA. *Regional Policy in EFTA. Industrial Mobility,* 1971.

Emanuel, A. *Issues of Regional Policies.* Paris: OECD, 1973.

Fester, F. "Alternativen der Entwicklungspolitik für periphere Regionen." *Stadtbauwelt* 52 December 1976.

———. "Entwicklungszentren—Urbanisierung peripherer Regionen statt Industriealisierung des ländlichen Raumes." *Informationen zur Raumentwicklung,* H. ⅔. Bonn 1976.

Hayward, J., and Watson, Michael, eds. *Planning, Politics and Public Policy: The British, French and Italian Experience.* Cambridge: Cambridge University Press, 1975.

Heidtmann, W.; Heumann, J. J.; and Altkrüger, W. "Entwicklungszentren in Schwerpunkträumen mit besonderen Struktruschwächen." Schriftenreihe "Raumordnung" des Bundesministers für Raumordnung, Bauwesen and Städtebau, 06.006. Bonn, 1976.

Heidtmann, W., et al. "Entwichlungsschwerpunkte in landlichen Problemgebieten." *Schriftenreihe "Raumordnung" des Bundesministers für Raumordnung, Bauwesen und Städtebau,* 06.001. Bonn, 1974.

Hellber, H.; Müller–Maas, D.; and Wullkopf, U., "Die Entwicklung der Siedlungstruktur in Europa." *Schriftenreihe "Raumordnung" des Bundesministers für Raumordnung, Bauwesen und Städtebau,* 06.015. Bonn, 1977.

Klemmer, P. and Kraemer, D. *Regionale Arbeitsmärkte.* Bochum: 1975.

Losch, A. *Die raumliche Ordning der Weltwirtschaft,* 3rd. ed. Stuttgart: 1962.

Marx, D. "Zur Konzeption ausgeglichener Funktionsräume als Grundlage einer Regionalpolitik des Mittleren Weges, *Forschungs- und Sitzungsberichte der Akademie fur Raumforschung und Landesplanning,* 94 (1975): 18.

OECD. *Re-appraisal of Regional Policies in OECD Countries.* Paris: OECD, 1974.

Pascalon, P. "Il faut envisager d'emblée une politique de developement rural modernisée soucieuse d'operer un couplage agriculture—industrie." *Bulletin de Conatef,* no. 253 (1978).

Perroux, L. "L'economie du XX Siècle," *Les Poles de Croissance,* 2 (1961).

Prud'homme, R. "Critique de la politique d'aménagement du territoire." *Revue d'Economie Politique,* no. 6 (1974): 921–935.

Rijksplanologische Dienst. *Ruimtelijke Vraagstukken van de Landelijke Gebieden.* Den Haag, 1977.

Part II
Bringing Jobs to People

6 Implications of the Dual Economy for Community Economic Change

Robert T. Averitt

The Emergence of an Urban Ebb Tide

Most Americans share a general impression that the decade of the 1960s represents a watershed in our social and economic lives. The 1970s are witnessing the emergence of new patterns. We have reached a turning point without a clear understanding of why we are turning and where we are going. The direction of American social life in the 1970s seems qualitatively different from the path we trod for over a century, yet the differences are difficult to pin down. The 1960s brought another major war, yet periodic wars are a well-established part of the American experience. The first half of the 1970s witnessed the beginning of a serious economic recession, but the recovery was relatively prompt and the severity of economic decline was no match for the misery of the 1930s. The economic influence of government continued to spread, but it had been growing for a generation. Still few can doubt that the 1970s mark a change in the way that Americans perceive their economic future.

One aspect of the changed American perception during the 1970s is statistically clear: big cities are losing their allure. Americans are moving back to the country and deserting the largest urban places for the first time in the nation's history. The migration from rural areas to American cities has a long history, but during the thirty years between 1940 and 1970, the shift to urban residence became a flood. The U.S. farm population dropped from 30 million in 1940 to 9 million in 1970.[1] For many rural communities, this massive human desertion was devastating. Farms lost a net of a million people annually through out-migration during the 1940s and 1950s. Because of low urban birthrates in the 1920s and 1930s and the virtual absence of foreign immigration, American cities lacked an ample supply of labor. Meanwhile the industrialization of agriculture was displacing millions. Yet the possibilities for migration from rural farming, mining, and forest areas were not unlimited. The last year that the farm population dropped by a million through net out-migration was 1962. The drop in coal mining employment had ended by 1969. By 1970 the urbanization process seemed to be exhausted, with but a fourth of the U.S. population remaining in rural areas. In 1920 roughly half of all Americans had called a rural area their home.

The urban tide began to flow out during the 1970s. From 1970 to 1975, nonmetropolitan population increased by 6.6 percent, while metropolitan growth was limited to a 4.1 percent rise. In addition, 40 percent of the total increase in nonfarm employment occured in nonmetropolitan areas, expanding their share of total employment to over 25 percent. (See table 6-1.) Even during the depression of the 1930s metropolitan growth exceeded the pace of nonmetropolitan growth. The recent expansion of nonmetropolitan areas cannot be explained by comparative rates of natural population increase. The bright lights of the largest American cities are simply growing dim. Nearly 2 million people moved from the metropolitan to nonmetropolitan areas during the first half of the 1970s. The urban tide is indeed flowing out. The same areas experienced a 3 million net migration to the cities from the countryside as recently as the 1960s. In every American region except the South, the nonmetropolitan population grew more rapidly than its metropolitan counterpart; its growth rate between 1970 and 1975 varied between 3.4 percent in the North Central states and 13.4 percent in the West (see figure 6-1.)

Table 6-1
Job Changes in Nonmetropolitan and Metropolitan Areas, 1970-1977 [a]

Designation	Nonmetropolitan [b]		Metropolitan	
	Thousands	*Percent*	*Thousands*	*Percent*
Mining	148	36	43	20
Construction	262	32	−47	−2
Manufacturing	323	6	−1,085	−7
Transportation, communications, and utilities	126	14	−14	[c]
Trade	1,007	30	2,039	18
Finance, insurance, and real estate	183	34	547	18
Services	916	39	2,562	28
Government	858	23	1,770	20
Total	3,823	22	5,815	11

Source: C. C. Haren, "Where the Jobs Are," *Farm Index,* Economic Research Service, U.S. Department of Agriculture (August 1977): 20-21. Reproduced from Kenneth L. Deavers, "Rural Conditions and Regional Differences" (prepared for a conference, "A National Policy toward Regional Change: Alternatives to Confrontation," Austin, Texas, September 24-27, 1977).

[a] Adapted from State Employment Security Agency estimates for March in respective years, seasonally adjusted.

[b] Includes some fifty smaller Standard Metropolitan Statistical Areas but excludes approximately 330 rural and other fringe counties.

[c] Less than 0.5 percent decrease.

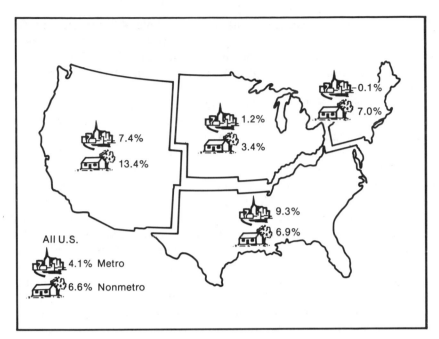

Source: Kenneth L. Deavers, "Rural Conditions and Regional Differences" (Prepared for "A National Policy toward Regional Change: Alternatives to Confrontation," Austin, Texas, September 24–27, 1977).

Figure 6–1. Regional Growth, 1970–1975 (Percentage Change).

In the Northeast, the movement is toward northern New England, the Catskills, the Poconos, and the Atlantic coast. In the North Central states, areas of rapid nonmetropolitan growth concentrate in north country counties, plus the Missouri Ozarks. Most counties in the Great Plains and western corn belt continue to lose population. Rapidly growing nonmetropolitan areas in the South include the northern Piedmont, the southern Appalachian coalfields, the Blue Ridge area, the Florida peninsula, the lower Tennessee Valley, the Arkansas Ozarks, the Oachita Mountains, and the central Texas hill country. Counties with high proportions of black residents, such as the delta and the Alabama black belt, continue to experience net out–migration. In 1970 about 44 percent of the nation's poor lived in nonmetropolitan areas. Between 1970 and 1974, the percentage of the poverty population residing in these areas decreased by about 20 percent.

From the beginning of World War II until 1970s, the American population became increasingly concentrated in cities. Now the population is sifting down; smaller urban areas and the countryside are gaining relative to large cities. The rate of population growth of rural areas (5.6 percent from

1970–1974) is greater than for the nation as a whole (4.7 percent) and for metropolitan areas 3.4 percent). The larger the city, the greater the magnitude of human retreat. The eight largest American cities alone lost 1.2 percent of their residents through net out-migration during the first four years of the 1970s.

How are we to explain the abrupt end of the American love affair with the city? One careful study suggests that the growth of nonmetropolitan areas can be explained along three basic dimensions.[2] The first is the increasing accessibility to the national system of cities provided by the recent advances in transportation and communication. The interstate highway system is now virtually complete, spanning the entire nation from East to West and North to South. The revolution in communications and data processing is even more impressive. The *Wall Street Journal* can transit news items from Chicopee, Massachusetts, to Hong Kong by satellite in a matter of seconds. A plastics plant in Northampton, Massachusetts, is in daily contact with its corporate owner in Sweden.

The technology of communications and the social capital of the interstate transportation network have corroded the geographic definition of city. Under this view, the question about why Americans and industrial jobs are leaving the city might be answered, "Because the terms *urban* and *rural* no longer have precise meanings." Geographic boundaries no longer separate the urban from the rural in terms of transportation time or communications access. Social and economic reality has outgrown our system of geographic classification.

A second commonly noted cause for the movement back to the countryside is a significant change in the American life–style. We now have a large and growing elderly population. In 1940 the average life expectancy was 62.5 years. It now stands at 69.0 for men and 77.0 for women. Furthermore the post–World War II baby boom will become a senior citizen boom during the next century. By 2030, some 55 million people, almost one person in five, will be 65 years old or older. Early retirement is expanding the number of older Americans who are free to live wherever they wish. Thirty years ago, almost half of all men over 65 were still working. Today only one man in five over 65 is still working or seeking work.

Demographic changes alone would enable a number of retirement communities to develop and prosper where the air is clear and the temperature mild. But the most significant economic change affecting most older Americans is the fact that the retirement years are now well funded. The six major programs for the elderly run by the Department of Health, Education, and Welfare—old age insurance, survivors' and disability insurance, Medicare and Medicaid, Supplemental Security Income, and black lung benefits—will pay out more than $94 billion to Americans over 65 this year. Another $14 billion will be paid to this group under civil service, railroad, and military retirement programs. These government programs alone add up to $112 billion, or 5 percent of the gross national product and 24 percent of the federal budget for 1978. When private retirement benefits are added to the state and federal funds flowing to the elderly, it is clear that we now have an enormous number of persons receiving significant incomes with a built-in partial protection from cost-of-living increases. When these persons choose to live in rural areas, they bring with them a large and growing market. If current policies remain unchanged, the elderly will be receiving 40 percent of the federal budget by 2025. Many of these persons are returning to the hamlets they knew during their childhood, but they are returning with the savings of a lifetime of urban and suburban work and the income promised them by four decades of social legislation.

That technological change has blurred the formerly clear boundaries between urban and rural life cannot be denied. The revolution in communications has been so complete that it is increasingly difficult to be truly out of touch with the urban world anywhere in America. Life-styles have also changed. The elderly are footloose, increasingly numerous, and comparatively prosperous. Rising incomes tend to increase the leisure activities orientation of most Americans, whatever their age. And a century of industrial growth has left a residue of inherited income that allows a large number of relatively young Americans to flee the city, seeking a refuge from stagflation. For a very large percentage of Americans, a livable level of income is no longer tied to active urban employment, or indeed to steady employment of any kind. When these persons leave the city, bringing their income with them, they unquestionably bring the impetus for a resurgence of rural and small-town prosperity.

Economic and Industrial Trends

I will devote my major attention here to the economic and industrial trends that underlie the return to the countryside. I do so because the first two factors, important as they are, can be called permissive in their influence. People and jobs may now move farther from the urban center without a loss of urban contact because of major improvements in transportation and communication advances. But the new technology and facilities do not compel individual persons or business firms to do so. The retired and the affluent young are free to migrate away from urban life, but during most of our history, they lacked the desire to do so. A shifting of migration patterns away from the trends that have prevailed throughout the United States' history must surely involve forces stronger than easy access to formerly remote areas and the ability to choose a place of residence without close regard for a source of sustaining income. Large numbers of individual

Americans are choosing to leave their urban residences of many years and establish a less urban existence. Industrial firms are choosing to expand outside the conveniences of urban and even suburban centers. The discovery that they can do so does not tell us why they are doing so.

Part of the answer to industrial relocation can be found in the emergence of OPEC and the quadrupling of oil prices. Large-scale, energy-related industrial development is reviving the local economies of several nonmetropolitan areas, most notably the Rocky Mountain states. Several researchers have studied the recent surge in industrial decentralization. Rodney Erickson and Thomas Leinbach assert that industrial activity tends to filter down through the system or urban places from cities of greater to places of lesser industrial sophistication.[3] They attribute this filtering-down phenomenon to the movement of the product cycle. According to this hypothesis, industrial products go through three distinct phases. The first phase is one of research and development. When new products are being developed, scientific and engineering skills are of critical importance, and these tend to concentrate in the city.

During the second or growth phase, markets must be established. Here the price elasticity of demand for the product takes center stage. Mass-production techniques are gradually introduced, and capital plays a growing role. A buyers' market slowly develops, the less efficient firms leave the market, and successful marketing techniques become decisive. Once again the city holds an edge. Sophisticated management personnel, like scientists and engineers, are found in abundance only in cities. In the third or mature phase, the technology of production stabilizes. The product emerges from long production runs characterized by capital-intensive techniques. Large capital requirements and highly sophisticated merchandizing dictate that only a small number of usually large firms survive. Finally unskilled and semiskilled labor emerge as the critical human elements. An urban environment is no longer essential to production, since low-skill labor is often abundant in the countryside.

What was once a new product becomes a commodity. In this final stage, the corporate hierarchy alters the geographic location of production to minimize costs and thereby ensure competitiveness and market share in a tightening commercial environment. Automobile assembly fits this broad pattern, as does the more recent evolution of hand-held calculators.

Erickson and Leinbach collected data on plant locations during the 1967-1976 period for nonmetropolitan counties in four states—Kentucky, New Mexico, Vermont, and Wisconsin. They found that only 14 percent of the branch plants filtered down to locations in the urban field. Less than 40 percent of the branch plants filtered down to nonmetropolitan locations within 250 miles. Approximately 60 percent were located within 500 miles of the corporate headquarters and/or main plants. Beyond the 500-mile radius, filtering-down plants tended to produce finished products, such as food and animal feeds, chemicals, machinery, building and construction products, and complete units of electrical equipment. The major cost savings came from labor and fixed operating expenses (such as land, buildings, and taxes). Locations were chosen with the intent to minimize competition for the available labor pool.

The Dual Economy and Geographic Dualism

By dividing the American geography into metropolitan and nonmetropolitan regions, we are postulating a geographic dualism. The metropolis is characterized by a large and dense population linked by a shared network of transportation and communication facilities. The city is roughly defined by a common public school system, police force and fire department, and the possibility of making toll-free telephone calls within the metropolitan boundary. The city has at least one and probably two major newspapers, several television stations, and large hospitals providing a broad range of medical care. It is the home of sophisticated goods and services of all kinds. Metropolitan America can be seen as a system of cities, with the level of sophistication and diversity declining as city size decreases. The largest cluster of American cities can be found in the manufacturing belt, which covers the Northeast quadrant of the United States and stretches from St. Louis and Minneapolis on the western edge to Baltimore and Boston on the eastern rim. The overwhelming majority of large American corporations have established their headquarters within this belt.

In *The Dual Economy* I pointed out that American manufacturing and retailing firms also fall easily into a dual pattern: the center business system and the periphery system.[4] Like the city, the center system is the home of economic sophistication. It is composed of very large corporations having numerous distinct operating units managed by a hierarchy of salaried executives. Center manufacturers employ the latest in research, product development, and advertising techniques. Their labor force is usually unionized and is well paid. These firms tend to dominate the key industries in manufacturing. They sell in national and international markets, and their superior credit rating makes both long-term and short-term borrowing relatively easy and inexpensive.

The periphery business system corresponds more closely to the relatively disadvantaged geography of nonmetropolitan areas. It is composed of comparatively small firms usually managed by a single individual or family. The periphery firm's sales are realized in a geographically restricted market. The most sophisticated techniques of research, innovation, and advertising are often beyond reach. Production is usually less capital intensive and less energy intensive. Before 1840 virtually all American business firms fit the periphery pattern, engaging in production techniques and selling in markets closely akin to those described by Adam Smith in *The Wealth of Nations.*

From Pheriphery to Center

The history of American business, then, is the history of the developing center system. The periphery economy represents the residue of economic activity not absorbed into the center, just as nonmetropolitan America represents the geography that remained after the American system of cities staked out its terrain. That the pattern of American urban geography coincides with the pattern of American industry is no coincidence. We did not, with rare exception, build our cities and then surround them with industrial parks. Instead we allowed linked industrial complexes to form, attracting to themselves large pools of laborers and dependents. In the manufacturing belt, a concentration of industry attracted the talent and facilities that we then recognized as constituting a city.

In *The Invisible Hand* our premier business historian, Alfred D. Chandler, Jr., has chronicled the evolution of the center economy.[5] The center business system replaced the periphery economy when administrative coordination permitted greater productivity, lower costs, and higher profits than did the coordination of economic activity through traditional market mechanisms. The center thrives on a high volume of production. Where nineteenth- and early twentieth-century technology increased the volume of productive activity in industries where enlarged markets could be created for the faster pace of goods throughout, the center firm appeared, expanded, and flourished. Where technology did not develop a sharp increase in output, thus allowing markets to remain small and specialized, the coordination of economic activity by markets composed of small firms remained viable.

In 1832 Louis McLane, the U.S. secretary of the treasury, authorized a survey of domestic manufacturing. The McLane report describes a system of production conducted by a large number of small units employing fewer than fifty workers still relying on traditional sources of energy—falling water, wind, amimals, and humans. Until the opening of the anthracite coalfields in eastern Pennsylvania, a lack of inexpensive coal constituted the major technological constraint to the production speed-up characterizing an industrial economy. The delivery of cheap coal on the eastern seaboard, first by canal and then by railraod, permitted the factory system to spread quickly among the metalworking industries. By the middle of the nineteenth century, the use of coal, iron, and machinery permitted the building of large steam-driven factories in commercial centers, forming urban markets and attracting large pools of labor. After the Civil War, the abundance of coal and the widening development of coal-using technologies accelerated the pace of production, just as the railroad and telegraph were beginning to transform the means of transportation and communication. The concurrent arrival of an abundant new source of energy and revolutionary means of transportation and communication created a fertile environment for the rise of the center business system.

We often associate the advantages enjoyed by big business with monopoly or with economies of scale, but the center economy relies largely upon economies of speed. A high volume of stock turnover ensures a steady cash flow, which permits the purchase of large quantities of inventory for cash and greatly reduces the cost of credit. These savings are possible only if the flow of goods through the enterprise is rapid and carefully coordinated. To be successful, the center enterprise must make internal transactions more quickly and in greater volume than would be possible if many small firms were producing for sale in isolated markets. Economies of speed result from the development of new machinery, a steady, assured flow of raw materials, and the intensified application of concentrated energy from fossil fuels. The center firm is an institution created to coordinate and control the high volume of input and output flowing through a linked production process and on to a multitude of consumers. It is increases in the volume and velocity of throughput, not the growth of factory or plant size, that increases the productivity of work and decreases unit costs.

Heirarchy of Production Types and Industry Shifts

For purposes of analysis, manufacturing can be broken down into three production types.[6] The earliest type is unit and small-batch production. Here production is predominantly craft oriented. Production schedules are based on orders received. Salespeople sell ideas and technical potential, not a finished product. The products are customized, so cost per unit is inevitably high. Before the middle of the nineteenth century, virtually all American manufacturing fell into this category, and many important industries still do. Examples include prototype aircraft and dies from the machine tool industry. As the market expands, the production of numerous products rises into a new category—large batch and mass production. Automobile production is probably the most familiar example in this class. The short-run profit of the firms in large-batch and mass-production markets depends largely on productive efficiency (reduction of costs), although long-run prosperity depends on creative development and marketing as well. Production becomes capital intensive and energy intensive, so that costs can be minimized by speeding the flow of product and thus lowering the fixed cost that must be borne by each unit. The newest production type, process production, becomes increasingly important in a fully industrialized economy. When a manufacturing procedure can be converted to continuous material flow, it is a candidate for process production. Originating with the manufacture of liquids, gases, and crystalline substances, it is now spreading to solid shapes—steel, aluminum, and engineering parts. Outside of manufacturing, the communications industry is a prime example of process production. The message flows through an extremely capital-intensive network. Unit costs, the cost per television program viewer or per minute of telephone conversation, can be extremely small when the network is used to capacity. Unskilled workers are not an important cost in process production.

When the product can be made to flow, the need for legions of low-skill labor is greatly reduced. Production becomes largely automatic (in the case of communications, delivery becomes automatic), so that cost reductions depend most heavily on plant load—another name for sales. The historic thrust in the American economy, as in any other industrializing system, has been away from unit and small-batch production into mass production and then onward to continuous-flow techniques. The ability of a specific industry to shift upward through the hierarchy of production types depends on the physical nature of the product. Automobiles and trucks can be placed on moving belts during assembly, but they cannot be made to flow like a liquid, a gas, or a radio wave. Thus automobile production remains lodged at the upper reaches of mass production, using a technique that is energy and capital intensive but at the same time using a large quantity of low-skill labor.

The product cycle as explored by Erickson and Leinbach charts the movement of a specific item—for example, automobiles or hand-held calculators—up the production hierarchy toward mass production or process production, with the upper limits of this journey determined by the physical characteristics of the item being produced and sold. Moving from the unit and small-batch stage to mass or process techniques, the item in question ceases to be a product and becomes a commodity. During the transition, the item slides down its demand curve, expanding its potential market and cutting production costs by utilizing the economies of speed. The industrial journey from product to commodity is a familiar one, which has touched a multitude of manufactured items.

But the evolution of a specific item is closely bounded by its physical characteristics. Petroleum can easily be made to flow through a refining complex, so its refining enjoys the economies of speed characteristic of process procedures. But trucks and automobiles cannot flow during manufacture, they must be pulled. Thus the final stage of the product cycle is determined for each product by its physical limitations. If the entire economic system is to continue its movement down the price curve because it is moving up the ladder of improving productivity, aggregate demand must shift from those products that have realized their cost-minimizing potential toward those areas where large productivity gains, and thus unit cost reductions, are still possible. Once the full economies of providing transportation have been realized, communication must be substituted for transportation if productivity is to continue its vigorous growth. The development of an information-rich economy simply represents the shift from physical goods to information as manufacturing techniques begin to realize their full physical potential.

Specific products do experience a kind of life cycle, moving from the research and development stage to the market introduction of a product to the final state of becoming a commonly used commodity. But some products cannot evolve to the final stage of process production. They never enjoy mass markets because of their physical characteristics and because they are not suited to mass consumption. Large corporate enterprises are most successful in those industries where high-volume stock turnover assures a steady cash flow and reduces borrowing needs while improving credit ratings and lowering the cost of the borrowing, which is unavoidable.

The Industrial Shift and Urban Retreat

The industrialization process produces its own long-run cycle, shifting the growth of final demand from one industry to another as products within each industry begin to reach maturity. The National Science Board of the National Science Foundation divided fifteen broad manufacturing industries into group I industries with high research and development intensity between 1961 and 1974, group II industries having medium R&D intensity, and group III industries with low R&D intensity.[7] (See table 6-2). Group I industries enjoyed total net sales over the thirteen-year period that were 23 percent above the sales of group II and 48 percent above group III sales. A high level of research and development is clearly associated with a high level of sales.

Throughout the history of American industry, the cities have served as the seedbeds of industrial development. If my industrial shift thesis is correct, we should expect that those cities most closely identified with the older industrial growth preceding the current revolution in chemicals and electrical equipment (particularly in electronics) should be undergoing a decline as a result of both filtering down, where producers seek cheap labor in the last phase of the product cycle, and the relative decline in traditional manufacturing sectors.

Table 6–2
Measures of Research and Development Intesity, by Industry, 1961–1974

	Mean over the 1961–1974 Period		
Manufacturing Industry	R&D Scientists and Engineers per 1,000 Employees	Total Funds For R&D as a Percent of Net Sales	Company Funds[a] for R&D as a Percent of Net Sales
Group I			
Chemicals and allied products	37.8	3.8	3.4
Machinery	26.1	3.9	3.2
Electrical equipment and communication	46.1	8.2	3.6
Aircraft and missiles[b]	85.4	19.1	3.3
Professional and scientific instruments	33.8	5.8	4.2
Mean for group 1	46.1	7.7	3.4
Group II			
Petroleum refining and extraction	15.8	0.8	0.8
Rubber products	17.4	1.9	1.6
Stone, clay, and glass products	10.8	1.6	1.5
Fabricated metal products	12.2	1.3	1.2
Motor vehicles and other transpor- transportation equipment	19.8	3.3	2.6
Mean for group II	14.4	1.9	1.2
Group III			
Food and kindred products	7.1	0.4	0.4
Textiles and apparel	3.1	0.5	0.4 [c]
Lumber, wood products, and furniture	5.0	0.5	0.4 [c]
Paper and allied products	8.3	0.8	0.8 [c]
Primary metals	5.5	0.7	0.7
Mean for group III	6.0	0.6	0.4

Source: National Science Board, National Science Foundation, *Science Indicators, 1976* (Washington, D.C.: NSF, 1976).

[a] Includes all sources other than the federal government.

[b] Includes ordnance.

[c] Data for company funds are not available for several years. Mean computed using only those years for which data are available.

R.D. Norton has dramatically illustrated the pronounced deterioration of the economic base of the older industrial cities located in the American manufacturing belt.[8] (See tables 6–3 and 6–4.) Professor Norton ranked the metropolitan areas of our thirty largest cities by the size of their population

Table 6–3
Estimated Real Per–Capita Income, 1974

City, by Size of Real Income	Real Income [a]	Intermediate Budget Index [b]	Per–Capita Money Income
Denver	$5,880	95	$5,585
Dallas	5,870	90	5,285
Seattle	5,740	101	5,800
Houston	5,680	90	5,110
San Francisco	5,650	106	5,990
Los Angeles	5,380	98	5,277
San Diego	5,120	98	5,016
Nashville	5,060	91	4,606
Atlanta	4,980	91	4,527
Indianapolis	4,890	99	4,843
Kansas City	4,740	97	4,601
Cincinnati [c]	4,700	96	4,517
Pittsburgh	4,560	97	4,426
Chicago	4,550	103	4,689
Detroit	4,460	100	4,463
Milwaukee	4,460	105	4,680
Baltimore	4,330	100	4,330
New York	4,260	116	4,939
Philadelphia	4,200	103	4,330
St. Louis	4,130	97	4,006
Cleveland	3,850	102	3,925
Buffalo	3,670	107	3,928
Boston	3,550	117	4,157

Source: R.D. Norton, *City Life–Cycles and American Urban Policy* (New York: Academic Press, forthcoming). Reprinted with permission.

[a] Equals column 3 divided by column 2 and rounded to the nearest $10.

[b] Urban United States equals 100.

[c] Cincinnati is the median.

in 1910. (See table 6–5 and figure 6–2.) The dozen cities having the largest populations in 1910 can be termed old industrial cities, since they served as focal centers for the industrialization of the late nineteenth century. The smallest cities in 1910 can be termed young, since their major development occurred after the major industrialization drive. A half-dozen cities are called anamalous, since they do not clearly belong to either period.

During the twenty–five years after 1947, the older Standard Metropolitan Statistical Areas (SMSAs) failed to generate a net addition to manufacturing employment, but the younger cities scored large gains in manufacturing and in private sector employment. Between 1950 and 1970, there was on balance no net migration of whites to the older cities, long before their

Table 6–4
A F D C Recipients in Large City–Counties, February 1977

City, by A F D C Share	Number[a]	Percentage of Estimated 1975 City Population[b]
St. Louis	86,000	16.4
Baltimore	133,000	15.7
Philadelphia	269,000	14.8
Boston	99,000	13.7
Washington	95,000	13.4
New York	844,000	11.3
New Orleans	61,000	11.0
San Francisco	50,000	7.6
Denver	35,000	7.3
Indianapolis	40,000	5.1
Jacksonville	26,000	4.7
Nashville	19,000	4.4

Source: R.D. Norton, *City Life–Cycles and American Urban Policy* (New York: Academic Press, forthcoming). Reprinted with permission.

[a]Numbers are rounded to the nearest thousand.

[b]The U.S. average is 5.3.

total population began to decline. As the older industries reach economic maturity, the cities that they supported begin to decline. Metropolitan areas of 3 million or more are experiencing net out–migration, as are cities of 1 to 3 million in the older manufacturing belt centered in the Northeast and North Central regions.

In a careful study of manufacturing employment over the 1939–1954 period, Perloff and associates found that the rapidly growing manufacturing industries continued to find their most favorable location in the old manufacturing belt.[9] But in a recent study of the 1963–1972 period, John Rees discovered that the manufacturing belt suffered in comparison with the newer peripheral regions.[10] The manufacturing seedbed seems to have shifted to the South and the West. The leading growth sector, electronics, experiences large competitive losses in both value added and employment from 1963 to 1972 in the New England, mid–Atlantic, and East North Central areas, as well as in the Pacific area, but large competitive gains in the South Atlantic, East South Central, and West South Central regions. The same was true for the other high–technology sectors—scientific instruments, transportation equipment, and plastics.

Table 6–5
Correlates of Population Growth in the Thirty Largest Cities, 1950–1975
(*Percentage Changes*)

Age Class	City, by 1910 Metropolitan Size	City Population	SMSA Population [a]	City Territory
Industrial	New York	− 5	5	0
	Chicago	− 14	35	7
	Philadelphia	− 12	31	1
	Boston	− 21	54	0
	Pittsburgh	− 32	5	2
	St. Louis	− 39	32	0
	San Francisco	− 14	46	2
	Baltimore	− 10	47	0
	Cleveland	− 30	29	1
	Buffalo	− 30	22	5
	Detroit	− 28	40	0
	Cincinnati	− 18	35	4
Anomalous	Los Angeles	38	67	3
	Washington	− 11	97	0
	Milwaukee	4	41	90
	Kansas City	3	4	292
	New Orleans	− 2	54	0
	Seattle	4	67	18
Young	Indianapolis	67	58	580
	Atlanta	32	104	256
	Denver	17	128	70
	Columbus	42	69	338
	Memphis	67	50	169
	Nashville	143	50	2208
	Dallas	87	110	176
	San Antonio	89	80	279
	Houston	123	142	206
	Jacksonville	162	93	2436
	San Diego	131	185	225
	Phoenix	522	267	1499
Means and Significance of Mean Differences				
Industrial Cities		− 21	32	2
Young cities		124	111	704
Differences		145	80	702
Significance		0.003	0.001	0.02

Source: R.D. Norton, *City Life-Cycles and American Urban Policy* (New York: Academic Press, forthcoming). Reprinted with permission.

[a]1975 SMSA territorial definitions have been used to measure 1950 as well as 1975 SMSA population.

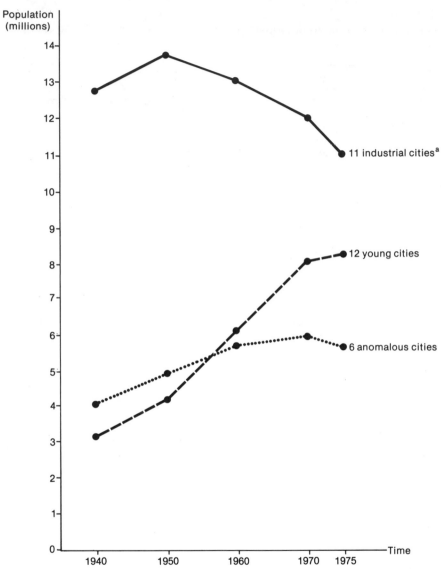

Source: R.D. Norton, *City Life–Cycles and American Urban Policy* (New York: Academic Press, forthcoming). Reprinted with permission.

[a]Excluding New York City.

Figure 6–2. Aggregated City Population Growth Trajectories, 1940–1975.

Public Sector Growth Effects

The public sector has grown rapidly in the recent period. In 1960, public spending at all levels of government—federal, state, and local—amounted to 32.8 percent of national income. By 1975, this proportion had increased to 43.4 percent. Since the 1964 federal tax reduction, increases in government spending have absorbed nearly 50 percent of the increases in national income. The rapid increase in government's share of national income has coincided with a very rapid rate of inflation. It is estimated that a 10 percent rate of general inflation generates roughly a 15 percent increase in federal tax collections.[11] Although the level of state and local taxation differs radically among states, Massachusetts provides a particularly vivid example of the tax lien on persons living in the older manufacturing belt. Massachusetts takes about 18 percent of the personal income of its residents. Before taxes, Massachusetts ranks tenth in personal income among the states. After taxes it ranks forty-eighth.

The combination of rapid inflation and high business taxes take a particularly heavy toll on the older, capital-intensive industrial sectors. The profits of these enterprises are taxed on the basis of the original cost of their capital. Since inflation has dramatically increased the replacement cost of capital equipment, these firms are being taxed on the basis of what might be termed phantom profits. As the capital goods currently in use depreciate, many large firms in older industries are unable to generate enough internal cash flow to finance the necessary capital replacement. We should not be surprised to discover that these firms are filtering down to states and localities where the cost of living is lower and where the state and local tax rate is less steep. What we are witnessing is the progressive capture by government of the economies of speed that enabled the large firms of the center economy to enjoy the advantages of a plentiful and assured cash flow during an earlier economic era. As a partial consequence, the stock market has become a one-tier market, with price-earnings ratios for a wide range of companies clustered in the mid-range, between five and fifteen. Over the past five years, the hundred largest companies in the Standard and Poors index of five hundred stocks increased their reported earnings per share at an annual rate of 12.1 percent, while the smallest hundred companies grew only 1.7 percent. Yet the stock market continues to cluster the value of their shares, apparently realizing that in an era of high taxation on phantom profits, the advantages of large size are more token than real.[12]

The Industrial Conference Board estimates that the cost of living in rural areas is about 20 percent lower than in urban areas, with most of the difference accounted for by less expensive housing and public services. The average rural dweller lives in a house that is but 64 percent as expensive as housing in the city. Given the level of marginal federal tax rates on money incomes bloated by inflation, the earnings necessary to pay a 20 percent higher living cost far exceeds 20 percent. For many Americans, the easiest avenue to an increased real standard of living is found in migrating back to the countryside. At the same time, the completion of the interstate highway system and the rate averaging practiced by regulated public utilities means that urban taxpayers are helping to enhance the attractiveness of rural and small-town life.

Most of my argument in explanation for the American retreat from the city can be contained in the phrase "escaping the social overhead cost of a mature industrial democracy." The political system is tied to geographic representation in the U.S. Senate, and even the U.S. House adjusts to population changes only after a considerable time lag. Most state legislatures follow the same pattern. The nonmetropolitan areas are well represented in the political process. As the percentage of personal income flowing to the public sector expands, this representation exerts a benign economic influence in the countryside. The social overhead cost of urban living has continued to grow, even as the recent inflation erodes the economies of speed for traditional industries firmly established in the older industrial cities.

The elderly and many of the young are more economically mobile than ever before because of the severing of income from work and the operation of inheritance laws on the fortunes accumulated during decades of industrialization. The revolution in communications and transportation has released the advantages of urban concentration, while traditional boundaries of state and local taxation still tend to localize the tax burden of urban crowding. To this must be added the impact of urban crime and school busing as factors that dim the perceived advantages of urban services once viewed as superior to those available in the countryside. The spillover of urban values has relaxed the moral rigidities of small towns, while the social cost of urban living has soared.

Summary

The older key manufacturing industries of the manufacturing belt were a response to the discovery of new and powerful prime movers in the form of cheap fossil fuels—first coal and then petroleum. The rural economy has taken advantage of these new energy sources, but the cities were based upon them in the most fundamental way. The development of modern heavy manufacturing can be viewed as nothing more than the increasingly sophisticated use of cheap and abundant fossil fuels for a multitude of purposes. The major nineteenth-century economists, from David Ricardo to Karl Marx, viewed goods as so many hours of embodied labor power. The raw materials were free in nature, but it took labor to make these materials available for their most suitable human use. With the discovery and utilization of coal and petroleum as substitute prime movers, the quantity of labor time necessary to produce a rapid outpouring of material goods declined dramatically. The center economy emerged as an institutional device for coordinating this transformation to more rapid product flows, creating large industrial cities in the process.

The social costs of sustaining ever-increasing cities grew from the beginning, but these rising costs were overcome at first by the increasing labor productivity flowing from the economies of speed.[13] A portion of these gains were directed to workers through labor unions and by the high wages made possible by a high-speed productive system. At the same time, government diverted an increasing portion of the nation's productivity gains for national defense and for the provision of social services, including large income transfers to the elderly and to the poor. Interest groups of many kinds formed institutional structures dedicated to directing more of the industrial gains to themselves. Mancur Olson describes the full flowering of this web of interlocking groups as "institutional arthritis."[14] The interlocking institutions that developed during generations of industrialization give up their gains slowly, if at all.

But the shifts of American industry have proceeded at a rapid pace during the 1970s. The energy crisis, marked by capture of petroleum pricing by the OPEC nations, has ended the era of falling energy prices. The new industrial thrust in electronics is potentially energy saving, not energy intensive. When information can be substituted for transportation, for example, the high cost of energy can be partially circumvented. And the peripheral, less-energy-intensive industries left behind by most of the economies of speed tend to reemerge as the cost of petroleum rises more rapidly than the cost of unskilled labor.

The older industrial economy and the older industrial cities face a new economic environment in the 1970s. Institutional arthritis cannot be easily cured; it can only be partially escaped by relatively footloose industries and mobile individuals. As industrial energy becomes increasingly expensive, even the most profitable manufacturing firms must seek to minimize whatever costs it can. With the rapid decline in the dollar since 1971, foreign labor becomes increasingly expensive. Thus the flight to the American countryside begins to emerge as the least-cost alternative in an increasingly costly economic world. The forces of OPEC, government tax and spending policies, the urbanization of the countryside, and the rising social cost of urban living sustained by the social paralysis of institutional arthritis have combined to implement a policy of population dispersal that seemed beyond our collective powers but a decade ago. The economies of speed, having powered the rise of the center economy that I described in 1968, have now shifted their thrust from the manufacturing sectors to the communication and data-processing sphere. The impact of this shift tends to favor geographic dispersal rather than concentration.

Notes

1. Most of the data contained in the next three paragraphs can be found in Kenneth L. Deavers, "Rural Conditions and Regional Differences" (prepared for a conference, "A National Policy toward Regional Change: Alternatives to Confrontation," Austin, Texas, September 24-27, 1977).

2. I refer here to Kevin F. McCarthy and Peter A. Morrison, *The Changing Demographic and Economic Structure of Nonmetropolitan Areas in the 1970's* (Santa Monica, Calif.: Rand Corporation, 1978). The study concludes (P. 47) that "the sharply altered recent patterns of nonmetropolitan migration do not mesh well with conventional theory, which seeks explanations for these patterns in the changing geography of economic opportunity. If migrants are opportunity-seekers in the conventional sense, the fact is not clearly evident in our data, and at least one other study has noted the same paradox."

3. The filtering-down thesis is described as the major influence attracting industrial activities to nonmetropolitan areas in Rodney A. Erickson and Thomas R. Leinbach, "The Filtering-Down Process: Characteristics and Contribution of Industrial Activities Attracted to Nonmetropolitan Areas," in Richard E. Lonsdale and H.L. Seyler, eds., *Nonmetro-industrialization,* (New York: Wiley-Halstead, forthcoming), chap. 4.

4. Robert T. Averitt, *The Dual Economy* (New York: W. W. Norton, 1968).

5. Alfred D. Chandler, Jr., *The Invisible Hand* (Cambridge: Harvard University Press, 1977).

6. An extensive discussion of production types in manufacturing and definition of key manufacturing industries can be found in Averitt, *Dual Economy.*

7. National Science Board, National Science Foundation, *Science Indicators 1976* (Washington, D.C.: Government Printing Office, 1977).

8. R. D. Norton, *City Life-Cycles and American Urban Policy* (New York: Academic Press, forthcoming).

9. According to Harvey S. Perloff, et al., *Regions, Resources, and Economic Growth* (Baltimore: Johns Hopkins University Press, 1960), p. 390, the American South suffered from slow-growth industrial specialization between 1939 and 1954; "the rapid-growth sectors, on the other hand, are concentrated in the Manufacturing Belt states plus Iowa, Minnesota, Arizona, and California."

10. John Rees, "Regional Industrial Shifts in the U.S. and the Internal Generation of Manufacturing Growth in the Southwest" (paper prepared for a conference on Regional Factor Mobility and Economic Development,

Johns Hopkins University, Baltimore, Maryland, May 1978). See also John Rees, "Technological Change and Regional Shifts in American Manufacturing" (paper prepared for the Association of American Geographers Annual Meeting, New Orleans, Louisiana, April 1978).

11. For a good discussion of the political economy of Keynesian inflation, see James N. Buchanan and Richard E. Wagner, *Democracy in Deficit* (New York: Academic Press, 1977). A fascinating analysis of inflation's impact on specific industries and on households can be found in Scott Burns, *Home, Inc.* (Garden City, N.Y.: Doubleday, 1975).

12. Carol J. Loomis, "The Irrational One-Tier Stock Market," *Fortune*, July 31, 1978. The stock market is a much maligned indicator of economic trends. This reputation is curious because the market provides a daily summation of the collective professional judgment rendered by a group of well-educated persons whose livelihood depends upon a generally correct forecast of our immediate economic future. *Fortune* calls the one-tier market "irrational" because the article is unable to come up with an explanation.

13. In 1960. Perloff et. al., *Regions*, p. 396, wrote: "Thus, the modern metropolitan region tends to develop magnet-like attributes. The polarity that it introduces into the nation's economic structure serves to explain why the Manufacturing Belt has remained dominant over a long period." The contemporary problem, of course, is to explain why cities in the manufacturing belt have developed a reverse direction in their magnetic field.

14. Mancur Olson, "The Causes and Quality of Southern Growth" (Research Triangle Park, N.C.: Southern Growth Policies Board, January 1977).

7

A Theory of Nonmetropolitan Growth

Jerald Hage

There is a large amount of work on urban ecology but much less on non-urban ecology, especially at the regional, or what I would like to call the macroecological, levels.[1] Generally researchers have studied how industry affects rural areas but not how an entire rural ecological space may change over time. Impact studies have generally not looked at much larger land areas, such as a third of a state.[2] Much work has been done on the penetration of rural areas by large central cities and the dependence of the former on the latter. It appears that much less has been done on how towns in nonmetropolitan areas are interpenetrating each other. My object here is to look at how large nonmetropolitan areas became integrated or organized and the consequences this has for life in small towns.

Probably the most common thesis about the relationships of cities to each other and of small communities or towns physically near to cities is the principle of hierarchy.[3] This principle has been slightly modified by a second one, called decentralization by ecologists or the process of suburbization. (It might also be called the shopping center thesis.) The idea I wish to advance is that the hierarchy of cities is breaking down; instead nonmetropolitan regions can be characterized by a set of interdependent communities with no single clearly dominant center city. Concomitantly dependence on rural areas in cities will become less. In one sense, this could be called a further step in the process of decentralization, but the real issue is the greater specialization and interdependence of rural communities in nonmetropolitan regions.

Much of the emphasis in urban ecology has been placed on the importance of economic factors. When economic growth takes place in a matrix of urban regions, it spreads from larger cities to smaller centers in a pattern of hierarchical diffusion.[4] Many of the causes of growth are political decisions made by states or the federal government. Beyond this, the advantages of scale, which has been an economic explanation for the concentration of populations in metropolitan areas, have been radically reduced and for a variety of reasons.

Postindustrial society had become a fashionable term, perhaps because the thesis is simple. There has been so much quantitative change with the general processes of urbanization, industrialization, and modernization that there is now a qualitative break with the past. Therefore all institutions of society—family, church, business, and government—must be reconstituted. The same can be said for our theories. Perhaps the word *rural* has no meaning in contemporary postindustrialized societies. Presumedly this is why we find *nonmetropolitan* more to our liking.

Ecological Integration

Defining a nonmetropolitan region is not an easy task. Berry and Kasarda have divided the United States into a series of greater and lesser metropolitan areas on the basis of the location of a central city.[5] But this kind of definition is too restrictive for my purpose. Ideally the definition should be of geographical areas that are larger and encompass several central cities.

This larger definition is true for a number of reasons. How one defines an ecological space has much to do with what results will be obtained. For example, if the emphasis is placed on a single central city, the one is likely to see only the dependence of the hinterland on the central city. But if the nonmetropolitan region includes more than just a few towns and small cities, one can begin to study the interaction patterns among all of the various concentrations of population. Organizational theory is increasingly shifting its emphasis from hierarchies to networks of communication, from vertical to horizontal communication.[6] In the study of nonmetropolitan regions, we at least know when to allow for the possibility of horizontal flows of goods and services between central cities and between towns that are dependent upon different central cities rather than assuming that regions must be defined a priori by hierarchical considerations.

In Europe, it is relatively easy to give a precise definition to the concept of a region because it usually has a geopolitical, linguistic, and/or cultural basis. Thus southern Italy has distinct dialects, and at the beginning of the nineteenth century, it was the Kingdom of Two Sicilies. Bavaria has had, and still has today, a distinct tradition within the context of Germany. Although France has probably done the most to eliminate regional cultural differences, Brittany, the Basque country, and a few other regions are still quite distinct areas.

But in the United States, geopolitical distances are much larger and regions have been arbitrarily defined as a group of states, so the delineation of regional boundaries is more difficult. France has nineteen major regions and eight or nine distinctive subcultural regions, and yet its physical space is equal to the combined size of Wisconsin, and Michigan.

One approach in the United States would be to define boundaries by somewhat similar topology rather than by political lines. For example, the northern half of Wisconsin, the upper peninsula of Michigan, and part of northern Minnesota might be considered a single ecological region. Delmar peninsula in the East is another obvious example. Using geographical similarity would not prejudge necessarily the flow of human beings. Naturally, this would be done only with countries not involving the major Standard Metropolitan Areas (SMAs).

The distance one can travel in two hours is a good rule of thumb for deciding the limits of region in the sense in which I am using the term. Most people find that an hour's trip one way is the upper limit to travel for work. Indeed it is this fact that in many ways sets an upper limit to the spread of the SMA. As long as governments do not improve the speed of public transportation and set limits on availability of roads to central cities, they affect the growth pattern. These guidelines do not solve all problems, but they at least indicate the approximate size of a nonmetropolitan region.

The general thesis is as follows: For a variety of reasons, towns and cities in nonmetropolitan regions are specializing and in the process breaking down the former hierarchy. Nonmetropolitan areas are becoming like wheels in communication networks rather than like trees.[7] As the number of links between various towns and cities increases, we can say that they are interdependent. This idea is interesting because there is a large amount of evidence for this process in communication networks in organizations and status systems in societies.[8] There would appear to be a movement everywhere—including at the level of nonmetropolitan areas—toward what Durkheim nearly a century ago called organic solidarity.[9]

The Political Economy of Nonmetropolitan Regions

The foremost factor causing this movement toward small-town specialization has been state and federal government decisions to establish small public service organizations, specifically university branches and hospitals, in nonmetropolitan areas. A second and almost equally important factor is the movement of manufacturing to small plants located in nonmetropolitan areas and the development of services, especially leisure-time ones, in these same areas. Although working quite independently of each other, both political and economic factors have operated to produce a considerable push to the development of jobs in small towns and cities, but perhaps because the influences are independent and uncoordinated, the growth of a central city has not resulted. Manufacturing plants, new resorts, and the like are *not* being built in a single town. This is the key force toward the development of multiple centers in nonmetropolitan regions as I have defined them.

Political decisions have been made on the basis of making services easily available to everyone. Beyond this, most or many public services do not have clear economies of scale. There are no or few efficiency gains to having a hundred thousand college students taught on a single campus, but there are many political gains to the voters in having a local campus where parents can see their children more often. The political decision is thus easy to make. The great growth in higher education has occurred largely in branch campuses located in small towns or cities. Welfare and health services, and especially hospitals, have equally been decentralized under the impetus of the Hill–Burton Act and for many of the same reasons. There are few economies of scale but great political capital if a hospital is readily available.

Still another growth area is research. Much of it is military in nature and is done by the government or in government–supported facilities that are located in nonmetropolitan communities. The location of the Oak Ridge National Laboratory in Oak Ridge, Tennessee, is well known. Less well known is the National Air Research Center outside Boulder, Colorado, and the *accelerator* in Wheaton, Illinois. Similarly, research centers of various major multinational corporations are being located in nonmetropolitan areas. When five hundred professionals and several thousand support personnel relocate to a rural area, the nature of that community is changed much more than it would be by the opening of a manufacturing plant that needs three thousand unskilled or semiskilled laborers.

During industrialization, plant sizes grow. Indeed the standard explanation for urbanization and the growth of large cities has been the necessity for and the efficiency of large–scale organizations that require large masses of unskilled labor. But large–scale organization is increasingly being conducted in multiple small–scale plants scattered in nonmetropolitan areas. Cars are no longer built only in Detroit, and the meat–packing industry is no longer concentrated in Chicago. Plant sizes have been steadily declining since the late 1950s, and the process does not seem likely to abate.

One reason for this trend is the continual search for cheap labor. Many industries have moved from one large geographical area to another for this reason. More critical has been the fact that as industry becomes technologically intensive, the need for masses of unskilled labor declines. In their stead are needed skilled labor in much smaller quantities, many sales personnel, and a more professional labor force of managers. In turn, smaller plants have become more feasible. Again it is hard to estimate the long–term impact of transportation costs and the energy crisis on the cost benefits of small plants rather than several large ones, but one suspects the trend toward smaller units will continue.

One factor that makes small plants more economical is differentiation of tastes. A college–educated population is concerned about quality of life, which is reflected in their demand for individualized services and a desire for quality above low cost. They want to avoid simple mass–produced items. The consequence for manufacturers is a highly differentiated market that remains small in size relative to any product.

Economic studies indicate that regional balance between the Northeast,

Midwest, South, and West had been largely achieved in the United States.[10] But in these studies, regions are artificial creations that have little to do with regions in Europe where imbalances are much greater. What has not been achieved is a balance between SMAs and rural counties. The logic of cheap labor and good transportation pushes industry from the metropolitan area (where their plants are probably outdated) into nonmetropolitan ones. If all the manufacturer needs is a small number of employees, which is typical of the cases I have shown above, then the choice, dictated by access to raw materials and markets, can be enormous. Therefore the same logic that previously made concentration in the cities desirable is now making movement to nonmetropolitan regions more desirable. Large labor pools are no longer important. The cost of new equipment and plants remains important. Taxes are an even more critical factor affecting costs. Lower costs in rural areas are the main economic inducement to move there; especially when plants become obsolete in metropolitan areas where replacement costs are extremely high. But even in large-scale industry that employs large numbers of semiskilled and unskilled labor (such as the automotive industry), the trend toward physical decentralization is quite profound.

It is in the area of highly technical and machine-intensive industries such as computers, electronics, precision instruments, and the like where I would expect to find the greatest number of small plants. And it is these that are being built in nonmetropolitan regions. There are exceptions, however, such as the concentration of small firms along route 128 outside of Boston and a similar phenomenon in the valley next to San Francisco, but the thrust of my thesis is that plants requiring the latest technology can be built anywhere, and the logic of economic factors gives—in many cases—preference to nonmetropolitan areas.

Nursing homes and retirement villages have been largely left to the private sector. They are an enormous growth industry given the shifting balance of the age structure of the population. For a variety of reasons, these are being located in nonmetropolitan regions in preference to cities, where land and labor costs are high.

Another area with growth, which is quite difficult to measure, is leisure-time activities. Increasingly people have bought cottages on lakes, boats, campers, and other expensive equipment specifically designed for pleasure in nonworking hours. The manufacturing of this equipment tend to be located in many instances in nonmetropolitan areas, and their use requires nonmetropolitan regions. Leisure-time activities are no longer confined to a once-a-year vacation; now they are a much larger part of the complete calendar year. Consequently more money is being pumped into rural communities, making more jobs available for the children who grow up there. They may choose to stay in these areas rather than migrate to larger towns because now various kinds of service employment are available.

· For a variety of political and economic reasons, a number of organizations—often branches of larger ones—have been created in nonmetropolitan regions. They are generally specialized or designed to make services available to the local community. Different organizations establish themselves in different communities and for two major kinds of reasons. Business firms prefer small towns without competing industry that will drive up wages. Political decision makers must try to balance political costs rather than economic ones. The town that gets the campus cannot get the next government facility. There is a need to spread the political bounty. Both forces drive toward nonconcentration of resources in a single central city. Clearly this dynamic means multiple centers in various regions. It has been further aided by the creation of an interstate highway system built more on a network flow of goods and services and the process of specialization.

All this implies a considerable modification of the Berry theory, which holds that cities are arranged in a hierarchy and that the dominant flows are from higher levels to lower levels.[11] It is not that these flows are not important; instead, multiple small towns and cities in nonmetropolitan areas and horizontal flows are now growing much faster than these other directions of influence. It is not that one system is replacing the other but rather that the logic of nonmetropolitan growth is overtaking that of metropolitan growth.

The Stages of Industralization

We can now stipulate that there is a postindustrial phase that is quite different from the industrial phase, a thesis that forms the basis for most ecological theory.

Stage theory is frequently criticized, and almost always is too simple a description of what process is occurring. Yet it offers a way to describe complex processes and is a way of orientating oneself in doing research. The concept of postindustrial society may be understood in this light. A large number of observers in the United States and in Western Europe have felt that the modern industrialized societies have moved to a new stage that is so qualitatively different that one must look for quite different causal laws or hypotheses. To put this new stage in perspective, we must review the existing theory.

Stage One

The first stage is the growth of a few cities outside the capital of the country. The rural–urban migrations are a well-known and much studied phenomenon. As part of the industrialization process, they can be conceptualized as the first stage in an overall process of urbanization. I suspect that within these overall population flows, there were separate and distinct moves, first from the farm to the towns of five thousand, to fifty thousand, then to the cities of fifty thousand and a hundred thousand, and finally to the metropolitan area. Naturally some people made the leap from rural farm to large metropolis in a single move, but this movement may not be the dominant pattern.

Stage Two

The second state of the process of urbanization is associated with the growth of the suburbs: a reduction in the concentration of population density in the central city and the spread of a number of small- to medium-size cities that are dependent upon the central city they surround. These are the familiar Standard Metropolitan Statistical Areas of the U.S. Bureau of the Census. The Bureau uses a central city population of at least fifty thousand for its standard. (I would prefer a larger center city to designate the metropolitan area, a minimum of a hundred thousand and perhaps even a quarter of a million.)

If we were to construct a set of regional or area maps of the United States, within each region we might draw a circle in scale to represent the city size and another circle to represent the surrounding metropolitan area. The process of urbanization at first meant a growth of the inner circle and then a decline or a halt of this growth, replaced by the growth in the second circle. It is useful to see this process in geopolitical terms as a deconcentration of population densities as a function of transportation and standard of living.

Stage Three

My prediction is that the growth of metropolitan areas, especially those with a central city of 250,000 or more, has largely stopped. Instead there is a flow toward nonmetropolitan regions. But instead of one small city's becoming a large metropoplitan area—that is, a continuation of the urbanization process— there will be a qualitative break in stage three. A number of small towns and cities in the same geopolitical area will grow apace, with specialization by each city or town, and each town will be connected by a good system of transportation to the other. Admittedly the energy crisis may force a return to the traditional urbanization process: one urban center offers the range of services to the surrounding hinterland, which remains dependent upon the center city.

There are, of course, innumerable examples of this stage three process in the Midwest. The quad–city area in western Illinois is one example. The building of the Chrysler plant in Bélvedeer, Illinois, had little impact on that town, but it did on the surrounding area, including Rockford, Illinois, and Janesville, Wisconsin. A similar process is happening in northern Wisconsin: the development of a nonmetropolitan geopolitical area with no dominant city but a wide range of services formerly associated only with large cities.

To provide some sense of quantification or a way of testing this hypothesis, I have suggested some crude measures of each stage. In table 7-1, the classic urbanization process, which is still going on, can be measured by the traditional indication of the proportion of the population in towns of two thousand or more. The more recent suburbanization process can be crudely measured by the percentage of the population in SMAs of a hundred thousand or more under the assumption (which is not completely true) that the metropolitan spread is found especially around the larger cities. A more sensitive measure of this process is the ratio of center city to surrounding population, but frequently these data are not available.

This ratio has become extreme in some areas. It is roughly one to two in New York City (7 million versus 15 million) and Chicago (3 million versus 6 million to 7 million) and even larger in Los Angeles and Paris. Part of the reason is a function of when additional areas were incorporated into the center city, the speed of growth, and when the growth occurred. But it seems likely that there is some upper limit in this ratio for larger cities. Furthermore, if the energy crisis continues, the upper limit may actually diminish. Energy consumption is quite technologically dependent even

Table 7-1
A Typology of Population Flows

Flow	Measure	Process	Stage
Rural to urban	Percent of population in towns of 2,000 or more	Classic urbanization	Early industrialization
Urban to suburban	Percent of population in SMAS of 100,000 or more, ratio of center city to total SMAs	Suburbanization	Late industrialization
Metropolitan to hinterland	Percent of population in towns of 5,000 to 50,000; ratio of SMAs' population to hinterland population	Deconcentration	Post industrialization

though it has not been up to now. The shifts to and from various sources as a function of price differential are very hard to predict.

However crude the indicator of the proportion of the population in cities of a hundred thousand or more is, it still can indicate some interesting and perhaps little appreciated facts. Britain, which pioneered first with urbanization and then suburbanization, is the first to enter the postindustrial demographic stage. The proportion of the population in large cities has been steadily declining. Admittedly this might be due entirely to the government's policy of new towns, but that policy itself is an important statement about postindustrial societies as they attempt to plan and regulate population flows.

The measure I would use for the last stage is the proportion of the population in towns of five thousand to fifty thousand. This is especially true if they continue to grow while the proportion of the population in cities of a hundred thousand or more stabilizes or declines. I believe that a reverse population flow has begun. This reversal does not mean that large metropolitan areas will decline in population size, but they will tend to stabilize and become less dominant in the regions in which they are located. Small-sized cities and towns will grow instead and become interdependent with rather than dependent upon the large SMAs.

Perhaps the most interesting change will occur in large metropolitan areas where there seems to be a tendency to develop multiple centers. This has already happened to a certain extent in Chicago and Los Angeles. Although it is hard to measure, a rough indicator is the location of night time entertainment. Previously, and consistent with the suburb–urban pattern, it was concentrated downtown in the central area of the city. This is no longer true. Conversely the old centers of the large metropolitan cities are somewhat deserted at night as new competing complexes in the suburbs have been created. Shopping centers are gradually getting their nighttime equivalent. Similarly the nonmetropolitan areas are developing their own networks of towns, one of which will specialize in evening entertainment.

Nonmetropolitan areas that become these new organic wholes with no central city but with a number of small- and medium-sized towns instead are not metropolitan areas in the normal sense of the term. Nor does it make sense to use the concept of SMA because the distinctive characteristic is that these areas cover a large number of counties and have a number of towns but no real central city of any dominant size. Their defining characteristic would be a cluster of towns and cities equal in size, with horizontal traffic flows moving between them. Transportation flows are hard to measure without specialized studies, and yet they would be a much more direct way of defining whether in fact the towns in a particular area did fit the idea of an organic whole.

Another critical indicator is specialization by service and industrial sectors. The more that this occurs, the more one can speak of some organic whole.

The Motivations in Location of Residence

So far my emphasis has been on macropolitical and economic forces that affect where organizations—and thus jobs—are located. But little has been said about macrofactors that influence population flows other than the availability of jobs. There are push as well as pull factors. Peoples' tastes are changing, and as these change, they affect the choice of residence. It is important to consider how these operate because it would be another test of the basic model. One can commit another kind of ecological fallacy by ignoring motivations. In some sense, decisions to migrate or not are industrial or family decisions that can be affected by factors other than work availability. Life–style is an important term.

Let us go back to the major changes occurring in postindustrial society.[12] The most critical is the growth in higher education and the development of the service sector. These have meant the creation of mass higher education systems. Presumedly this educational change means some dramatic shifts in values as well:

1. A preference for quality over cost of a product or a service.
2. A preference for quality of life over amount of income earned.
3. A preference for time saved over money saved as a key indicator of efficiency.

These central assumptions suggest the preference for a wide variety of different kinds of products and services that are highly individualized. Thus where one lives becomes a more important and personal question of taste and results in a continual movement toward small plant size where production is limited in quantity but perhaps distributed nationwide.

Travel and mass communication facilitate this process of individualized tastes. As one sees the great variety of possibilities—including places to live—one can more correctly understand what one wants. Highly educated people are more likely to weigh the costs and benefits of metropolitan versus nonmetropolitan living carefully and may find the latter much more attractive. The discussion of life–style and of alternative communities has been commonplace in the literature. Although most hippie communities of the 1960s have not survived, a desire for a sense of community–gemeinschaft—and an increasing preference for nonmetropolitan areas (provided sufficient services and jobs are available)—did survive.

These desires for more personalized services have manifested themselves in a wide variety of ways. Part of the critique of bureaucracy is because of its perceived impersonality. Part of the appeal of towns and small cities is the sense of being a person, achieved by having many acquaintances, neighbors, and friends. Part of the preference for small specialty shops over supermarkets stems from the same desire—to be perceived and treated as an individual. Many of these observations are commonplace and well known; it is simply their implication for migration between metropolitan and nonmetropolitan areas that I am stressing here.

Interestingly this same process is affecting the nature of metropolitan areas as well. The desire to create communities within cities and their suburbs is much stronger. One of the most interesting statistics that reflects this pattern is the increasing average length of residence. Increasingly people prefer to stay in the same area and have continuity in their neighborhood relationships. This increased drive for quality of life and gemeinschaft, which is a function of increasing levels of education in the society, thus not only affects flows from metropolitan to nonmetropolitan areas but it also encourages people to settle in both places, changing the nature of the communities and indeed creating them.

Although it is difficult to explain why education has this impact on values or taste preferences, it appears to stem from a progression of needs. When a basic income level is achieved, concerns turn to the search for interesting work. In particular, professionals, managers, and others who have received a college education have carefully considered what they want to do and why. Their choice of an occupational career is a serious investment decision. In sum, individuals weigh a number of factors concerning employment and do so on a cost–benefit analysis. They then apply this same procedure to choice of location.

Part of the attraction of large cities as places to live was that they offered a distinctive set of services that could not be obtained elsewhere. Mass communication, especially cable television, has made many of the leisure-time activities previously available only in a few places now within reach of the smallest town. One can now enjoy an off–Broadway play without leaving one's town. And if one really wants to see a live production, one can do it on any of the many long holiday weekends by taking one of the specialized cheap tour tickets available. Low-cost air transportation has moved the few remaining critical distinctions of large metropolitan areas within easy reach of the nonmetropolitan regions. Even the capital cities of Europe are now readily accessible to Americans. Mass communication and cheap air transportation—despite the energy crisis—have made specialized services available to those living outside metropolitan areas.

Even cultural activities long concentrated in large metropolitan areas are increasingly being located in nonmetropolitan ones. Sometimes it happens because of the whim of a benefactor; Getty and his art museum on the southern California coast is an example. More often the founder of a ballet, opera, or theater may prefer a simple life-style. The government has been encouraging the development of new centers of excellence outside the standard metropolitan areas.

Beyond this, many standard services frequently found only in cities of a hundred thousand or more are now available in much smaller towns and medium-sized cities. The real issue in the development of services is not population but the number of people who want a service. Previously population figures have been used as an indicator of the latter, but in postindustrial society, this simple equation breaks down. With a college-educated labor force, there is a proliferation of tastes, and quality rather than cost becomes critical, resulting in a demand for individualized products and services. Admittedly the duplication of specialty shops in small towns and cities is expensive in one sense, but if people continue to value quick availability, then the growth in demand means proliferation of these shops.

Notes

1. Brian J. L. Berry and John D. Kasarda, *Contemporary Urban Ecology* (New York: Macmillan, 1977).

2. Kurt Finsterbush, personal communication, 1978.

3. Berry and Kasarda, *Contemporary Urban Ecology.*

4. Brian J. L. Berry, *Geography of Market Centers and Retail Distribution* (Englewood Cliffs, N.J.: Prentice-Hall, 1967).

5. Berry and Kasarda, *Contemporary Urban Ecology.*

6. Tom Burns and G. M. Stalker, *The Management of Innovations* (London: Tavistock Publications, 1961): Jerald Hage, *Communication and Organizational Control* (New York: Wiley, 1974).

7. Alex Bavelas, "Communications Patterns in Task-oriented Groups," *Journal of the Acoustical Society of America* 22 (1950): 725-730.

8. Hage, *Communication.*

9. Emile Durkheim, *De la division du travail social* (Paris, 1893).

10. Jeffrey Williamson, "Regional Inequity and the Process of National Development: A Description of the Patterns," *Economic Development and Social Change* 8 (July 1965).

11. Brian J. L. Berry, *Essays on Commodity Flows and the Spatial Structure of the Indian Economy* (Chicago: University of Chicago, Department of Geography, 1966).

12. Daniel Bell, "The Measurement of Knowledge and Technology," in Eleanor B. Sheldon and Wilbert E. Moore, ed., *Indicators of Social Change* (New York: Russell Sage Foundation, 1968), and *The Coming of Post-industrial Society* (New York: Basic Books, 1973).

8

A Theoretical Framework for the Analysis of Community Economic Development Policy Options

Glen C. Pulver

For many years, developers have placed almost total reliance on increased productivity in agriculture, greater exploitation of natural resources, and the addition of new manufacturing industries as strategies for community economic development in nonmetropolitan areas. A study of secondary date from the International Labor Office and the U.S. Bureau of Labor Statistics indicates that the rate of job growth in goods-producing industries is declining rapidly in highly developed countries. In contrast, employment in the service sector is increasing. As a consequence, alternative strategies for economic growth must be found in postindustrial economies.

My theoretical framework for the analysis of community economic development policy options presented here indicates that the existing concentration on expanding goods-producing industries is unnecessarily narrow. Improving the efficiency of existing firms, attracting new basic employers from the nonmanufacturing sector, encouraging business formation, capturing more of the existing income, and increasing the aids received from broader governmental levels are all viable community economic development alternatives. A comprehensive policy that considers all options may allow nonmetropolitan areas to participate fully in future economic growth.

Overview

Improved community economic well-being as measured by individual income and employment is of concern to policy makers throughout the world. In spite of numerous governmental programs, including developmental credit, income maintenance, public education, affirmative action in employment, job training, and trade protection, a large portion of the world's people suffer the problems associated with low family income. In lesser-developed countries, the problems are widespread. In more-developed countries, a smaller proportion of the people may be directly affected, but broad concern for income and employment is fueled by rising taxes, higher rates of inflation, and expanded unemployment.

National, subnational (state and provincial), and local policy makers are of necessity attempting to outline strategies aimed at optimizing opportunities for economic development at the community level. Locally industrial development organizations, economic development committees, business groups, and government officials develop industrial parks, prepare promotional brochures, and sponsor special events in an effort to attract more income and employment to their community. State and provincial officials employ industrial developers, provide special tax incentives, and produce tourism promotional programs in a similar effort. On a national level, mechanisms for improving both individual and community income and employment include regional development commissions, direct credit or guarantees to businesses, protective tariffs, and assistance to individuals.

But rarely are public investments in economic well-being based on comprehensive analysis of the opportunities that communities have for development. Instead most are connected to a historic preoccupation with goods-producing industries, especially manufacturing. Manufacturing has been viewed by many as the most effective vehicle for creating jobs and providing a long-term basis for income growth. This bias is derived from the perception that manufacturing has been the major source of economic growth in modern Western development. Although the common assumption seems to be that this will continue in the near future, there are strong indications that this may not be the case.

The U.S. economy has changed substantially recently. Since World War II, the historic dominance of goods-producing industries (agriculture, forestry, fishing, mining, construction, and manufacturing) has been replaced by the service sector. In 1947, employment was almost evenly distributed between the goods-producing and service-producing sectors. By 1970, service industries had increased their share to approximately two-thirds of total national employment. The projection for 1985 is that only 29 percent of the United States employment will be in goods-producing industries. Manufacturing is not among the ten industries projected to show the largest increases in number of jobs between 1968 and 1985. The only goods-producing industry to appear on the list is construction, and it ranks eighth.[1]

Similar conclusions might be drawn from statistics on the employment structure of other countries. The more developed an economy, the greater the proportion of employment in service-producing industries. Employment by economic sector in a number of countries is presented in table 8-1. For example, 13.2 percent of those employed in Mozambique in 1976 were in the service-producing sector. In india, 16.5 percent were thus employed. In Egypt, 30.5 percent of those employed were in the service-producing sector. In Brazil, service-producing industries employed 37.8 percent of the workers. In contrast 51.5 percent in Japan, 57.2 percent in Sweden, and 64.3 percent in the United States worked in these industries.

It is important to note that more highly developed countries are also

Table 8-1
World Employment by Economic Sector

	Egypt	Mozam-bique	Brazil	U.S.	India	Japan	Sweden	U.S.S.R. [Russia][a]	
	(as percent of total employment)								
								[productive]	
Agriculture, hunting, forestry, fishing	53.3	73.4	44.3	3.8	72.0	12.5	6.4	26.3	same as #1
Mining, quarrying	0.2	4.3	0.6	0.8	0.5	0.3	0.5	45.1	industry, construction, transport, communications
Manufacturing	12.9	5.4	11.0	22.7	9.5	25.2	28.0		
Electric, gas, water	0.6	0.1	0.5	1.3	0.3	0.6	0.8	6.7	trade, public dining, material–technical supply
Construction	2.5	2.8	5.8	6.2	1.2	9.0	7.1		
Wholesale/retail trade, restaurants, hotels	7.2	2.8	7.7	20.0	4.9	21.1	14.4	0.5	other productive
								[non-productive]	
Transport, storage, and communications	4.1	2.2	4.2	5.0	2.4	6.2	6.7		
Finance, insurance, real estate, business services	14.9	0.2	1.5	5.2	0.7	3.2	5.3	14.2	educational, cultural, scientific and research institutes and public health
Community, social and personal services		7.9	22.0	31.8	7.8	20.8	30.8	6.8	administration, communications, housing services, banking and insurance
Other	4.3	0.1	2.4		0.7	0.2			
1st time seeking work				0.9					
Unemployed						1.9			
Military Service				2.3					

Source: *1976, Yearbook of Labour Statistics* (Geneva: International Labour Office, Switzerland, pp. 50–166. Note: Data are not necessarily comparable or completely accurate but are the best available. Some figures are based on census data, others on statistical samples. "Employed" equals employers, self–employed and wage earners, *plus* unemployed, unless specifically broken out into separate category.
[a] Russian data are organized differently from primary categories in the table; they have been grouped in a way that most nearly corresponds to the other table entries.

characterized by larger percentages of people employed in manufacturing. In Mozambique, 5.4 percent were employed in manufacturing in 1976. In India, 9.5 percent were thus employed, in Brazil, 11.0 percent and in Egypt, 12.9 percent. In the more highly developed economies, the statistics were as follows: United States, 22.7 percent; Japan, 25.2 percent; and Sweden, 28.0 percent. There is little doubt that the development of manufacturing industries remains a prime consideration in any national development strategy. The point is that manufacturing should be only one part of such a strategy.

A comprehensive strategy aimed at the economic well-being of any community should recognize the unique opportunities that each community has for development. Each possesses a special combination of natural and human resources, market conditions, and institutional factors. If local policy makers are to maximize economic well-being in their communities, they should carefully analyze all opportunities available and invest in those with the greatest potential. State or provincial policy makers should also be aware of the options open to communities within their influence. National lawmakers interested in developing specific regions or aiding particular groups of people need to recognize what can and cannot be accomplished by various programs.

It seems clear that any community economic development strategy should be based on a careful analysis of unique needs, resource availability, market conditions, and citizen goals. Considerable time could be given to analyzing the needs and goals of people. Are the citizens of the community seeking supplementary household income? Are they interested in economic growth or stability? Is there a highly skilled but unemployed segment in the population? Similar time could be given the subject of resource availability and market conditions. Is there much unused land suitable for irrigation? Does a significant mineral deposit lie unexploited beneath the soil? Is there a strong demand for a manufactured good in a nearby community? Much has been written on these topics. For my purposes here, I will assume that an analysis of the realistic economic potential of a community is the first step in the creation of any development strategy.

The next step in policy development should use a theoretical framework for examining community economic policy options that can be set next to this primary analysis (needs, resources, markets, goals) in order to chart a realistic strategy for development. The basic community economic policy options considered here are attracting new basic employers, improving the efficiency of existing firms, improving the ability to capture dollars, encouraging the formation of new businesses, and increasing the aids received from broader governments.

Attracting New Basic Employers

The most common effort of local leaders hoping to improve employment and income in their community is the pursuit of new basic employers: Basic employers are essentially those industries that produce goods or services for which payments are received from outside the community. The rationale is that basic industries will more fully utilize local resources, which in turn will bring income into the community to be dispersed among those who already live there. People who are unemployed or underemployed will receive wages for their labor and management skills. Natural resources such as agricultural lands, forests, and mineral deposits that are not fully exploited will generate greater income for the community. Through the multiplier effect, this income in turn will be spent on goods and services in the community, producing still more income and employment.

Historically much effort has been aimed at attracting new manufacturing firms, expanding arable agricultural lands through irrigation, and developing extractive industries such as mining and forestry. More recently it has been recognized that certain nonmanufacturing industries are also basic employers (among them insurance companies, nonresidential construction firms, wholesaling businesses, computer services, and the hospitality industry). In addition, many nonlocal government offices in the community are basic employers; they more fully utilize the labor and management resources of a community, export services beyond the community, and in turn expand the income available for dispersal among the people already present. There are an ever-growing number of future employment opportunities in more developed economies.

A number of options are available to policy makers interested in attracting new basic employers. None will ensure that new basic employment occurs unless the policy makers themselves initiate the development. Most of the options propose action aimed at creating an atmosphere that provides positive incentives for new businesses. In all cases, the terms *industry* and *industrial* are to be defined broadly to include insurance companies, nonresidential construction firms, wholesaling businesses, and other basic industries.

1. Communities may expedite the introduction of new employers through the development of industrial sites, the extension of sewer, water, rail, and power lines, investments in speculative buildings, and labor force surveys. None guarantees new industry, but all facilitate movement to the community and, at minimum, evidence community interest.

2. Collective action can be encouraged through the formation of organizations such as industrial development corporations. These corporations

may provide the organizational and financial base necessary for an effective industrial development program, including a program of search and reception of potential businesses.

3. Community and regional infrastructure may need to be developed if new employers are to be attracted. Transportation facilities such as airports, highways, railroads, and ports may need modernization. Inadequate banking, accounting, computer services, communication mechanisms, and legal assistance may inhibit development in some communities. Community services are increasingly important in industrial location. Schools, parks, restaurants, and health care facilities all play a strong part in a community's ability to attract new basic employers.

4. The availability of capital can attract business. Community leaders can do much to help utilize local capital resources. Many states in the United States have authorized community industrial bonding programs. A mechanism is provided by which the local government can indicate that the bonds of a specific company have special status, providing for some tax exemption on interest paid the bondholder. The bonds are generally sold privately, and the funds are used for investment in new plants and equipment. In some communities, low bank lending limits may restrict capital availability to only the smallest businesses. In these cases, joint lending relationships can be developed. Direct public loans are sometimes provided to individual businesses when capital is otherwise unavailable.

5. Another option available to policy makers interested in attracting new basic employers is to indentify specific public programs, projects, offices, and services that could be located in the community and then organize politically to secure them. For example, staff salaries, expenses, and office space costs of a regional development office may represent significant economic development to the community where it is located. Services are exported to surrounding communities, and tax dollars from other communities represent real income to the community of location. The same can be said for state or provincial governmental units, such as district highway offices, or regional or local offices of national agencies, such as agricultural experiment stations. Government is a prime employer not to be overlooked.

Improving the Efficiency of Existing Firms

The continued good health of businesses already located in a community is vital. The more efficient they are, the more competitive they can be in the long run in regional, state, national, and world markets. Existing firms that remain competitive provide continuing income and employment. If the firms are locally owned, the expenditure of increased profits and costs of financing bring even greater benefit to the community.

The expansion of existing businesses is a major source of employment growth and often the basis for greater exploitation of natural resources. For example, the Wisconsin Department of Business Development reports that from 1970 to 1976, 590 plant locations new to the community occurred in Wisconsin. During the same period, 2,993 firms reported plant expansions in communities where they were already located.[2]

Policy makers interested in improving the efficiency of existing firms have a number of options.

1. The management capacity of existing firms can be strengthened through educational programs. Special courses in finance, personnel administration, business organization, marketing, and other related areas can be developed for the managers of manufacturing and other basic industries, as well as service and retail outlets. Expanded public investment in university outreach and vocational-technical adult education programs can be effective if properly encouraged by local leaders.

2. Courses at technical schools could be helpful in keeping business abreast of the latest developments in technology. Once again this option may require an expanded public investment to make such facilities available on a widespread basis.

3. The community might aid employers in improving work-force quality through educational program, employment counseling, and social services. Vocational education programs can significantly improve the skills of potential employees, thereby improving product and service quality and reducing costs per unit of output. Effective employment counseling programs can speed up the process of filling vacant positions and can improve the fit between worker interest and ability and the job. Social services of several types are of direct aid in improving business efficiency. For example, alcohol counseling can reduce business losses from worker absenteeism, and day-care facilities can reduce the incidence of parents not reporting to work because of child-care problems.

4. The identification and organization of capital resources may be of even greater importance to existing businesses than to those being sought from outside the community. Business growth generally requires capital investment in new technology, market development, and physical facilities. In smaller communities, the funds required may be beyond the single-loan limit of local banks. Firms headquartered in larger cities may have ready access to large financial institutions with a ready capacity to analyze and support loans for business expansion, but this may not be the case in many communities. Passing comfort resolutions for industrial revenue bonding, creating small business investment corporations, and being aware of resources available from and contacts with national agencies are important activities. (U.S. federal agencies, such as the Small Business Administration, Farmers Home Administration, and the Economic Development Administration, all engage in credit extension.)

5. As in the case of attracting new businesses, investments in community and regional facilities may improve local business efficiency and access to nonlocal markets. Transportation, service, and communications infrastructure should be as efficient as possible. For example, an order lost because of telephone or postal service breakdown is a lost income and employment opportunity. It is clear that taxpayers in a community should not be expected to pay all of the cost of investments that improve local business profits, but basic services that are not competitive with those of other communities place any firm at a disadvantage.

Improving Ability to Capture Income

The citizens of every community receive income in the form of wages, interest, dividends, rental receipts, insurance benefits, and government payments. Businesses receive income from product and service sales, rental payments, and other sources. Local governments receive income from property taxes, services provided, and aids from state or provincial and national sources. All of this income that is expended within the community for retail or wholesale goods, services, and industrial inputs adds to the employment and income of the community. It is clear that not all community income can be expended locally. Nonetheless the larger the percentage spent locally, the better off the community.

Not only may effort be made to capture monies generated within a community, but the opportunity to acquire monies generated in other places exists. Tourist-oriented activities and establishments may attract people from a wide geographic area, thereby functioning much like a basic industry in expanding income and employment. Shopping centers in larger cities have much the same effect insofar as they draw shoppers and their resources from neighboring municipalities.

Those interested in expanding a community's ability to capture income may choose from several options.

1. The market potential of existing retail outlets may be identified through surveys aimed at determining consumer needs and buying habits in a specific trade area. If stores are open during hours that are inconvenient to potential customers or desired goods and services are missing or presented in an improper fashion, income will be spent in other communities. Another problem is that products may be stocked that no one desires. Changes in buying patterns need to be identified. Customer surveys have a limited life and need repetition over time to be most useful.

2. A community may improve the share of the retail market captured through downtown analysis and renewal. Business districts in parts of the world are hundreds of years old. Over time nearly all have been modified,

usually one business at a time. In many cases, some stores may be rundown, empty, or unsightly, causing all to suffer when shoppers turn instead to modern, attractive, highly capitalized shopping centers. If small-town, neighborhood, or downtown retail outlets expect to remain profitable, they must know and understand their competition. In addition, they must undoubtedly support a well-thought-out plan of merchandizing, advertising, and physical plant design.

3. The quality of service offered by a community's businesses is vital to the capture of income. Belligerent, unresponsive, or ineffectual behavior by employees can drive customers away. Policy makers can aid firms in developing employee training programs to improve service quality.

4. Purchases by nonlocal people (tourists, neighbors, and passersby) are a vital part of the economy of many communities. Indeed the economies of some countries (Monaco, for example) are almost entirely dependent upon these revenue sources. Advertising and promotion programs are vital in most of these cases. Successful programs generally require considerable collective effort. Joint funding by individual businesses, communities, and units of government of a major annual event or ongoing advertising and promotion is an opportunity.

5. Concentrated effort aimed at encouraging citizens and business people to buy locally may also have some effect. The importance of consumer buying within the community is usually recognized, and regular sales events are often held. But sometimes overlooked is the importance of industrial purchase. The support of local supply houses, business service agencies, transportation, and communication firms may be as important to the local economy as employing local people. Emphasis on these aspects in local information campaigns may have some effect.

6. Nearly all of the options suggested in this area will be enhanced by the collective action of a local business organization. This type of organization can provide the needed direction and sense of participation that generates broad involvement in development. Without it, little is apt to happen.

Encouraging Business Formation

There is a continuing need for the creation of new businesses to meet the shifting demands of people. As populations grow, new businesses are required to service the expanding demand for goods and services. And as people move from one geographic area to another, they force a shift in the quantity and quality of products that each community must provide. In addition, technological change generates products and services that are often of a completely different type. New businesses must be created to fill the gaps. A shift in consumer preference or business methods may have a similar effect. All of these forces represent an economic growth opportunity for someone or some community. There are policy options open to those interested in encouraging business formation.

1. A major problem in the formation of most new businesses is the lack of adequate capital. Policy makers at all levels have several options to aid in the provision of capital to the local entrepreneur. Locally, they can encourage investment of private funds through the formation of capital groups. Small business investment corporations, community development corporations, and other forms of venture capital institutions are examples. More direct assistance may also be provided through loans and loan guarantees especially tailored to emerging businesses or to specific client groups (such as racial minorities or depressed regions). Other mechanisms for organizing community capital are possible.

2. Individual counsel and intensive education in advanced technology, business methods, and law may also be provided to those interested in forming new businesses. In some parts of the world, major public investment provides considerable individual counsel to those interested in farming, while little public support is provided other economic sectors. Much could be done by community leaders and other policy makers to prevent the failure that all too often accompanies those attempting to create new businesses.

3. The market potential for new retail, wholesale, and input–providing businesses could be identified by careful analysis. For example, it is conceivable that a local firm is purchasing raw materials that it needs that are produced at a distant point. Market demand projections might indicate significant economic advantage for its local production and supply. This kind of research may be beyond the scope of an existing firm that would be quite anxious to be the supplier. Public–financed market analysis can often lead to the development of new local businesses.

4. Many of the policy options that are effective in attracting businesses and improving business efficiency are basic necessities in the formation of new businesses.

The entire concept of encouraging business formation is unacceptable to some, who may view these policy options as undue public interference with the private sector. Or they may believe that aid in business formation is fostering unfair competition. The matter can be resolved only by the policy makers.

Increasing Aids from Broader Governments

Citizens and businesses within a community are usually subject to taxation by a number of governmental units. These taxes are used to support local government services, public schools, regional commissions, state or provincial government programs, and national activities such as health care and national defense. It is clear that a taxation system is necessary to provide public services. Nonetheless assuming an established structure of taxation, it is to the short-run economic advantage of a community to reacquire funds taxed away by broader governmental units and, if possible, to acquire monies taxed in wealthier communities.

Most public expenditures in a community from broader units of government have the same general effect as purchases by other external entities. These expenditures may range from the purchase of a meal or supplies by a government employee to the massive infusion of government transfer payments, such as old age and survivor's insurance, aid for dependent children, and school lunch programs. Luther Tweeten states: "Welfare reform, with federal takeover of public assistance programs, would bring in dollars and as such, public assistance may be defined as an 'export industry.' The argument for reform rests on grounds of efficiency as well as equity. On efficiency grounds, a given real income to those receiving public assistance can be provided at lower costs in a rural area than in the metropolis."[3]

In recent years, increasing the population of elderly has been viewed as a developmental opportunity more frequently. Historically the elderly required significant public financial support, and community leaders judged a large elderly population to be a drag on a community's economy because they were considered a dependent population. Today with substantial social security payments, medical assistance, and strong pension programs, the retired people in a community may possess a higher-than-average income. This is particularly true if they move from larger cities to smaller towns at retirement.

Public policy makers can play a direct role in increasing aids from broader governments.

1. Educational and other program efforts can be organized to ensure the correct use of public assistance for the elderly, handicapped, and others who cannot work. A recent study by Peter Helmberger found that if the citizens of Dane County, Wisconsin, who were eligible for food stamps (a national program) used stamps at the national average rate, income in Dane County would increase by $1 million annually.[4] This income would represent the equivalency of a significant job growth. Government transfer payments are a major share of income in many communities, and the general economic well-being of people in some wide geographic areas is more dependent on this income than on private sector activity.

2. A large number of aids from national or state government are often available to assist local governments in development. These might include monies to support street or highway construction, park and recreation development, sewer and water systems, school improvement, and other

forms of infrastructure. This infrastructure is essential to economic development, but it should be remembered that the injection of capital to bring about the improvement is itself a mechanism for raising economic well-being. Thus, aids such as funds for emergency employment that do not provide long-run infrastructure improvements should also be viewed as positive economic activity. The programs of broader governments should be actively monitored and utilized by local governmental officials interested in economic improvement.

3. Policy makers interested in the economic well-being of their people also have the option of direct political activity. They can support political activities aimed at ensuring fair treatment of community concerns by broader governmental units.

Conclusion

A wide spectrum of options is available to policy makers at all levels of government. At the national level, the decision might be made to provide special tax incentives to encourage business expansion in areas of high unemployment. Funds might be provided for counseling people interested in starting new businesses in low-income areas. Special infrastructure aids might be provided depressed communities.

At the state or provincial level, business efficiency might be encouraged by providing educational programs in business management. Tourism promotion organizations might be partially financed to help capture dollars from other states or nations. Direct loans might be provided to firms attempting to comply with changing environmental standards. Income transfer programs might be developed to assist financially disadvantaged groups.

In most cases, action by local policy makers is vital if real community economic well-being is to be achieved. A myriad of opportunities may be provided by broader governments. Without local initiative, however, little will be accomplished. Many of the development options available involve no aid from other governments, but simply local decision and action.

Those interested in community economic development should first examine the goals, needs, resources, and market conditions of the people and areas concerned. These factors form the base on which development policy must be built. The framework for analysis of development options is wide. In selecting programs aimed at improving income and employment, policy makers need not be restricted to historic efforts directed at expansion of the goods-producing sector. A sound developmental policy must be comprehensive and consider all available options.

Notes

1. U.S. Department of Labor, Bureau of Labor Statistics, *The Structure of the U.S. Economy in 1980 and 1985,* Bulletin 1831 (Washington, D.C.: Government Printing Office, 1975).

2. "Report on New Industries and Plant Expansions in Wisconsin," *Community Economics,* no. 11 (Madison: Department of Agricultural Economics, University of Wisconsin, August 1977).

3. Luther Tweeten, "Enhancing Economic Opportunity," pp. 91–107 in L. R. Whiting (ed.) *Communities Left Behind—Alternatives for Development,* North Central Regional Center for Rural Development, Iowa State University Press, Ames, Iowa, 1974.

4. "Farms and Food Stamps—The 1977 Farm Bill," *Economic Issues,* (Madison: Department of Agricultural Economics, University of Wisconsin, December 1977).

Part III
Issues of Community Change

9

In Search of Community Power

Howard Newby,
Peter Saunders, David Rose,
and *Colin Bell*

In the twenty-five years since Floyd Hunter published his famous study of Atlanta, *Community Power Structure,* the investigation of the contours of power in local communities has become almost a subdiscipline in its own right. An exhaustive bibliography would contain hundreds of titles, particularly in the United States, where the study of community power has generated a fascinating debate from which general lessons can be learned about the close relationship of ideology, theory, methodology, and empirical findings.[1] The study of community power has become an arena within which fundamental epistemological issues, which go far beyond the substantive problem to which they are related, have been fought. Despite the prodigious amount of work carried out on the study of community power and despite the increasing sophistication and rigor that many of these studies have manifested, many of the important issues remain no less contentious. Indeed the difficulties involved in studying power relationships empirically remain stubbornly intractable to the kind of techniques that have become the standard apparatus of sociological investigation.

Some of these difficulties are even more apparent outside North America, where systematic studies of local power are relatively few. In Britain, for example, the methodological problems of attempting merely to gain access to the locally powerful can be considerable, for a pall of secrecy frequently surrounds the dealings of even the smallest local council.[2] In addition, the greater degree of centralization of decision making and homogeneity of political culture in Britain has been reflected in a greater predisposition among sociologists and political scientists to regard community power as not worth studying. There has been a widespread belief that most local authorities do not possess sufficient autonomy to determine their own affairs in any significant manner, that the "eclipse of community" has progressed to the extent that most of the important decisions now lie in the hands of extralocal agencies.[3]

Most of these points have been well founded, and it is therefore not surprising that the study of community power in Britain has been somewhat moribund, particularly when the theoretical problems generated by the

---

This chapter is based on research financed by the British Social Science Research Council.

121

American community power debate have been enough to intimidate many researchers otherwise inclined to replicate these studies in a different political culture. Nevertheless, the issue of whether community power is worthy of serious consideration is an empirical matter and not something that can be legislated a priori. Without denying the centripetal tendencies of advanced industrial societies, there is much evidence to show that the immediate locality remains the focus of many people's lives and that local political processes have retained an important significance in the determination of their life changes—and this applies as much in Britain as in the United States. Not only can community power research be justified on these grounds, but it can also advance our theoretical understanding of power. This point needs to be stressed, for problems of the state loom so large in current sociological thinking (at least, as far as European sociology is concerned) as to obscure the issue of local power and how it is possible to study the locally powerful.

Nevertheless the formidable epistemological problems remain. One of our purposes is therefore to review the current state of the art in the empirical study of power, particularly as found in Steven Lukes's *Power: A Radical View.*[4] A further aim, however, is to indicate how many of the practical problems involved in the study of community power were encountered during an investigation of rural class relations in England. This study, although not primarily directed at examining community power, involved an assessment of the local political power retained by farmers and landowners in the face of recent changes in the social composition of the English countryside (most notably, the arrival of a substantial number of ex-urban professional and managerial middle-class commuters and second-home owners) and the extent to which their traditional political hegemony of the countryside had been weakened by such changes. The problems encountered in such an ostensibly straightforward task have led to a reexamination of some of the orthodox conceptual notions in the study of power. Some of the conclusions, we hope, will provide a useful entree into the study of power elsewhere.

Background

The study under consideration concerned a long-standing analysis of class relations in East Anglia, the most highly commercialized agricultural area of England. It began with the study of agricultural workers and continued with a somewhat broader-ranging investigation of farmers and landowners.[5] (A more detailed description of this study, together with an extensive presentation of empirical findings, is presented in a forthcoming book.[6])

Although the study stretched across the entire East Anglian region of

England, as far as the study of local political power was concerned, we concentrated upon the county of Suffolk, a primarily agricultural county comprising much of the southern half of the area. Farming in Suffolk is almost entirely arable, and agricultural units are on average relatively large in scale by European and British standards. The county is one of what Frankenberg has called "the capitalist-organized business farming areas of Britain."[7] The county, along with East Anglia generally, has a very high concentration of hired labor, both because of the nature of the farming and the size of the farms that typify the area. Land is mostly owner occupied (over 70 percent according to official statistics, which are an underestimate for various technical reasons), and since good arable land is currently worth approximately four thousand dollars per acre, the amount of capital required to purchase (or even lease) a viable farm of three hundred acres or more is considerable.[8] The class division between farmers and farm workers is both clearcut and pervasive, especially by comparison with other areas of Britain where family farms predominate. There is little or no interclass mobility for no farm worker can hope to amass the capital necessary to acquire his own farm, particularly since the wages paid to farm workers in the area are among the lowest of any other group in the entire British economy.[9] Agriculture in the area is very capital intensive. It is often in the vanguard of agricultural technology, particularly in the field of mechanization, and as a consequence the number of workers employed has declined by nearly two-thirds since the late 1940s. Productivity per man is consequently very high (approximately $40,000 per man-year compared with wages of approximately $5,000 to $6,000). Agriculture in the region is one of the most prosperous in the United Kingdom and has been enhanced since entry into the European Economic Community.

This highly capitalized, commercial farming dominates the economic activity of Suffolk. Even the manufacturing and service industries in the local towns tend to be agriculturally related; machinery and fertilizer production, food processing, and grain milling are examples. Agriculture is very much a highly specialized and rational means of making money (agribusiness in a slightly looser sense than the customary American usage) rather than a dignified and arcadian way of life. Even the traditional aristocratic elite of the region have been forced to come to terms with the exigencies of modern agricultural economics. Indeed in many cases, they have been in the forefront of innovation and commercial enterprise.

Despite the consequent loss of labor from agriculture, Suffolk is an expanding county in terms of number of inhabitants. The population has been increasing by ten thousand per year during the 1970s, and recent planning forecasts envisage a continuing expansion. This growth may seem surprising, given the agricultural base of the local economy and the continuing drift from the land of rural workers. This net increase is, however, largely accounted for by a continuing influx of urban and overwhelmingly middle-class newcomers from London and elsewhere in southeast England: business commuters, rural retreaters, weekend cottagers, and retired professionals. This horizontal local/newcomer cleavage has been of considerable significance for it has crosscut the vertical economic and social divisions based upon class interests among the locals themselves.

Despite (or, perhaps, because of) the deprivation that the rural working class of Suffolk has suffered, particularly until World War II, agricultural workers in the area are not noted for their radicalism or for their overt acts of opposition to the prevailing social and economic order. Trade unionism among farm workers is weak, both in Suffolk and nationally, and there has been no strike in agriculture since 1923, even though the so-called wages gap between agricultural and industrial workers has widened, on both an absolute and percentage basis, since the war. To some extent farm workers have been inhibited in expressing any opposition by their dependence upon farmers and landowners for both employment and housing. In Suffolk over two-thirds of farm workers live in housing tied to the job, and in a situation of chronic housing shortage such tied cottages have provided a powerful disincentive to opposing the locally powerful. Indeed from time to time tied-cottage evictions have been used as a powerful antiunion weapon by farmers, although legislation passed in 1976 has prevented the worst abuses of the system. The lack of overt opposition and even positive identification with the ideology and actions of the locally powerful has often led farm workers to be regarded as deferential workers.[10] (There are some interesting parallels here with the American literature concerning the ideology of slaves.[11]) Initally the study of farm workers in the area was carried out in order to investigate the nature of deference and the structural causes of deferential interaction. Although this reputation of farm workers often mistakes their powerlessness for deference, the success of the locally powerful in maintaining at the very least the acquiescence and acceptance of a rural social structure among those whose inferiority is created and endorsed by it is quite remarkable.[12]

It was in order to investigate the parameters of social control in this highly polarized rural class structure that we established our research project of farmers and landowners. As well as offering an opportunity to study the same class structure from the other side and thereby obtain directly comparable material to that gathered from farm workers, such a study also enabled us to add to the hitherto meager literature on the entrepreneurial British middle and even upper classes. It is therefore within a very wide-ranging investigation of such issues as landownership, tenure, inheritance patterns, entrepreneurial behavior, labor relations on the farm, relationships with the local village community, environmental changes, political ideology and behavior, and the changing nature of private property relationship that the information presented here on community power (which has been somewhat artificially abstracted from this context) must be understood.

At an early stage in the research, we recognized that some of the most important factors that helped to regulate the rural class relationships that we were studying occurred beyond the farm gate. We realized that a study of class relations on the farm, for example, had to take account of the pervasive political control that farmers exercised in the locality and that informed the political culture within which this relationship was located. Moreover, it was a possibility that local political control would have a considerable impact upon such factors as the provision of employment opportunities (through planning policies relating to industrial development), housing, education, welfare services, and so on. Consequently we decided from the outset to conduct an investigation of community power in Suffolk.

One hundred, or even fifty, years ago, the question of who held power in Suffolk (and in rural England in general) would hardly have been regarded as problematic. Whatever their internal differences of opinion, landowners and farmers formed a coherent and easily identifiable rural ruling class that retained a firm grip upon all of the important institutions of English rural society—the land, employment, housing, education, and the law. At the apex of this ruling class stood the traditional English landowning aristocracy, which together with the landed gentry and titled families of county society, dominated the social and political order of rural areas. For generations their power and benevolence had enveloped all aspects of rural life, personified by the imposing figure of the local squire, who until World War I was a seemingly permanent and enduring fixture on the rural scene. In the last fifty years or more, however, such squirearchical rule has come under severe attack, first, as Thompson had documented, from a farming tenantry impatient with their economic and political omnipotence and ready to take advantage of the break-up of the landed estates between 1918 and 1923 to consolidate their position as commercial owner-occupiers.[13] More recently, both farmers and the remnants of the traditional squirearchy have seen their local political power threatened by the arrival in the countryside of articulate and independent middle-class exurbanites.

Taken together these two changes suggest that the class domination of rural England, which was so manifest during the nineteenth century, has become less coherent and less personalized. At the very least, such changes suggest that the nature and mechanisms of political power in a rural area like Suffolk are a matter for serious empirical investigation rather than a priori assumption. Of considerable significance here has been the growing bureaucratization of local government and the democratization of local politics in England since 1888. Both have resulted in the development of an increasingly formal and impersonal structure of local administration in which public persons have largely replaced traditional social leaders in positions of local power.[14] The spread of citizenship rights, especially the right to vote, into even the most remote rural areas has ensured that the economic power and social status traditionally associated with the landed upper class is no longer an automatic passport to political dominance because of the necessity for modern political leaders to cultivate electoral support.

It is possible to summarize these formal institutional changes by stating that there has been a slow, but progressive shift in the mode of local political authority from that deriving out of tradition and custom toward that vested in formal office as legally defined.[15] Since the turn of the century, power in rural England has become less and less associated with particular individuals and families and more and more the property of certain bureaucratically defined positions. So that the personnel should not change, or that their interests should continue to be served, the locally powerful in rural England have been forced to adapt to these changed political circumstances. The latest in this series of administrative reforms concerns the reorganization of local government in England and Wales in 1974; it is the most recent in a series of changes that have served to weaken particularistic modes of control and to rationalize the government of rural areas, thereby impelling a further dependence on the occupancy of formal office in order to retain local political power.

Since 1974 Suffolk's local government structure has been divided into three levels. At the lowest level are the parish councils, each with a membership of around ten or twelve local villagers. Elections for parish councils are often spasmodic and frequently uncontested, reflecting the paucity of their power and responsibilities. At the middle level are the district councils, each with around fifty members. There are seven district councils in Suffolk, each representing some eighty thousand people, and each is responsible for the provision of public housing, development control of planning, and various local services such as refuse collection, public parks, and other civic amenities. At the third and highest level is the Suffolk County Council whose eighty-two members are responsible for strategic planning, education, highways, police, social services, and a range of minor functions. Before the 1974 reforms, the county functions had been divided between two county councils (East and West Suffolk) and a county borough council (Ipswich). In the middle range, a larger number of smaller rural district councils shared rather fewer responsibilities than do their successors. Our period of observation of local politics in Suffolk covered the changeover from the old to the new system.

As a first step in analyzing the political strength of farmers and landowners in Suffolk, we ascertained the extent to which they had achieved positions of dominance within the local authorities now ruling the area. We did so in the full knowledge that the parameters of local power were largely set by the central institutions of the state, over which local political leaders had little control. However, we wished to argue that regarding the provision of two crucial resources—employment opportunities (through local planning policies) and housing—the control of local authorities provides a key to a considerable degree of control over the life chances of rural workers. A survey that we conducted of councillors in Suffolk confirmed the findings of an earlier national study showing that farmers were by far the most numerous group on rural councils before reorganization.[16] On average they were 35 percent of members nationally, compared with less than 0.1 percent farm workers and twice as many as the next most prominent group. However, reorganization had been widely opposed by rural councillors who feared the consequences of being amalgamated with neighboring urban districts, and indeed reorganization significantly affected the level of farmers' representatives on the new authorities. On the Suffolk County Council, for example, the proportion of councillors who were farmers was 16 percent, rising to an average of 23 percent of the district councils.

These figures imply that farmers are in a considerable minority in local government in Suffolk, but they require careful interpretation. For example, farmers remained considerably overrepresented in the positions of greatest potential power: the chairmanship of council committees. Thus although farmers accounted for only 16 percent of the county council membership in Suffolk, they enjoyed something approaching a monopoly over key positions. The chairman and vice-chairman of the county council were both farmers, and so too was the leader of the majority conservative group. The chairmen of the Planning Committee and the Education Committee were both large-scale farmers, and so were the chairmen of the key finance and policy subcommittees. The chairman of the Social Services Committee was also a farmer. In fact, no major committees on the county council were not chaired by farmers or landowners. Such evidence, though of interest, needs to be treated with caution, however. Clearly numerical representation of itself may mean little. The point here is that power has a potential quality. Political positions represent only one type of potential power resource, which must nevertheless be used before power can be said to have been exercised. This is important in order to avoid any naive positional approach to the analysis of community power.[17] Too many elite studies have taken the positional definition of powerful groups for granted, yet power cannot adequately be studied from any such static and formalistic perspective.

Furthermore, even if farmers are seen to occupy and to use key positions within local councils, it should not be assumed that they are exercising power in their own interests. Many farmers, for example, cite altruism, philanthropy, and public service as their motives for becoming involved in local government, values that are often ingrained in the gentlemanly ethic traditionally associated with the rural squirearchy.[18] Such articulated motives should not lightly be ignored, for as Giddens has pointed out:

> We are surely not justified in making direct inferences from the social background, or even the educational experience, of elite groups to the way in which they employ whatever power they possess once they attain positions of eminence. Because a man emanates from a specific type of class background, it does not inevitably follow that he will later adopt policies which are designed to promote class interests corresponding to that background.[19]

It is not enough, then, to look simply at who is exercising power or who is in a position that entails the right to exercise power without also considering the question of who is benefiting as a result. One group may, in principle, exercise power in the interests of another, making the final test of power not so much who decides but what is decided—and, of course, not decided.

Political Stability and Rural Community Power: Some Problems

It was with these familiar prescriptions in mind that we set out to observe the local elite in action by analyzing important political issues, the decision-making process surrounding them, and who gains and who loses thereby—in other words the time-honored procedure suggested by Dahl, Polsby, Laumann, and others. We therefore began by scanning local and regional newspapers dating back to 1960 and talking to selected informants who had access to the local political process. Our intention was to discover a number of political issues that could form a basis of our analysis. Following Dahl's prescriptions, we intended to assess the power of the farming and landowning interests in Suffolk by analyzing the course and outcome of those issues where these interests had been mobilized against opposition.[20] Yet after some diligent searching, it became apparent that Suffolk's recent political history was remarkably devoid of issues or indeed of any outward manifestations of political conflict. With one or two exceptions, Suffolk's politics appeared remarkably noncontentious. Nothing, it seemed, happened to disturb the calm surface of social relations in the county. We, therefore, encountered the phenomenon of deference from the obverse side. Despite a hierarchical class structure and plenty of plausible issues over which conflict could occur, we found a decidedly tranquil situation of political harmony. So it was that our chief research objective shifted from the analysis of issues to the explanation of political tranquility. Why were there so few issues?

At this point we were forced to face some epistemological problems. In the light of previous research on agricultural workers that had established that their class situation was characterized by extreme powerlessness, poor pay and conditions, a high degree of insecurity, and lack of alternative opportunities in both housing and employment, we were reluctant to take this apparent tranquility at face value. Farm workers were characterized not so much by an identification with the prevailing political and social order as by a somewhat fatalistic acceptance of it—an ambivalent accommodation to the realities of the class structure as they perceived them.[21] But how could we question the validity of this political stability in Suffolk, particularly when local farmers and landowners themselves portrayed local politics in terms of harmony and consensus? For Dahl, such a question would be regarded as either meaningless or irrelevant.[22] According to him, a situation of political stability such as this can be explained only in terms of a theoretical model of democratic pluralism, and the assertion of any interests independently of, and in contradiction to, the subjects' own interpretation of their interests is untenable. Thus what an individual asserts or believes to be his interests (and we should note that the two may not be synonymous) are therefore his interests "even though from the point of view of observers, his belief is false or ethically wrong."[23] For Dahl, although power may be unevenly distributed within a given political system among the leaders and the led, the latter nevertheless retain the crucial power to vote their leaders in and out of office and to organize politically to defend or sponsor their interests. If they are dissatisfied with the way in which their leaders are using their power, they enjoy both the right and the capacity to do something about it. A corollary is that if people do not act in defense or pursuit of their interests, they must be reasonably satisfied with the way in which power has been exercised on their behalf. Mass political inaction, such as we found in Suffolk, is thus for Dahl indicative of a well–integrated and smoothly running system of local representative democracy.

Fundamental to this model are the twin concepts of legitimacy and community. Thus power is seen to be exercised with the consent of those subject to it (in other words it is legitimated), and to the benefit of collective rather than narrow sectional interests (that is, it is communal in benefit). Thus, power relationships, according to this model, involve moral obligations of deference on the part of subordinates and of altruism on the part of superordinates. As Parsons has expressed it, power is "a means of effectively mobilizing obligations in the interests of collective goals."[24] Although such mutual obligations may have to be enforced at times (for example, by subordinates pressuring their leaders or by leaders invoking the law against recalcitrant subordinates), they are more generally morally binding. Thus, people accept the actions of their leaders because they recognize their legitimate right to take such actions on their behalf. It need hardly be added that such a theoretical formulation appears particularly apposite to rural politics where relations of domination may still be morally sanctioned according to the traditions of upper–class philanthropy as much as to office. Despite the diminishing importance of traditional forms of authority in local politics, the notion of noblesse oblige with regard to public service has remained remarkably resilient and provides an excellent example of Parsons's emphasis on the moral character of power relations.

Two major problems with the Dahl–Parsons pluralist explanatory model arise, however. The first concerns the fact that it can take no account of the possibility that power may be used amorally to prevent opposition from arising. There is, in other words, a second face of power.[25] The powerful may be in a position to mask or preempt the emergence of any issues that appear to threaten their dominance and thereby avoid any visible manifestation of class antagonisms. In this sense political stability may be the consequence of a prior exercise of manipulative power rather than the continuing exerice of any truly authoritative power.

Bachrach and Baratz suggest three ways in which such manipulative power may be exercised. First, potentially contentious issues may be excluded from the political agenda by defining them out as nonpolitical or illegitimate demands. Second, there is a problem of anticipated reaction: the power of the dominant group may be such that potential opponents consider it wise not to raise complaints, perhaps because they fear repercussions. Clearly, where (as in many parts of Suffolk, for example) the same individuals dominate the local political system, the local employment market, the distribution of local public housing, the local legal institutions, such as the magistracy, and are still sources of local welfare and patronage, there is likely to be a strong disincentive for less powerful and more dependent groups to mount a challenge against them.[26] Third, inaction may indicate the power exercised by dominant groups over the political consciousness of their subordinates. There is, in Schattschneider's terms, a "mobilization of bias" prompted by the dominance of the locally powerful. The conditions of the rural class structure are frequently conducive to the exercise of power in this manner. For example, the work situation on most farms is small scale and has a particularistic rather than bureaucratic management structure.[27] Thus the spatial location of the different classes is likely to bring them into geographically (though not necessarily socially) close proximity. Social cohesion and control may therefore be ensured through personal ties, and a spurious legitimacy is achieved by those in power through the effective transmission or imposition of their values, rationalizations, and ideologies to subordinate groups.[28] Instead of legitimacy springing spontaneously from below as the source of power for community leaders, it may be imposed from above as a consequence of their hegemony. As Gouldner has observed, it is always possible for the powerful to "enforce their moral claims and conventionalize their moral defaults.[29]

Bachrach and Baratz, therefore, suggest that nondecision making presents a second face of power, which must be taken into account. They offer a critique of the Dahl–Parsons approach, which had placed a concept of articulated preference at the center of any empirical study of power. Faced with the same empirical observation—an absence of political conflict—Bachrach and Baratz open the way to an entirely opposite theoretical interpretation. They question the adequacy of articulated preference as the basis of any conclusive proof of the distribution and legitimacy of local political power. Nevertheless they wish to operate within the same epistemological paradigm as Dahl and Parsons do; they are simply pointing out that the power to make and enforce a decision also includes the power not to make and enforce such decisions (hence the term *nondecision making* is applied to their approach). Unfortunately, it is much more difficult to demonstrate the nonexistence of something than it is to demonstrate its existence, and although some ingenious attempts have been made to circumvent this problem, they have not been very successful.[30] As our experience in Suffolk demonstrates, there is nothing to observe in a situation where nondecision making is suspected of being a widespread political phenomenon.

Bachrach and Baratz themselves shy away from the possible consequences of their own critique where, by definition, nonarticulated preferences will not be amenable to orthodox research strategies. Thus even they suggest that where there is no observable evidence of a conflict or subjectively recognized goals, "the presumption must be that there is a consensus on the prevailing allocation of values."[31] This, however, is an assumption that recent empirical evidence on lower-class political ideologies renders somewhat questionable. For example Converse and, more recently, Mann have demonstrated that working–class consciousness is characterized more by ambivalence and pragmatism toward the dominant values in society and that they frequently lack any coherent set of beliefs that would lend legitimacy to the prevailing social and political order.[32]

Bachrach and Baratz therefore do not specify how precisely nondecision making is to be demonstrated. Although they offer a means of escaping from the teleology of the Dahl–Parsons model and hence some of its tautological aspects (the proof that the powerless have nothing to complain about is that they complain so little), they have few methodological prescriptions to offer and leave the benefit of the doubt with the pluralist/consensualist model.

How, then, are we to assess our two conflicting explanations of political inaction? Given the fact of political stability in Suffolk, is it to be explained in terms of the altruistic use of legitimate power or the self–interested use of manipulative power? If the former, then it is necessary to demonstrate both the existence of attributed legitimacy and the generation of communal benefit. It the latter, it is necessary to demonstrate the generation of sectional bias and the means whereby inaction has been maintained

in the face of this bias.[33] Since power involves causality, it becomes necessary to demonstrate the causal means by which power is used either for the
benefit of the community as a whole or for the benefit of those who hold
power. This leads to the second major difficulty of the Dahl–Parsons
approach: how are such benefits to be assessed?

Dahl argues that if an individual believes that he has benefited from a
given exercise of power, then he has so benefited, but this position begs the
crucial questions raised by Bachrach and Baratz. Dahl's position assumes
both that we are all in the same position to assess what is in our interests (we
are not ignorant of possible alternatives) and that what people believe to be
in their interests is what they state to be in their interests. For Dahl, there is
nothing useful to be said about interests beyond what is reported on a questionnaire return, for articulated preferences and interests are synonymous.
Against this, however, Lukes has argued that objective interests may be dis-
cerned in a given situation, even against the articulated preferences of those
to whom they are applied.[34] Lukes takes as indicative evidence of this Matthew Crenson's study of air pollution controls in Gary, Indiana, and elsewhere.[35] Using Crenson's study as an example, Lukes seeks to show how
self–evident interests may be imputed to those affected. Thus, he concludes,
"There is good reason to expect that, other things being equal, people
would rather not be poisoned (assuming in particular that pollution control
does not mean unemployment)—*even where they may not articulate this
preference.*"[36]

Lukes then shows how political inaction over the use of air controls
cannot be taken as evidence of either articulated or nonarticulated preference but is a result of the false consciousness of the inhabitants of Gary.
Lukes therefore seeks to replace the notion of articulated preference with
that of objective interest and the subjective assessment of benefit with an
externally available calculus of benefit according to some universal rationality. The pursuit of objective interests through the imposition of false consciousness is what Lukes calls the "third face" of power.

There are two reasonably obvious objections to Lukes's approach.
First, there is ultimately no philosophical justification for his assumption
that people would rather not be poisoned by air pollution, any more than
there is any ultimate philosophical justification for the pleasure principle,
which formed the basis of utilitarianism. We cannot take for granted what
in Weberian terms can be called a formal rationality of human behavior,
which would assume some universal human nature. We are, rather, limited
to the elucidation of a causally adequate form of substantive rationality
derived from the society in which they are located. Second, on a more practical level, it is by no means clear how widely applicable Crenson's example
is. Most studies of community power (and certainly not our own in Suffolk)
do not deal with such life–and–death issues; the stuff of most local politics

is of a much less dramatic, though nonetheless decisive, character. Despite these objections, however, Lukes's approach, suitably modified to take account of its inherent weaknesses, can be a useful methodological tool in the investigation of political passivity. For example, it is both methodologically viable and theoretically justifiable to infer interests contextually, without subscribing to any universalistic notion of objective interest. In the context of the formal rationality of a capitalist economy, for instance, it can be argued that it is in people's interests to maximize their economic returns and minimize their costs, other things being equal. This is not to deny the substantive rationality of altruistic behavior within a market system, but it is to recognize that the function of the ideal–type market lies in allocating values such that the functionally rational goals of actors operating within the market lies in the maximization of returns. In this way, the contextual interests of two parties to a transaction may be deduced independently of the subjective meanings that they attribute to their actions.

On the basis of this argument, it may be suggested that it is in the interests of, say, employers to sponsor and support such policies that result in the maintenance of cheap labor supplies. This is not to argue that those employers who do in fact support such policies do so for this expressed purpose; they may have other subjective motives entirely. In other words, we may draw a distinction between what the powerful state as their motives for acting (and of course there is no check on whether these actually are their motives) and the consequences that follow from this with regard to their own contextually defined material and political interests. We can say something about objective effects as well as subjective motives, but since power is concerned with causality, it is, arguably, the former that are politically the most significant. Thus it can be argued that, irrespective of their aims and motives, the effect of employers' support for policies that perpetuate a low–wage economy advances their own interests as employers. Similarly when property owners combine to prevent any further residential development in their locality (especially public housing development, which might threaten their property values), we can argue that irrespective of their stated intentions, their interests are furthered in that the resultant scarcity of housing in the countryside serves to inflate the market value of existing dwellings. Or again, we can argue that it is in the interests of those relatively prosperous sections of a local population to support low public expenditure policies by their local councils, for this ensures low rates (local property taxes), while such a policy will disadvantage the least prosperous sections who may be expected to benefit most from increased public expenditure on welfare and other similar services. In all three of these examples, the interests of employers, house owners, and ratepayers respectively can be inferred contextually, independently of any professed motives and preferences which these groups may voice. Such assertions cannot be quantified, but all may be justified with reference to functionally rational modes of behavior within the context of a market economy.

The concept of contextual interest thus provides a way out of the impasse threatened by the existing three faces of power. First, it enables some assessment of benefit to be made on an objective—that is, external—basis. Second, and consequently, it enables the balance of political power to be assessed even in a situation of total political inaction and where no issues are politically contested.

The Mobilization of Bias in
Suffolk Politics

We bagan our analysis of political inaction in Suffolk by considering the outcomes of the routine exercise of political power and assessing their relative costs and benefits for the various sections of the country's population. The overall pattern soon became clear: a persistent and pervasive bias had been, and continued to be, generated through county and district council policies to the cumulative advantage of the relatively prosperous and to the distinct disadvantage of the already disadvantaged local inhabitants. For example, the county maintained an exceedingly low level of public expenditure and therefore had low rates. Only six other counties in England and Wales levied a lower rate than Suffolk. In the new county council's first year of operation (1974–1975), only four of thirty-seven counties in England and Wales spent less per capita on education and only four spent less per capita on social services. In the field of housing, the county and district councils over the years had pursued a policy of encouraging high-priced, low-density private housing development and severely restricting public housing development schemes. Between 1966 and 1973, for example, the district councils that comprised the old East Suffolk County had built an average 1.3 local authority dwellings per 1,000 population per year, compared with 2.7 for the East Anglian region as a whole; private dwellings were constructed at a rate of 5.6 per 1,000 population per year (6.6 for East Anglia as a whole). This lack of public housing development cannot be explained by any lack of demand. We estimated that at least ten thousand families were waiting for houses in Suffolk, and these figures do not take account of those who fatalistically did not bother to register or the substantial number of local farm workers in tied cottages whom the councils deemed unqualified because they were already adequately housed. Rather, it reflects both the low expenditure policies of the councils concerned and county council planning policy, which stipulates that housing development in rural areas should be of low density and very high quality (and hence price).

Planning policies are significant beyond their effect on the provision of working-class housing. Suffolk County Council strategic planning policy contains an explicit and traditional principle of opposing any large-scale development scheme, whether it involves council housing estates or the introduction of new industries into the rural parts of the county. These policies have been cloaked in a rhetoric of environmentalism and opposition to the so-called desecration of the Suffolk countryside by any large-scale housing or industrial development. But as our review of council expenditure indicated, such a concern appeared somewhat passive and negative rather than active and positive. Expenditure on the preservation of buildings and other rural amenities, for example, was less than three-quarters of the national average (despite Suffolk's containing two officially designated areas of outstanding natural beauty and being famed for the antiquity and beauty of its villages and churches, celebrated in the paintings of John Constable). Nor is the public encouraged to come and view the environment that has been preserved; expenditure on the promotion of tourism was also less than three-quarters of the national average. Indeed many councillors were openly hostile to the promotion of tourism, wishing to preserve the countryside from the public rather than for the public.

On these two major aspects of local political policy—low rates and preservationist planning—there was a complete political consensus between farmers and landowners on the one hand and the representatives of exurban middle-class newcomers on the other, and this coalition in part accounted for the lack of contentious political issues. It is possible to explain this consensus at two levels. At the level of *verstehen,* it is possible to assume that those who have sought to live in an aesthetically pleasing rural environment will quite rationally seek to preserve it from encroachment. This will apply to both local landowners and farmers, who seek to preserve their businesses but whose heritage is the land, and to the middle-class newcomers, who have moved into the countryside primarily as a retreat from the urban world and who seek peace, tranquility, and an idyllic setting for what they regard as a more authentic and a more harmonious life-style.[38] A further influx of new housing and/or industry would not only destroy this arcadian "village in the mind" but would spoil the somewhat static and sentimental vision of rural life that most newcomers possess.[39] There is therefore a quite understandable desire to preserve the quality of the rural environment.

This policy may also be assessed at the level of causality, and it is here that the most significant bias is revealed. In pursuing a strategy of rural preservation, council policies also reproduce a low-wage rural economy based on agriculture. This outcome has not necessarily been intentional, but whatever their motives, Suffolk's politicians have succeeded in generating an environmental policy with clear economic advantages for local employers of labor. Preservation of the rural status quo has necessarily involved the preservation of existing restricted labor market opportunities and depressed wages structures. Industry, in other words, represents more than a possible blot on the landscape. It is a potential source of competition for cheap labor. It is no coincidence that although East Anglia has been one of the most prosperous farming areas in Britain, local farm workers have remained among the lowest paid in the country.[40]

We carried out a similar exercise on the patterns of local public expenditure. Expenditures were generally at a low level, but on two items—the police and highways—they were above the national average. It was our belief that in the routine operation of established and publicly noncontentious policies, the pattern of benefits generated was clearly in favor of local agricultural and middle-class interests and to the detriment of the rural working class. In this context at least, the potential threat to the traditional political domination of local farmers and landowners by the arrival of a substantial number of newcomers had easily been absorbed; indeed no conflict on these issues had ever emerged. Faced with this evidence of mobilized bias through local council expenditure, housing, and planning policies, it was apparent to us that the pluralist explanation of political inaction, based as it is upon the assumption of communality as well as legitimacy, was largely inapplicable. Where it did provide a useful explanation of inaction was in relation to the relatively privileged groups in the county—farmers, landowners, and middle-class newcomers—who clearly had little to complain about. But as an explanation of working-class passivity, the Dahl-Parsons model was considered invalid. If, however, we were to explain the passivity of the Suffolk working class in terms of a model of political manipulation, then it was equally apparent that we needed to demonstrate not only that sectional bias was operating but also how opposition to this bias was effectively prevented from emerging. Having considered outcomes, we next had to consider causes.

The first point to note here is that even most sectionally biased policies are often presented by those responsible for them as being in the public interest. It is not, however, that political leaders (at least, in our view, as far as Suffolk is concerned) deliberately misrepresent the nature of the policies they pursue, but rather that the public interest and their sectional interest are congruent. Accusations of deliberate self-interest on the part of Suffolk's political representatives are likely to meet with ridicule, for as they see it, they are giving freely of their time on behalf of the community to develop and execute policies from which everyone may benefit. Thus, explaining the county council's planning policy, one member (himself a farmer and landowner) observed: "The lack of industry does help farmers, but this is an agricultural county. It's always been the county council's priority—you don't build on good agricultural land. It does help farmers, but that's incidental." And one of his colleagues suggested: "We are all mixed up with the agricultural thing. I mean, when you boil it down, the towns and villages and what–have–you in Suffolk in the main are dependent on agriculture, so that we really have all got the same ends all the time."

These arguments, of course, have something of a self–fulfilling element, for the people of Suffolk remain dependent upon agriculture only to the extent that planning policies inhibit industries from locating in the county. We are not arguing that Suffolk's political leaders are being cynically hypocritical; rather it is the effect of the dominance of their values, within which is embedded their definitions of what constitute the public interest, that has perpetuated the marked mobilization of bias in local planning and other policies.

This being the case, we were still faced with the problem of explaining how such sectional policies had been routinely pursued under the guise of communal benefit with virtually no challenge from those most disadvantaged. We found that the causal mechanisms that account for the lack of opposition in Suffolk included all three of those types of nondecision making that Bachrach and Baratz listed. Thus opposition was avoided by defining out certain issues from the political agenda, prevented through the anticipated reactions of politically fatalistic working class, and suppressed through the transmission of certain ideologies and definitions of the situation.

Certain political issues remain unvoiced in the formal political arena by the extraordinary emphasis that leading local politicians in Suffolk place upon what they term "keeping politics out of local government." Before the 1974 reorganization, for example, over half of all council members in the East Anglian region claimed to be independent of any political party (the proportion reached 68 percent among those with an agricultural interest). Indeed the reorganization of local government was widely condemned for stimulating the party–political institutionalization of local government in the area. The significance of this entrenched value of nonpolitics is that it not only derives from but in turn perpetuates and strengthens the prevailing definition of the political situation of Suffolk as one of consensus. It enables sectional policies to be presented as being in the public interest because there is a general acceptance that local governmental affairs are apolitical in character. If decision making can be represented as the implementation of the obvious and if everybody is assumed to be on the same side, then the task of councillors becomes merely the pursuit of a nonproblematically defined public interest. In consequence, those who refuse to accept the normative convention of nonpolitics can find themselves labeled as troublemakers or extremists and thus unworthy of serious political attention because their views so clearly lack the legitimacy of common acceptance. In this way political conflict can be defined out as the work of politically motivated, and therefore illegitimate, agitators pursuing their own selfish and sectional interests against the common good. Party politics thus becomes defined as irrelevant and, in the absence of party politics, conflicts of interest generally fail to become manifest. A belief in nonpolitical local government both obscures an essential conservatism and also effectively blocks the fundamental means by which opposition may come to be voiced.

The second cause of nondecision making refers to the fact that disadvantaged groups may fail to act out of anticipation that their proposed actions may prove to be fruitless or costly. According to Parry and Morriss, such cases may be amenable to study only insofar as tentative demands are initially made by subordinate groups as a means of assessing which way the political wind is blowing, with these demands only later being withdrawn or aborted.[41] Clearly, however, cases of inaction stemming from anticipated reactions will more usually be routinized, for subordinate groups are likely to be only too familiar with the direction of the prevailing political wind—and in Suffolk, at least, it rarely wavers. Consequently inaction may often follow anticipated reactions with no outward and visible sign that nondecision making has occurred, and in such cases it will appear indistinct from the inaction that stems from political satisfaction, for in neither case will subordinate groups actually do anything. This outcome is significant for it allows those in power to impute satisfaction in a situation of working–class passivity, as in Suffolk. A district council chairman put it thus:

> It's because of the type of people who live in Suffolk—they're people of the land, but they're no fools. They're very astute people. But they don't get terribly involved—no, that's not the right way to say it—they feel strongly, and they expect their representatives to know what they're feeling strongly about, almost instinctively without writing it down or without saying it. . . . I suppose, being facetious they choose the right people, and the right people do the right things for them. It can't be like that, but it almost looks like that, doesn't it?

The problem with this explanation—apart from the plethora of causes of militancy that exist in the county—is that there are occasions when pluralist democracy is supposed to exhibit healthy opposition and competition among its members. On such occasions in Suffolk, however—such as local elections and participation exercises by local planning authorities—it has proved extremely difficult to excite any political involvement on the part of the population. Unopposed elections are commonplace, turnout at elections that do take place is abysmally low, and public reaction to participatory planning experiments has disappointed local planning officers. The problem is that for the bulk of the Suffolk population, inaction has become the standard and routinized response to a situation of continuing political exclusion. For most of the time, they neither expect nor are expected to play any part in policy making, and when structured opportunities to participate are offered them in order to maintain the image of a healthy democratic process, they react as they have always reacted—by doing nothing. Most people in Suffolk recognize, consciously or implicitly, that politics is not their game and that they cannot change the rules.

This leads us to consider the third area of nondecision making identified by Bachrach and Baratz and referred to by Lukes as the third face of power: the situation where inaction results from the prior manipulation of the beliefs, values, and information available to subordinate groups by powerful elites. A consideration of this issue takes us far beyond an examination of local politics in Suffolk, but it is possible to indicate how these mechanisms operate within the context of rural politics and the rural class structure of the area. The key to this issue lies in the particularism that characterizes local class relationships both inside and outside the institutionalized political system. Power is often personalized and nonbureaucratic. The result is that political issues become individualized and personalized, and the transmission of elite ideologies across class boundaries is considerably eased. For example, many councillors claim a personal rather than a party-political following. One said: "In rural areas the individual carries more weight. If he's well known, irrespective of his politics, a local man has an advantage over a non-local man, especially in Suffolk. It's a personal following."

As a result, influence is expected to be exerted at the individual rather than the collective level. (There are some obvious parallels here with patron–clientelist politics.) Councillors see only personal problems—such as the inability of a particular family to obtain a house—rather than political issues—the planning and budgetary policies that produce a housing shortage. Thus by fragmenting issues into problems, the particularism of power relationship inhibits collective mobilization and prevents generalized complaints from being raised through the orthodox political channels.

Such particularisms is not limited to the politics of Suffolk; it pervades the whole of local class relationships. For example, the direction of technological change in the agriculture of the county has also tended to make relationships between farmers and farm workers more particularistic and diffuse. By drastically reducing the number of farm workers employed and increasingly isolating those who remain, mechanization has reduced any collectivist impulse that might have emerged in the past from the frequent and pervasive contact between workers on the land. Furthermore, the continuing outflow of labor from agriculture, often accompanied in the past by rural depopulation, has undermined the solidarities of whatever rural working–class subculture formerly existed in rural communities in an era when labor was more numerous on the land.[42] Thus, while agricultural workers in Suffolk in the past often developed a strong, if covert, sense of group identity based upon their shared experience with workmates and neighbors, it seems likely that this bond has declined.[43]

Relationships with farmers have also been affected by these changes. The debureaucratization of farms that has been a consequence of the diminution of the labor force has simultaneously allowed interaction between employer and employees to take place on a more informal and personal basis. Changes in the work situation have therefore encouraged a more particularistic and paternalistic mode of control.[44] In addition the former communal solidarities of the rural village have been disrupted by the arrival in most parts of Suffolk of the new, nonagricultural, adventitious mostly urban middle-class population. One consequence has been that new status divisions have been created between locals and newcomers. These cut across class lines, encouraging a solidarity among locals (both farmers and farm workers) against such unfamiliar interlopers. This cohesiveness has been exacerbated by the impact of the newcomers on the local housing market. Farm workers have gravitated to tied cottages, located mostly on the farms (rather than in the villages), which leads to even more pervasive contact between employer and employee.[45] Taken together, these changes have encouraged particularistic vertical ties while providing a set of conditions under which the beliefs and values of local farmers and landowners are more easily transmitted to their employees, and isolation from alternative belief systems is more easily ensured.

Both the local political process and the surrounding social structure therefore encourage identification and solidarity along a local–nonlocal, rural–urban cleavage rather than along class lines (insofar as they encourage collective action at all). In Suffolk, indeed, there is an entrenched ideology of antiurbanism. Outsiders provide the focus in terms of which internal solidarity may be generated, and stereotyped urbanites, with their demands for cheap food, their disregard for the countryside, and their ignorance of country folk, provide the ideal source of internal cohesion among the locals. This ideology is not deliberately fostered as some kind of shrewd diversionary tactic. By and large, the farmers and landowners of Suffolk maintain a genuine antipathy to urban ways and urban values (as they perceive them), and the hostility of farm workers to their village's being taken over by outsiders is real enough. However, such an ideology does promote cross-class solidarity by blurring class divisions as subjectively perceived and helping to perpetuate local working-class acceptance of the values and beliefs of the local gentry.

One objection to our argument is possible. It could be suggested that if a particular group is so dominant that it can successfully prevent opposition before it becomes articulated, then no opposition and no contentious issues would ever develop. Does our model explain too much, therefore, rather than too little? Some political conflicts have occurred from time to time in Suffolk, so how can public issues arise in a situation of pervasive political domination? From the evidence that we collected, three possibilities suggest themselves. First, conflict may arise as a result of a split within the local ruling group. In Suffolk, for example, a cause célébre concerns the antipathy of the newcomers toward the effects of modern farming practice on the environment. A good deal of conflict has been generated between farmers and newcomers over such matters as hedgerow removal, aerial spraying, straw and stubble burning, the diversion of public footpaths, and so on. This conflict is a focus of much local–newcomer antagonism. It is, however, very localized in extent—almost literally parochial—and although much friction is created locally over these issues, they rarely enter the formal political arena and certainly have no observable effect on the consensus over political policies at county and district level between the two groups. Second, conflict is generated where an outside agency attempts to impose a policy on the county against the will of those in power locally. There are numerous examples of political issues being generated in this way, mostly against central government proposals for the county. These are not conflicts generated from within the local political system and indeed merely serve to enhance the sense of local consensus against outside interference. The third area where contentious issues arise concerns situations where no one's interests are affected and therefore where conflict is not a threat. In Suffolk, these issues include such matters as fluoridation of the local water supply and a heated conflict over whether council meetings should open with prayers. It is possible to suggest, therefore, that the political significance (in terms of its effect on the overall pattern of resource distribution) of any given issue varies in inverse proportion to the publicity that it receives.

It would appear, therefore, that an analysis of the contentious issues that have arisen in Suffolk politics, far from casting doubt upon our assertions of political dominance by the farming and landowning interests in the county, strengthens them. The situation in Suffolk seems analogous to that found in rural Wales by Madgwick and his colleagues in what remains virtually the only other British rural community power study. Noting the local domination of the farming interest, they conclude: "No other class is coherent enough to operate as a group. . . . The views of the elites tend to confirm both the existence of some stresses and tensions and the absence of widespread and overt class hostility."[46] Or as one of our respondents, a small holder, put it: "It's the big people who get on these councils so there's no one left to pressure the council. It's their decisions, not the decisions of the small people. They pretend to give you a say, but what they say, goes." This, in just three sentences, is how we would summarize the situation in Suffolk, too.

Conclusion

We hope that this analysis has some relevance beyond local politics in Suffolk. We were forced to confront some of the key problems faced by any analysis of political stability in advanced industrial societies. We have treated the lack of discontent, the quiescence, the absence of rancor, as problematic in their own right within the context of a hierarchical social and political structure. Dogs that do not bark in the night are in some ways even more interesting than dogs that do. Are they contentedly asleep as the Dahl-Parsons pluralist model would suggest? Are they muzzled as the Bachrach and Baratz approach maintains? Or have they been doped as some Marxist models might lead us to believe and, as Lukes suggests, ought to be allowed as a possibility? These three models do not, as most commentators seem to have concluded, have to be taken as mutually exclusive. All political systems maintain a certain minimum consensus, yet many procedures and mechanisms prevent the articulation of the interests of nonpowerful groups. It is possible to refer to contextual interests in any political and social system and hence to cut through epistemological problems of investigating empirically a system of political dominance from which contentious issues rarely or never emerge.

Notes

1. See Colin Bell and Howard Newby, *Community Studies* (London: Allen and Unwin, 1971), chap. 7.

2. See P. Stanworth and Anthony Giddens, eds., *Elites and Power in British Society* (Cambridge: Cambridge University Press, 1974).

3. Maurice Stein, *The Eclipse of Community* (New York: Harper and Row, 1964).

4. Steven Lukes, *Power: A Radical View* (London: Macmillan, 1975).

5. For agricultural workers, see especially Howard Newby, *The Deferential Worker* (London: Allen Lane, 1977). Also see Howard Newby, "The Low Earnings of Agricultural Workers: A Sociological Approach," *Journal of Agricultural Economics* 23 (1972): 15-24, and "Agricultural Workers in the Class Structure," *Sociological Review* 20 (1972): 413-439; and Colin Bell and Howard Newby, "The Sources of Variation in Agricultural Workers' Images of Society," *Sociological Review* 21 (1973): 229-253.

For farmers and landowners, see Colin Bell and Howard Newby, "Capitalist Farmers in the British Class Structure," *Sociologia Ruralis* 14 (1974): 86-107; David Rose, Peter Saunders, Howard Newby, and Colin Bell, "Ideologies of Property: A Case Study," *Sociological Review* 24 (1976): 699-731: and Peter Saunders, Howard Newby, David Rose, and Colin Bell, "Rural Community and Rural Community Power," in Howard Newby, ed., *International Perspectives in Rural Sociology* (London: Allen Lane, 1978), which also contains some of the material presented in this chapter.

6. Howard Newby, Colin Bell, David Rose, and Peter Saunders, *Property Paternalism and Power* (London: Hutchinson, and Madison: University of Wisconsin Press, forthcoming).

7. Ronald Frankenberg, *Communities in Britain* (Hammondsworth: Penguin Books, 1966) p. 252.

8. See David Rose, Howard Newby, Peter Saunders, and Colin Bell, "Land Tenure and Official Statistics," *Journal of Agricultural Economics* 25 (1977): 68–75.

9. See Newby, "Low Earnings," and "Agricultural Workers."

10. See Newby, "Agricultural Workers," and *Deferential Worker.*

11. For examples, see Stanley Elkins, *Slavery* (Chicago: University of Chicago Press, 1958), and E.D. Genovese, *In Red and Black* (London: Allen Lane, 1971) and *Roll, Jordan, Roll* (New York: Pantheon, 1974).

12. See Howard Newby, "The Deferential Dialectic," *Comparative Studies in Society and History* 17 (1975): 139–164, and *Deferential Worker.*

13. F.M.L. Thompson, *English Landed Society in the Nineteenth Century* (London: Routledge and Kegan Paul, 1963).

14. J.M. Lee, *Social Leaders and Public Persons* (Oxford: Oxford University Press, 1963).

15. Cf. Max Weber, *The Theory of Social and Economic Organization* (Glencoe, Illinois: Free Press, 1947).

16. For full details, see Newby et al., *Property Paternalism,* chap. 6; L. Moss and S. Parker, *The Local Government Councillor* (London: MMSO, 1967).

17. See Bell and Newby, *Community Studies,* chap. 7.

18. See Newby, "Deferential Dialectic."

19. Anthony Giddens, *The Class Structures of Advanced Societies* (London: Hutchinson, 1974) p. xii.

20. Robert Dahl, *Who Governs?* (New Haven: Yale University Press, 1961), and Nelson W. Polsby, *Community Power and Political Theory* (New Haven: Yale University Press, 1963).

21. See Newby, *Deferential Worker,* chap. 7.

22. Dahl, *Who Governs?*

23. Ibid., p. 52n.

24. Talcott Parsons, *Societies: Evolutionary and Comparative Perspectives* (Englewood Cliffs, N.J.: Prentice-Hall, 1966) p. 85.

25. P. Bachrach and M.S. Baratz, "The Two Faces of Power," in their *Power and Poverty* (New York: Oxford University Press, 1970).

26. See also the discussion of the power of "Jones" in Springdale by Arthur J. Vidich and Joseph Bensman, *Small Town in Mass Society* (Princeton, N.J.: Princeton University Press, 1958).

27. Newby, "Agricultural Workers," and *Deferential Worker,* chap. 5.

28. See, for example, Bell and Newby, "Sources of Variation," and Rose et al., "Ideologies of Property."

29. Alvin W. Gouldner, *The Coming Crisis of Western Sociology* (New York: Basic Books, 1970) p. 297.

30. G. Parry and P. Morriss, "When Is a Decision Not a Decision?" in Ivon Crewe, ed., *British Political Sociology Yearbook,* 1: *Elites in Western Democracy* (London: Croom Helm, 1974), pp. 317–366.

31. Bachrach and Baratz, "Two Faces of Power," p. 49.

32. Michael Mann, "The Social Cohesion of Liberal Democracy," *American Sociological Review* 35 (June 1970): 455–470.

33. See Lukes, *Power.*

34. Ibid.

35. Matthew Crenson, *The Unpolitics of Air Polution* (Baltimore: Johns Hopkins University Press, 1971).

36. Lukes, *Power,* p. 45. Emphasis added.

37. The chapter dealing with local politics in Newby et al., *Property Paternalism,* runs to over seventy pages; a more abbreviated summary appears in Saunders et al., "Rural Community."

38. On the significance of notions of heritage and stewardship, see Rose et al., "Ideologies of Property."

39. R.E. Pahl, *Urbs in Rure* (London: Weidenfeld and Nicolson, 1965).

40. For data, see Newby, "Low Earnings."

41. Parry and Morriss, "When Is a Decision Not a Decision?"

42. See Howard Newby, "The Changing Sociological Environment of the Farm," *Journal of Farm Management* 2 (1974): 474–487.

43. Newby, *Deferential Worker.*

44. Howard Newby, "Paternalism and Capitalism," in Richard Scase, ed., *Industrial Society: Class Cleavage and Control* (London: Allen and Unwin, 1976).

45. This highly abbreviated account is elaborated in Newby, *Deferential Worker.*

46. Peter Madgwick et al., *The Politics of Rural Wales* (Cardiff: University of Wales Press, 1973), p. 156.

10 Local Corporatism

Gudmund Hernes and Arne Selvik

Corporatism increasingly has become the focus of social research.[1] Loosely defined, it describes a system of interest intermediation between organized groups, particularly in the economic area, and the state apparatus. This interpenetration can take many forms; examples are representation on public committees or consultation before new legislation is proposed.

Rokkan has argued that the multifarious interaction of government agencies and interest organizations—what he calls corporate pluralism—supplements, and to some extent supplants, territorial representation through the electoral process—what he calls numerical democracy.[2] His thesis is that votes count in regular elections and determine who shall be the members of representative bodies. But organized interest groups, with their permanent and full-time staffs, manned by experts on par with those found in specialized state agencies, provide the more important premises for political decisions, and hence to a large extent determine what the content of public policy will be. "Votes count, but resources decide."

Originally corporatism was considered primarily a system for the political representation of economic interests. In contrast to Marxist theory, which bases its vertical theory on the conflicting interests of workers and capitalists generated in the labor market and in the authority relations of production, corporatism sought to reduce this conflict through horizontal interest representation encompassing both employers and employees in the different sectors of the economy. Several corporatism theorists, of different political persuasions, envisioned a central body composed of representatives from the organized interests in the different sectors. Its purpose was partly to coordinate economic decisions in the various branches of the economy, partly to resolve their conflicting claims on factors of production, and partly to set levels of remuneration for workers and employers in the various sectors.

Viewed in this way, a corporate system could partly supplement and partly replace the market as the automatic regulator of decentralized economic decisions. Increased monetarization and extended markets led to an increasing division of labor but also to a greater potential for direct and indirect economic repercussions, which might widen and amplify local or sectoral crises. Differentiated manufacturing produces not only goods but also groups lodged in different economic positions that became carriers of different and potentially conflicting economic interests.

Hence the market was not only a mechanism for decentralized coordination, it was also a major source of social conflict requiring organized resolution. By joint action between the affected interests and political authorities, the free price formation could be modified (for example, by public guarantees of minimum prices), free entry on the market could be limited (so as to prevent overcapacity or price wars), free establishment of firms could be confined (so as to secure balanced growth), and free commercial activities could be regulated (so as to reduce wide fluctuations in income). Under this perspective, corporatism can be considered as a way of systematically modifying the free operation of the market; it incorporates into the public decision-making apparatus those groups that are affected by the unhampered operation of the market—groups that also to a large extent organize in response to their market conditions.

Practically the whole literature on corporatism focuses on interest intermediation at the national level. The main thesis we present here is that corporate systems are now rapidly growing at the local level, at least in the Scandinavian countries. Hence we will ask whether the same causal processes are at work here as at the national level and what the consequences of this development are likely to be. We will also present the preliminary results of data pertaining to this development for Norway.

Theories of Growth of Corporatism:
The Effects of Market Conditions

Based on a thorough review of the literature, Schmitter has given an elaborate definition of corporatism:

> Corporatism can be defined as a system of interest representation in which the constituent units are organized into a limited number of singular, compulsory, noncompetitive, hierarchically ordered and functionally differentiated categories, recognized or licensed (if not created) by the state and granted a deliberate representational monopoly within their respective categories in exchange for observing certain controls on their selection of leaders and articulation of demands and supports.[3]

However, drawing on Manoilesco, Schmitter also distinguishes between societal corporatism, usually organized from below, with autonomous and penetrative organizations, and state corporatism, often organized from above, with dependent and penetrated organizations. In the former case, the characteristics of the formal definition are less exact than in the latter—for example, by the noncompetitive aspect's not being very strict or by its being the result of voluntary agreements among associations. Examples of societal corporatism are found in Switzerland, the Netherlands and Scandinavia; examples of state corporatism in Portugal, Spain, Brazil, Peru, Mexico, and Greece.

> Societal corporatism is found imbedded in political systems with relatively autonomous, multilayered territorial units: open competitive electoral processes and party systems; ideologically varied, coalitionally based ececutive authorities—even with highly "layered" or "pillared" political subcultures. State corporatism tends to be associated with political systems in which the territorial subunits are tightly subordinated to central bureaucratic power; elections are nonexistent or plebiscitary; party systems are dominated or monopolized by a weak single party; executive authorities are ideologically exclusive or more narrowly recruited and are such that political subcultures based on class, ethnicity, language, or regionalism are repressed. Societal corporatism appears to be the concomitant, if not ineluctable, component of the postliberal, advanced capitalist, organized democratic welfare state; state corporatism seems to be a defining element of, if not structural necessity for, the antiliberal, delayed capitalist, authoritarian, neomercantilist state.[4]

Since our empirical focus is on Norway, societal corporatism will be our concern here.

In *Modern Capitalism*, Shonfield views the expansion of the state as a way of correcting deficiencies of the market. The modern state finds itself simultaneously trying to accomplish several important goals: to foster full employment, to promote economic growth, to regulate working conditions, to smooth business cycles, to cover individual and social risks, to resolve labor conflicts, and to prevent inflation. Governments attempt to attain these goals through bargaining with and between organized groups about their future behavior in order to move economic conditions along the desired or agreed path.[5]

The first six of the items on the list also are goals of public policy at the local level. Municipalities try to secure full employment within their boundaries, to some extent by subsidies or even by running businesses themselves. In Norway there have been many examples of the latter during the recent recession. Many also have adopted growth-promoting policies, both by investments in infrastructure, like communication and educational facilities, and also by constructing industrial parks and plants available for firms that may locate production units there. This is also a form of subsidy, which in part is funded by the national government, the so-called *SIVA-anlegg* (industrial parks). Communities have also improved their educational systems in order to increase the skills of the local labor force. Institutional reforms have furthermore taken the form of establishing new positions, the most important of which is the *tiltaksshef* (director of initiatives). His chief task is to attract new industry and to advance the working conditions of already established firms.

Local ordinances to some extent have been adopted to affect working conditions. Many municipalities have also tried to reduce the impact of the recent downswing in the business cycle by temporary measures and appropriations of exemptions from standard rules. Some elements of the social security system are financed at the local level, with considerable variations between municipalities. For example, disability benefits (*uføretrygd*) are national, but some communities, especially the larger urban ones, appropriate additional funds. The same holds for pension programs or medicare. Finally, municipal authorities have on occasions tried to mediate in local labor disputes, albeit mostly informally.

Schmitter and Solvang and Moren have emphasized that growth of corporatist structures, such as public committees with interest group representation, has been characterized by spurts in response to economic crises.[6] No doubt the same tendency has been observed during the recent slump at the community level in that many more initiatives in the political arena have been taken, partly from local authorities, partly from business, and partly from trade unions. Often they operate as a team, directing their efforts toward the national government.

Lobbying can be documented by the response to a question asked of all 155 members of Parliament in the spring of 1977.[7] The answers to the question, "Has there during the last few years been any tendency toward more joint initiatives from communities, in which local politicians, administrators, trade union officials, business executives or organizations operate together?" follow:

A marked tendency toward more joint initiatives: 25.2 percent.

A certain tendency: 51.0 percent.

No change: 22.6 percent.

Rather fewer such initiatives: 0.6 percent.

No answer: 0.6 percent.

Clearly the tendency is marked: three–quarters of the representatives have taken note of it, and one quarter call it a marked tendency. In a questionnaire mailed to the chief executives of eight hundred of the largest corporations in Norway (response rate 72 percent), 11 percent responded that employee representatives had on one or more occasions participated in contacts directed toward the Parliament. However, the corresponding percentages were 24.4 with respect to contacts with the executive branch of ministries and 29.7 for contacts with municipal authorities. Of these who have had such contacts, 55 percent say that they have increased over the last five years, and only 1.9 percent say they have decreased. In sum, it seems safe to say that there has been a marked tendency toward more joint initiatives from firms, employees, and municipal authorities directed toward the national political system and more efforts by business leaders and worker representatives invested toward the local political system.

The same trend can be observed from the municipal side. In 1977 a questionnaire was mailed to all 360 mayors in Norway. Among the questions, they were asked whether contacts with firms about the location of new or the protection of existing jobs had become more or less frequent, and more or less important over the last few years. To the question of whether contact were more frequent during the past five years, 57.0 percent replied that they were more frequent, 38.8 percent about the same, 3.9 percent less frequent, and 0.3 percent reported no contact. To the question of whether contacts were more important for the municipality during the past five years, 75.2 percent said they were more important, 22.9 percent the same as before, 1.5 percent said they were less important, and 0.3 percent reported no contact. The tendency is quite clear: contacts have on the whole become more frequent and are definitely judged more important.

The same questions were asked of the 383 highest administrative officials in the municipalities, and the distribution is about the same. However, on another question there was a marked difference. They were asked whether the initiative of such contacts comes primarily from the municipality or from the firms. The responses follow:

Mostly from the municipality: mayors, 27.6 percent; highest officials, 16.8 percent.

Mostly from firms: mayors, 20.9 percent; highest officials, 39.4 percent.

Evenly divided: mayors, 51.5 percent; highest officials, 43.8 percent.

We find that the same tendency has been reported in many other studies of corporatism at the national level. More initiatives from the outside are directed to administrative officials than to elected representatives.

Other factors of course, may explain the difference, such as the fact that administrative officials may define their own role as more passive than politicians do. A final question is of interest in this context. The mayors were asked how they viewed more organized cooperation between the municipality and the organizations in the local economic and work life, such as trade unions, agricultural and fishing industry organizations, industry and trade associations, and the like. They answered thus:

Of very great importance of the municipality: 24.6 percent.

Of fairly great importance: 34.0 percent.

Of some importance: 29.7 percent.

Of little importance: 4.2 percent.

Hard to say: 7.4 percent.

Clearly mayors on the whole are in favor of more organized contacts of a corporatist nature. In sum, therefore, the contacts with individual firms have increased in frequency and importance, and the need for more structured contacts with local interests organizations is generally deemed more timely.

Another way of stating this is to say that there are more reactions in the political arena to turbulence created by the market. There are several reasons for this.[8] The operation of the market is based on the principles of self-interest and competition. But if competition hurts the interests of a firm, it need not restrict its activities to market-oriented action. Firms are political actors whose returns, conditions of expansion, and possibilities for survival to a great extent are decided within the political system. Self-interest does not end at the boundaries of the market. Particularly when a firm is threatened by loss or bankruptcy, its executives are likely to look for political solutions to its economic problems. This response is strengthened because of the increase of the political self-confidence of trade and industry. Second, several forms of public support for entrepreneurial and industrial activity have been established, ranging from special state banks to funds for retooling or financial support for relocation. Thus, not only is there a demand for public support; there is also a supply. Third, workers have more at stake. A large part of the labor force has invested income, time, and effort in capital goods or durables (such as homes, cottages, and boats) that are mortgaged and require a stable flow of income. When these investments are threatened by adverse market conditions, the reaction is political. Not surprisingly, the closest cooperation between labor and capital is found in firms that are in difficulties. Fourth, many municipalities and local governments are dependent on regular tax revenues for meeting their increasing commitments to education, care for the aged, welfare measures, and development of infrastructure, among others. When the sources of revenue are jeopardized, municipal authorities are likely to turn to the state for assistance to the firms that provide its tax base. In short, there is greater demand for assistance than the national state is willing to provide; and in crises there are more firms in trouble, more workers with personal investments, and more municipalities with greater commitments. "They all have more at stake, and in difficulties it is therefore natural that they stick together."[9]

Expansion of Public Authority and
Institutional Innovations

These developments to a large extent have the character of ad hoc reactions to market conditions that produce temporary coalitions for political action. Nevertheless, the aggregate of such actions, which are increasing and increasingly becoming a regular part of everyday political life, should be considered a definite corporatist trend emanating from local communities.

The development of local corporatism, however, is not only a reaction to variable economic conditions, but also to political changes. Since the mid-1960s, a wide array of new legislation more strictly regulates the conditions under which businesses may operate. Politics affects profits; hence business leaders and industrial organizations have to follow more closely and try to influence the laws that are enacted. They also must affect how the new legislation is implemented.

Much of this legislation leaves discretionary power to administrative agencies in the public sector. Because policy decisions are not entirely programmed by the legislation itself, it becomes relatively more important to keep a sharp eye on what their contents are and to do so on a continuing basis. We offer two illustrations of this development, the first pertaining to corporatist development at the national level. The managing director of the Norwegian Mercantile Association in 1974 argued:

> Our firms are no longer primarily interested in their particular product group, but concentrate more on the common objectives of the industry. This is a result of recent developments and a question which recently came up: What is the government's intentions? It is important that trade associations have proposals regarding policy decisions in the business area. If the government wants more to regulate trade, it will first have to learn what it is all about, which we can teach. In this I am not differentiating between conservative and socialist governments.[10]

The year before, the assistant manager of the Norwegian Industrial Association argued for strengthening local member organizations, primarily because industry would increasingly be affected by the government's new planning system:

> As regards public planning, industry has realized that such activity is of vital importance for the conditions required by the firm to operate at the community, county or regional level. This may be questions of land use, expansion of parts of the educational system, and a number of public activities essential to the environment in which firms and people have to operate. Industry realizes more and more that its interests have to be incor-

porated and heeded in the public planning process. Those who do not make their demands and points of view felt, won't be heard. . . .

During the sixties the government has attempted to develop legislation for an administrative organization which can carry out major physical and economic planning. I don't describe this in detail, but mention briefly the new building legislation, which outlines the directions for regional and local planning. The bill was proposed by the government in the fall of 1964 and passed by the parliament the following spring. The legislation is the basis for physical planning and zoning, where regional plans and municipal plans are essential aspects. § 20 of the law states: "The municipality shall as early as possible seek cooperation with public authorities, organizations, etc. which have an interest in the planning." If industry is to assert itself in this planning, it needs organs or organizations which can coordinate the interests of the industry, formulate them, and present them to the government. . . .

The Industrial Association will give high priority to developing industrial organizations which can serve as opposite numbers to the governmental planning agencies. The Industrial Association should coordinate industry's efforts on a national level, and certain means should be given to local and regional organs. But we have to realize that the Association is not able to carry out the day-to-day work at every point in the country. It is probably useful for industry first to organize at the district level, and that modes of work are developed which ensure coordination and articulation of industry's interests. The next step is to ensure that contacts with the county authorities are established which enable us to promote the interests as well as possible.[11]

In short, there is an increasingly felt need to manage the uncertainty created by the expansion of the public sector and discretionary power at the local level. The regulated want to regulate the regulators. The chairman of the Industrial Association in the county of Vestfold (Norway is divided into nineteen such counties) illustrate the extent of this desire:

I believe I have noticed a new understanding of the fact that industry has to work closely with the local authorities. We may say that until now we have been too concerned with the internal workings of the firm. When it comes to solving "external" problems such as land use, communications, housing, etc., we have been ill prepared to handle them. I believe that the involvement by many of the industrial leaders in the country in these areas will affect the working conditions of the firms. By gaining insight, knowledge and personal contacts with a broader social and political milieu, we will in the future be able to solve the problems of firms in simpler and better ways. By investing time in these problems today, we will secure the interests of industry in the general plans that set the framework for industrial development in the years ahead. Put another way, one can say it is preventive work for industry that is being done by today actively participating in the planning process at the county level.[12]

The Industrial Association in Vestfold County introduced an institutional innovation: it took the initiative for establishing a public position for an industrial consultant at the district level, and in 1973 it set up the Industrial Advisory Board, clearly a corporatist structure, with representatives from the Industrial Association, the county's Trade Union Council, and county authorities.

In short, the sequence of development seems to have been first the establishment of more authority and discretionary power for planning and development at the county and municipal level. Second, industrial organizations have reacted to the expansion of local public authority by internal organizational development to strengthen their capacity for exerting influence and to attempt to establish public positions and advisory boards with industrial representation so that their views are taken into account.[13] Hence not only fluctuating or changing market conditions are behind the growth in local corporatism. Another important impetus comes from the expansion of local public authority and discretionary power.

The local initiative was followed up at the national level. The Norwegian Industrial Association established a special committee to suggest a general system for industrial consultants. Its point of departure was the system existing in the agricultural sector, which for a long time has had an arrangement with public agronomists serving as consultants at both the county and municipal level. The arrangement came to serve as a model for the proposals put forward by the special committee of the Industrial Association. Hence it is not unreasonable to speak of cross–sectoral political learning in this context.[14] That is, institutional development can be considered a learning process.

The proposals of the special committee were relayed by the Industrial Association to the government, which in 1977 hired industrial consultants in five counties as an experiment. In addition, four other counties hired industrial consultants on their own, so that nine now function. Almost half of the nineteen counties are so represented. In five of the counties where the new positions have been set up, Industrial Councils have been established to serve in an advisory capacity to the industrial consultant; members represent the Industrial Association and the trade unions in the county. These are clearly corporatist creations; interest aggregation and articulation takes place within sectoral public bodies. No doubt this system is likely to grow in the next few years. Examples of other such corporatist organs at the district level could be given in both the industrial and agricultural areas.

Indeed the system with industrial consultants is now being expanded to encompass municipalities as well as counties. In 1977 funds were appropriated by the Parliament for the establishment of industrial consultants in three municipalities in each of five counties. Their main function is to provide information and guidance, particularly for smaller firms and especially about legislation, regulations, and funds that may be available to them through public banks and financial institutions. Also for these lower–level industrial consultants, advisory boards with representatives from both trade unions and the Industrial Association of the county have been set up. The county industrial consultant is a member of the board to facilitate county-wide coordination.

Corporatist structures, in the form of public agencies or boards with political representation from economic sectors, have existed for agriculture and fisheries for some time. Some have also been found in the industrial sector (like the municipal *tiltaksnemd*). On all levels they are rapidly expanding. The driving forces behind this growth have been changing market conditions, expansion of local authority and discretionary power, particularly over planning, and cross-sectoral learning. Local reactions to changing market conditions to a large extent have taken the form of ad hoc activities and coalition formation, whereas the reaction to the expanding public authority at the local level has been institutional innovations that are now spreading. The particularistic reactions to market conditions are probably due to the fact that their impact is particularistic, affecting firms differentially. In contrast, new laws and regulations represent permanently altered conditions and regular decision making, which requires continuous attention if specific interests are to be taken into account routinely. Hence they call for changes in institutional arrangements and interest representation on a stable basis.

The extent to which firms or their employees act directly toward the political system, or pass their initiatives through interest organizations, should be considered a variable, or rather two variables, since direct and indirect action in different amounts may be combined.

Consequences of the Development
of Local Corporatism

Several consequences flow from the development of local corporatism. First, the business community, by making demands for industrial consultants, representative boards, and the like, in effect is arguing in favor of the expansion of state power. However, it hopes to use this state power to further its sectoral interests, if possible by cooperating with the trade union movement—and to a large extent that is possible.

Second, political decisions in the economic area at the local level become more visible. But different sectoral agencies may sometimes act at cross-purposes. Hence we expect that there is a built-in tendency toward expanding boards with sectoral representation or to create new bodies on which several sectors can be represented and through bargaining resolve differences. In other words, it may lead to increased demands for corporatist participation in local administration.[15] Corporatism to some extent therefore feeds on itself. However, some may argue that by removing many important economic decisions from democratically elected bodies, decisions are likely to become more technocratic and depoliticized, leading to greater voter apathy. Which of these two trends is likely to be strongest remains to be seen.

Third, the fact that specialists on industrial policy, such as the industrial consultants and their advisory boards, become situated at the local level implies a potential source of conflict with the central administrative apparatus of the state. They may counter the decisions of public officials and policy makers in the industrial sector at the national level.

It is customary to distinguish between the territorial representation through the electoral channel and the functional representation through public committees encompassing spokesmen for organized interest groups at the national level. The new system of industrial consultants and their advisory boards at the county level provides a merger or fusion of territorial and functional representation. Local economic interests are given a better political foundation through new public programs, positions, and agencies at the county and municipal level.

The growth of strength at these lower levels may result in greater pressure for the use of more selective economic incentives. The new experts on local economic conditions will have few difficulties in mobilizing political arguments for why special supports, subsidies, differential taxes, or recompensation for general taxes for particular industries should be provided for their districts in order to maintain employment or to aid depressed areas. Such measures, whereby the national government intervenes selectively and discriminantly to assist or foster certain regions or industries, have been called neomercantilist. And the development of local corporatist structures no doubt will be an impetus for more neomercantilist measures, particularly since the assistance given to one district provides an incentive for countervailing relief in others.

Hence we may expect the central administrative apparatus to an increasing extent to have to take on the role of defenders of the market. As Berrefjord has stated, we may come to observe what at first may look like an idiological paradox: the bureaucrats in the ministries become the advocates for the economic efficiency and impersonal operation of competition and the price mechanism.[16] No doubt this may also add to the potential for conflict between local and national levels of policy making.

Finally, we are likely to find increasing competition between local communities vying for the location of plants from the same firms. They are caught in the prisoner's dilemma: all municipalities are forced to invest in industrial parks, which leads to an overcapacity and little comparative advantage. All invest more, but their relative position remains roughly the same. This phenomenon could be called market inversion, since it is political units that contend and economic organizations that can choose. In the questionnaire sent to all mayors in Norway, they were asked: "How strong is the competition with other municipalities about firms (factories, plants, hotels, etc.) for locating their establishment in your community?'' The responses follow:

Severe competition: 27.8 percent.

Fairly severe: 31.9 percent.

Fairly little: 26.9 percent.

Insignificant: 13.5 percent.

Almost 60 percent of the mayors experience this competition, and more than a quarter of them find it severe. No doubt the amount of competition has increased, evidenced by such developments as the establishment of factory halls and the growth of infrastructure.

Further analysis of these data to indentify the characteristics of those communities that face the greatest competition is in order—and is in progress. Because such direct and indirect subventions have to be funded largely by local taxpayers, a paradoxical result may be to put already established firms in a less favorable position. That is, the older cohorts of companies may have to support infant industry. So while local corporatist structures encourage neomercantilist policies from the national government, against which its officials have to defend the operation of the market and of free competition, local communities have to compete in a political market and woo firms with special favors to make themselves economically attractive.

Conclusion

Although most of the literature on corporatism focuses on the national level, in several countries there is a trend toward the development of corporatist structures at the local level. This has come about partly as a result of changing market conditions, often expressed politically in ad hoc coalitions of business executives, trade unionists, and local officials. But in part it is also due to new legislation aimed at regulating economic activity and putting more discretionary power at the county and municipal level, providing an incentive for institutional innovations to affect the use of the new authority. The response has been an offensive to strengthen the local branches of industrial associations, so that they can more effectively cope with the new challenges and opportunities, and the establishment of new public positions, such as industrial consultants and advisory boards with functional representation. The important actual and potential consequences range from growth of neomercantilist policies to increased community competition for industrial establishments. Further analysis is needed both to map differences between countries and to identify the processes that cause variations in local adaptations.

Notes

1. See, for example, Stein Rokkan, "Numerical Democracy and Corporate Pluralism," in Robert A Dahl, ed., *Political Oppositions in Western Democracies* (New Haven: Yale University Press, 1966), and Fredrick B. Pike and Thomas Stritch, eds., *The New Corporatism* (Notre Dame: University of Notre Dame Press, 1974).

2. Rokkan, "Numerical Democracy."

3. Philippe Schmitter, "Still a Century of Corporatism?" in Pike and Stritch, *New Corporatism,* p. 93.

4. Ibid., p. 105.

5. Andrew Shonfield, *Modern Capitalism* (New York: Oxford University Press, 1965), p. 231.

6. Schmitter, "Still a Century," and Bernt Krohn Solvang and Jorolv Moren, "Partsreprestasjon i Komieer: Litt om Utviklingen over Tid [Representation on public committees: A historical sketch]," in Jorolv Moren, ed., *Den Kollegiale Forvaltning* (Oslo: Universitets forlaget, 1974).

7. The questionnaires referred to here are among those administered in connection with the study of the distribution of power in Norway. This study, commissioned by the Prime Minister's Office, was funded by appropriations directly from the Norwegian Parliament. It is directed by Gudmund Hernes.

8. Compare Gudmund Hernes, "Markedet som Domstol (The market as a court of law)," *Norges Industri,* no. 20 (1976): 20–23.

9. Ibid., p. 22.

10. Interview in *NHST* (December 1974).

11. *Norges Industri,* no. 8 (1973), p. 15.

12. Ibid., no. 21 (1974), pp. 6–8.

13. Compare Ole Berrefjord og Gudmund Hernes, "Markedsforvitring og Statsbygging (The withering away of the market and state–building)," *Sosialøkonomen,* no. 7 (1974): 3–16.

14. Ibid.

15. Ibid.

16. Ole Berrefjord, "Fra Embetsmannsstat til Embetsmannsstat (From the Officials' state to the officials' state)," in Gudmund Hernes, ed., *Forhandlingsøkonomi og Blandingsadministrasjon* (Oslo: Universitetsforlaget, 1978), pp. 134–159.

11 Growth and the Quality of Life: Some Logical and Methodological Issues

Paul R. Eberts

It is my impression that to most people, the question of whether growth is necessary to improved quality of life is silly. The answer is obvious; it is a resounding "yes." To some extent the answer to the question is a matter of definition. The precise meanings of the words *growth* and *quality of life* color any definitive response to the question. If growth is defined in economic terms—the most common definition—and if "quality of life" has anything to do with things or facilities bought with money—the most common definition—then it is reasonably certain that economic growth precedes and is a necessary (although probably not a sufficient) condition for development toward a better quality of life, both on the individual and collective levels.

Still growth in economic terms (income, employment, and institutions) alone is not enough to improve quality of life. Most social scientists recognize this as fact, even if many economists seem impervious to it. Parke and Seidman maintain that "doubts about the easy equation of economic growth and social progress led, in the 1960's, to a renewed interest in social measurement and to the birth of the 'social indicators movement.'"[1] This renewed interest generated a number of U.S. government reports, including *Toward a Social Report, Social Indicators,* 1973, and *Social Indicators, 1976.*[2] Summers et al. also demonstrate that rural industrialization as the impetus to economic growth in rural localities has been of some benefit in certain rural localities, but has been a mixed blessing in some other areas and a demonstrable curse in still others.[3] Among other things, industrial plants locating in rural areas:

1. May not be interested in retraining or hiring low-skilled persons;
2. May not be interested in and consequently may depress other forms of local development;
3. May not draw their labor force from the immediate community in which they locate;
4. May be low-wage operations;
5. May attract additional unemployable people who eventually inflate local welfare rolls; or
6. May force other economic externalities onto the local community which

are not compensated for by the increased industrial activities, especially in terms of additional educational facilities, public utilities, taxes, and other subsidies.[4]

Thus, economic benefits from rural industrialization may not meet the expectations necessary for certain aspects of quality of life to appear, even if most people in most localities that have experienced rural industrialization favor its occurrence.[5] In addition, effects of changes in rural economic structures may have negative by-products on other noneconomic indicators of quality of life, such as crimes, suicides, mortality, marital disruptions, poor housing conditions, and so forth.[6]

One further issue underscores the importance of carefully examining the effects of economic growth on quality of life. For the last decade, U.S. economic growth has been operating at a lower rate than previously (approximately 2.5 percent instead of the previous 5 percent). Indeed, the U.S. growth rate problem appears to baffle even the experts as world resources and markets become tighter and as automated technological changes force more workers into the labor-intensive and expensive service sector. Thus, most localities in the United States may have to deal with the prospects of reduced or at least stagnant growth. Analysis of economic growth and quality of life issues is important, therefore, to set the stage for what the future portends.

Final agreement on the effects of economic, industrial, and population growth is quite complex and needs further examination. Perhaps growth should not be defined only in these three terms. Perhaps quality of life should also be defined differently. Perhaps both indirect as well as direct effects need to be analyzed. In any case, findings such as those above suggest that the controversy is not resolved and that considerable theoretical and methodological work must be completed before the controversy will diminish. In the meantime, most economic and political leaders, both national and local, will probably persist in adhering to the simple hypothesis that economic growth is necessary to increase local quality of life.

Logical and Methodological Issues in Relating Growth to Quality of Life

Although this study seems to require a simple two-variable model—growth being the independent variable and quality of life the dependent one—the multiple theoretical and methodological (operational) definitions of both concepts make the study much more complex. In fact, the major problem in dealing with these two concepts is to handle their multiple indicators. Whether such a problem is more theoretical or more methodological is a matter of semantics.[7] Indeed, at the present stage in analyses of social indicators, the relation of indicators to each other and to general concepts is so unclear that specification of a theory of social indicators is premature.[8] The process of relating social indicators to general concepts, therefore, is both theoretical in abstractly defining the concept and methodological in understanding the interrelation of multiple indicators to each other.[9] Both aspects will be considered here. Their considerations will also raise a number of subissues relating to such things as clustering techniques, collinearity, significance, and direct and indirect effects.

Quality of Life

Quality of life refers to almost as many different subconcepts as there are people working on the subject.[10] The range of definitions includes everything from the purely subjective to the broadly institutional, and the objective aggregated personal characteristics accumulated from the census such as the U.S. Government's Office of Management and Budget's *Social Indicators, 1973*, and *Social Indicators, 1976.*''[11] Thus, quality of life has been used to refer to such disparate things as general feelings about life and society, infant mortality, the general differentiation of institutions in a set of localities, and the interrelations of these institutions as in input–output and systems analysis.[12]

A first key conclusion from these considerations is that any comprehensive study of quality of life must certainly include most of these three general theoretical types of multiple indicators: the subjective, objective, and institutional.[13] The present study contains a number of the last two indicators. It includes none on the subjective feelings of people about their lives and conditions. Fortunately, Christenson documents that the subjective feelings of people about their local institutions are strongly and positively related to the availability and quality of the local institutions.[14] Such a finding obviates the absolute necessity for combining subjective with objective and institutional measures of quality of life in the same study, especially in a study such as this one, which includes a number of institutional and objective indicators used by researchers in the last decade and a half.

A second key issue is to determine which unit of observation will be used as the basis for collecting the indicators. The choice largely determines the nature of the available indicators, as well as the level of comprehensiveness in generalizations made from their analysis. As Summers et al. point out, different individuals in communities often have different reactions to the effects of rural industrialization.[15] Most of the middle and leadership classes feel it is good, while some other individuals (the older, low skilled, and nonindustrially employed) hold considerable reservations. Other contenders as units of observation besides individual persons include communities, counties, regions, states, and nations. As soon as such aggregations occur, then problems of ecological correlations are more likely to arise.[16] At the same time, usefulness in terms of trend and comparative analysis for various localities' policy purposes becomes more possible.[17] Any choice of unit of observation, therefore, has its advantages and disadvantages.

Unit of Analysis

I use indicators based on small macrosystems (counties, specifically those rural and urban counties—in contrast to metropolitan and suburban—in the twelve states of the U.S. Northeast) as primary units of observation. All data items are aggregated to this level, even if some data sources are individuals as citizens of these counties or individuals as representatives of organizations in the counties. I chose the county as the unit of observation because it emcompasses places with both rural and urban characteristics and hence gives a more comprehensive picture of life in these places than does any other unit. In addition, probably more secondary data are available for counties than for any other similar unit, especially if certain larger communities located within the counties' borders may be considered as nodes of these counties, and if their data can be combined and used judiciously as part of the county data.[18]

Since these units are subject to problems of ecological correlations, analyses based on them must also be judicious. Still, such analyses are possible, and certain questions, in my judgment including the one relating growth to quality of life, can be answered only by using locality type data.[19] Moreover, my study uses all 196 of the urban and rural counties in the Northeast (as well as some data obtained on the two largest communities in each county), so that certain statistical problems in claiming generality of the findings can be avoided. In this way, indicators of both an objective nature, as aggregated from the personal characteristics of individuals through census-type materials, and of an institutional nature, as based on the characteristics of public and private organizations and associations and obtained through a variety of sources, can be combined for the descriptive as well as the model-building types of analyses necessary for illuminating the question of the relation of growth to quality of life.

Given the county as a unit and the rationale for focusing on institutional and objective indicators, it is now possible to consider the third key issue: the choice of specific indicators for each concept from the multiple possible alternatives. Quality-of-life indicators are reasonably subjective. In fact, the January 1978 review of *Social Indicators, 1976,* in the *Annals of* the *American Academy of Political and Social Science* contains many criticisms of the available indicators, as well as many suggestions for new ones.[20] Currently available ones serve both the interests of public policy makers concerned with obtaining information on which to base their decisions and of public and private researchers whetting their scientific appetites. Consequently, they are quite disparate and subjective, even if not chosen capriciously.

Social Indicators

I will use a set of these indicators, including those that have recieved attention by other researchers. My primary justification for their choice is either their representativeness (face validity) as a type of indicator or their commonness of use by others. At this point in quality-of-life and social indicator research, such procedure seems a sensible strategy.

The indicators are not simply subjective. They do represent sets of values. Public policy makers request certain kinds of information because they value certain things (such as reduction in poverty levels) and would like to see the system change in order to produce their conception of a better life. Social scientists also value certain things, or they would not devote a considerable portion of their lives to studying them. At the very least, the indicators chosen are used for explicating a better understanding of some aspects of human existence. Although the list of indicators may not be very coherent, it cannot be said that it is wholly subjective and represents merely the values of a set of random individuals. In other words, although the indicators may be ethically relative, they are not ethically neutral; some people do believe in their importance and relevance.

Table 11-1 presents the list of major concepts and specific indicators used in this study. The table itself is an intercorrelation matrix of thirty-six key indicators of growth and quality of life. In some ways all thirty-six, including the ones on economic and population growth, can be considered quality-of-life indicators since some people view growth itself as part of quality of life. For present purposes, however, the operational indicators of growth will be those in the major category of economic (or export) base indicators, numbers 13 through 20.[21] These eight include most of the major categories of export base: public administration, large manufacturing, colleges and universities, agriculture, and transportation (which in this case is a Guttman scale and includes trucking, railroads, and airlines). In addition, the growth indicators also include at least population size and median family income in the general category of local resources, indicators 26 and 27. Greater median family income perhaps should also be considered a quality-of-life indicator. It has been consistently demonstrated that people

Table 11-1
Correlation Matrix of Key Indicators of the Infrastructural and Aggregate Quality of Life Variables, 196 Northeast U.S. Rural and Urban Counties, c. 1970.

		1.	2.	3.	4.	5.	6.	7.	8.	9.	10.	11.	12.	13.	14.
Local public agencies and budgets															
Local institutional structures															
1. Total per–capita expenditures	1966	—													
2. Per–capita expenditures, education	1966	.88	—												
3. Per–capita expenditures, welfare	1966	.82	.67	—											
4. Per–capita expenditures, health & hospitals	1966	.26	.16	.24	—										
5. Per–capita expenditures, police	1966	.55	.30	.53	.08	—									
6. Per–capita expenditures, highways	1966	.83	.65	.64	.14	.37	—								
7. Per–capita expenditures, government employees	1967	.37	.34	.26	.14	.48	.13	—							
8. Public planning scale	1970	.27	.19	.22	.08	.43	.07	.60	—						
Local public political processes															
9. No. elected officials	1967	.25	.38	.32	.20	-.02	.07	.22	.07	—					
10. % voting	1968	-.10	-.07	-.06	.12	-.12	-.05	-.13	-.27	.19	—				
11. Two–party competition	1968	-.10	-.12	.02	.01	.12	-.24	.10	.17	-.07	-.12	—			
12. Mobilization–competition typology	1968	-.16	-.18	-.07	-.06	.10	-.21	.07	.17	-.07	.06	.73	—		
Local public and private economic bases															
13. Diversity economic base	1970	.18	.17	.20	.13	.18	.04	.51	.46	.06	-.33	.24	.14	—	
14. No. public administration employees	1970	.24	.21	.13	.02	.46	.04	.86	.47	.01	-.22	.16	.11	.44	—
15. No. manufacturing units with 100+ employees	1967	.14	.10	.06	-.01	.30	.01	.81	.56	.02	-.14	.15	.10	.49	.65
16. Per–capita value added, manufacturing	1967	.08	.03	.03	.02	.14	.03	.25	.39	-.08	-.16	.12	.10	.22	.11
17. Total college enrollment	1970	.10	.09	.06	.10	.19	-.02	.59	.32	.10	-.13	.05	.05	.47	.45
18. % land in agriculture	1970	.05	.13	.13	-.01	-.17	-.01	-.04	.00	.07	-.18	.18	.04	.62	-.02
19. Average market value agricultural product sold	1969	.35	.34	.33	-.02	.12	.31	.32	.27	.14	-.29	.03	-.05	.46	.28
20. Transportation scale	1970	.14	.05	.14	.19	.28	.08	.33	.45	-.02	-.26	.12	.14	.65	.27
Local service differentiation															
21. Commercial services scale	1970	.09	.04	.07	-.04	.32	-.07	.37	.60	.11	-.33	.05	.01	.37	.28
22. Medical specialties scale	1970	.26	.17	.20	.07	.42	.06	.59	.69	.14	-.18	.07	.10	.42	.51
23. Mass media communications scale	1970	.15	.11	.08	.06	.27	-.06	.49	.67	.16	-.33	.10	.09	.38	.40
Local equity															
24. Gini coefficient of income :(inequality)	1970	-.16	-.14	-.01	.07	-.05	-.18	-.23	-.34	.12	.24	.05	.08	-.11	-.15
25. Affluence–poverty ratio	1970	.36	.30	.23	.02	.43	.23	.54	.41	-.11	-.16	.06	.06	.33	.48
Aggregated characteristics of population															
Local resources															
26. Population size	1970	.22	.20	.11	.03	.44	.02	.97	.60	.07	-.18	.13	.10	.50	.89
27. Median family income	1970	.50	.44	.33	-.04	.52	.36	.54	.56	-.09	-.31	.03	-.03	.37	.50
28. Median school years (education)"	1970	.49	.37	.32	-.07	.45	.48	.34	.46	-.17	-.32	-.11	-.10	.23	.30
29. % professional & technical in labor force	1970	.34	.30	.18	.06	.39	.19	.45	.45	.03	-.24	.07	.10	.34	.45
30. Median age	1970	-.10	-.22	.00	.00	.03	.03	-.16	-.12	-.15	.34	.00	.10	-.19	-.18
Disrupted personal & social well-being															
31. % poverty among families	1970	-.49	-.36	-.36	.04	-.42	-.46	-.38	-.50	.18	.40	.05	.09	-.36	-.32
32. % unemployed	1970	-.18	-.11	-.11	.06	-.33	-.13	-.25	-.32	.18	.33	.04	.12	-.31	-.28
33. % disrupted marriages	1970	.06	.03	.03	.01	.20	.00	.42	.12	-.05	-.02	.04	.03	.11	.66
34. Per–capita suicides	1967	-.03	-.11	-.02	-.01	-.01	.16	-.16	-.12	-.06	.10	-.06	.00	-.09	-.14
35. Per–capita homicides	1967	-.19	-.16	-.14	-.07	-.04	-.23	-.10	-.03	.09	-.09	.22	.17	-.04	-.06
36. Per–capita infant mortality	1967	-.01	-.05	.03	.01	-.04	.04	-.13	-.18	.03	-.02	.07	.05	-.12	-.10

15.	16.	17.	18.	19.	20.	21.	22.	23.	24.	25.	26.	27.	28.	29.	30.	31.	32.	33.	34.	35.	36.
.43	—																				
.59	.12	—																			
.00	.07	-.07	—																		
.27	.20	.09	.41	—																	
.23	.11	.24	-.05	.17																	
.35	.29	.16	.05	.26	.39	—															
.51	32	.27	.07	.22	.33	.63	—														
.46	.36	.25	.02	.21	.35	.68	.69	—													
-.38	-.51	-.11	.05	-.10	-.09	-.26	-.22	-.30	—												
.47	.21	.38	.03	.17	.19	.17	.39	.15	-.23	—											
.84	.24	.61	-.06	.31	.32	.39	.59	.49	-.25	.57	—										
.47	.40	.32	.03	.29	.27	.37	.51	.36	-.55	.76	.55	—									
.31	.43	.20	-.07	.25	.28	.40	.43	.39	-.56	.43	.33	.79	—								
.29	.20	.49	-.02	.13	.28	.26	.48	.35	-.19	.64	.47	.70	.55	—							
-.05	-.04	-.31	-.07	-.21	-.09	-.20	-.07	-.16	.10	-.18	-.16	-.28	-.21	-.43	—						
-.40	-.46	-.22	-.07	-.32	-.30	-.36	-.44	-.34	.61	-.63	-.39	-.85	-.82	-.49	.14	—					
-.28	-.31	-.14	-.13	-.28	-.22	-.39	-.37	-.26	.39	-.39	-.28	-.66	-.60	-.36	.15	.66	—				
.17	-.04	.05	-.02	.06	.04	-.03	.21	.09	.06	.19	.46	.16	.06	.16	-.02	-.08	-.04	—			
-.11	.08	-.13	-.03	.03	-.03	-.04	-.08	-.11	.10	-.13	-.17	-.15	.00	-.12	.10	.07	.06	-.03	—		
-.11	-.13	-.07	.05	.02	-.05	-.07	-.07	-.05	.31	-.12	-.09	-.26	-.38	-.14	.08	.32	.19	.00	.10	—	
-.15	-.09	-.09	-.01	.00	-.10	-.17	-.13	-.16	.20	-.15	-.14	-.20	-.26	-.20	.09	.16	.16	.01	-.01	.23	—

with more income feel better about themselves, their environment, and even their interpersonal situations.[22]

The other indicators in local resources—median school years (education), percentage professional, technical, and kindred in the labor force, and median age—could also be considered either as quality-of-life indicators or as growth indicators. Most lists generated for quality of life, such as *Social Indicators, 1973* and *Social Indicators, 1976*, include all of these local resource indicators as quality-of-life indicators. But since they are also indicators generally recognized as growth producing, it can be argued that they should be considered growth indicators.

Such a discussion over which indicators belong to which variable in the model underscores the notion that social indicators are often ambiguous.[23] It also reinforces Land's notion that the more important social scientific work on social indicators is model building.[24] Certainly the latter can inform the former. When indicators are related to each other in similar ways, then there must be similarities between them, and they should be grouped accordingly.[25] But often there is no way to discover such similarities without treating each indicator as if it is distinct from every other. In Lundberg's sense, then, "one indicator, one variable."[26]

Certain other indicators may also be grouped with quality-of-life concepts. Clark has used per-capita expenditures for a number of government functions (welfare, education, and so forth) as key indicators of contributions of government to quality of life.[27] These are indicators 1 through 6 in the table. These same indicators could also be used as independent or input variables for the level of government effort to affect other kinds of development and quality of life.[28] Thus, these indicators are somewhat ambiguous and can be connected to several types of concepts. In any case, I will use them because they are too important to omit.

Indicators 7 and 8, number of local government employees and a Guttman scale of local planning activities, are also indicators of local effort to deal with local problems. Christenson and Christenson and Sachs document the strong positive relation of objective and subjective indicators in terms of the affirmative responses of local people to their local institutions and their less affirmative responses to institutions more distant from them.[29] These two indicators are proxies for all local government institutions.

Participation in community affairs is also considered an important indicator of quality of life.[30] The four indicators under local public political processes intend to capture this notion. Indicators 9 through 12—more elected officials, greater percentage of the population voting in presidential elections, greater competition between the two parties in presidential elections and a typology combining participation-mobilization and competition—are all indicators of greater participation of people and ideas in the

local political process.[31] The notion of participation, of course, is fundamental to the democratic political process on which U.S. society is based.

Greater differentiation in private sector local services also has been
deemed an indicator of greater quality of life.[32] Presumably a greater
number of different types of services provides a greater number of options
for local populations in choosing their services and obtaining employment.
Each of the indicators is a Guttman scale—of commercial services, of
medical specialties, and of mass communication facilities (newspapers,
radio, and television).

It is possible, of course, that the commercial services scale could be
considered with population size at a reasonably high level (it is 0.39 in Table
11-1 for 1970, 0.41 for 1960, and log of population size with commercial
services is 0.71 for 1970 on these 196 counties). Again we are in a position of
ambiguity of determining what the indicator indicates. In general, the
commercial services scale is too important to be overlooked; therefore, its
behavior vis-a-vis other variables must be closely observed. As with other
cases only further empirical analysis can inform us of its similarities and
differences with other variables.

In passing, it should be noted that the export base of public and private
agencies might also be considered quality-of-life indicators as well as
growth indicators. Certainly the export base is fundamental in sustaining
the viability of localities and in providing employment for the local population.[33] Employment, of course, is crucial for quality of life.[34] In any case,
the distinction between the two sets of indicators for the two concepts does
seem ambiguous and somewhat subjective.

The distribution of income is recognized as an important indicator of
quality of life.[35] Equality in the distribution of income is fundamental to the
operation of a democratic system. The Gini coefficient of income distribution (indicators 24) and affluence/poverty ratio (indicator 25), where the
percentage in the top quartile of the general population (in the case for
1970, $15,000) is divided by the percentage in the bottom quartile (for 1970,
$5,000), are both intended to capture the equality notion. Both are widely
used by a number of economic researchers.[36]

The final set of quality-of-life indicators relates to the disruption of
personal and social well-being. They are indicators 31 through 36: percentage of local families in poverty (U.S. Census definition), percentage unemployed, percentage of people who are currently disrupted in their marital
life (percentage widowed, separated, and divorced), and per-capita suicides, homicides, and infant mortality. Other mortality and crime statistics
would certainly be appropriate here, as well as indicators on housing
conditions.[37] Still the present set of indicators seems reasonably representative of the quality-of-life issues involved; it is used extensively in social
indicator research and therefore is the set on which this study is based.[38]

Additional indicators would be expected to relate to each other in ways essentially similar to those presented here.

To summarize the third issue on the choice of specific indicators for each concept, the major observation is that the choice often seems ambiguous and arbitrary. Each indicator has to be interpreted within the context of other similar ones. At one time a given indicator can be interpreted as a quality-of-life indicator, and at another it seems appropriate to call is a growth indicator. The indicators that most clearly (or at least ambiguously) relate to quality of life are those associated with the subconcepts of disrupted personal and social well-being and local political processes. As we shall see, most of these (with the exception of poverty and unemployment) are also the ones least related empirically to the growth indicators. An interpretation that would relate only these two sets of indicators to the notion of quality of life, whereas all other indicators would relate to growth, would not be wholly unreasonable, even if it might be unpopular.

Clustering of Indicators

A fourth, more methodological issue in relating growth to quality of life is whether there are just a few key clusters of relations that might arise from the intercorrelation of all these indicators. That there are thirty-six indicators in this list suggests that it could perhaps be reduced through factor or some other cluster type of analysis.[39]

The intercorrelations in table 11-1 shows how relatively impervious these indicators are to such reducing techniques. In the set of intercorrelations on local public Agencies and budgets, the first three indicators are all intercorrelated at over 0.50, and would probably form a factor. Moreover, indicators 5 and 6, although correlated with each other at only 0.37, are also intercorrelated with these first three at over 0.50 in all but one instance (per-capita police and per-capita highway expenditures would probably also be part of the general-expenditures factor. But per-capita expenditures for health and hospitals does not correlate with the others and would probably have to be considered separately from them.

Similarly number of local government employees and the planning scale correlate at 0.60 but do not intercorrelate at over 0.50 with any of the per-capita expenditures. Thus, they too might form a factor of their own but would be on the periphery of any factor with local budgets (their correlations with per-capita police expenditures do reach 0.48 and 0.43).

In fact, in table 11-1, number of local government employees and the planning scale, along with population size, median family income, median education, and the medical specialties scale, have more correlations over 0.50 than any of the other indicators. Median family income has thirteen correlations over 0.50, population size has nine, median education has five (and eight more over 0.40), number local government employees has nine, the medical specialties scale has nine, and the planning scale has eight. None of the others has more than five (total per–capita government expenditures, with four of these five appearing with other per capita expenditures indicators).

These findings indicate that there are seven overlapping clusters in the data:

1. Per–capita expenditures: Total, education, welfare, police, highways.
2. Population, social and economic status: Population size, median income, median education level, number of local government employees, professional-technicals in the labor force, the two equality indexes, fewer poverty families, less unemployment, and perhaps the planning scale.
3. The Guttman scales of differentiation: Commercial services, medical specialties, mass communications, and the planning scale (but not the transportation scale), along with number of local government employees.
4. Disadvantaged people: Percentage of families in poverty and percentage unemployed (0.66).
5. Economic base: Number of public administration employees, number of firms employing more than a hundred people, number of local government employees, and total college enrollment.
6. Diversity of economic base: Diversity itself, percentage of land in agriculture, and the transportation scale, as well as manufacturing, public administration, college enrollments, and number of local government employees (from cluster 5).
7. Political competition: Two party-competition and mobilization (participation)—competition topology (0.73).

These seven clusters encompass twenty–six of the thirty–six indicators and hence summarize these twenty–six, even if certain clusters overlap. Cluster 5 is almost, but not quite, identical to cluster 6. Percentage of poverty families appears in two clusters (2 and 4), as does the planning scale (2 and 3). Number of local government employees appears in four clusters (2, 3, 5, and 6). Thus some ambiguity exists in these interrelations. Relationships are not as clear–cut as researchers would like them to be. Moreover, similar relations are found for the 1950 and 1960 data as for the 1970 data shown in table 11–1.

Ten indicators do not appear in any cluster: four of the six indexes or disrupted personal and social well–being, two of the four local political process indicators, per–capita value added by manufacturing, average market value of agricultural products sold, per–capita expenditures for health and hospital, and median age. Several of these correlate with some in the six clusters at over the 0.40 level. Per–capita valued added by manufacturing correlates 0.45 with number of manufacturing plants employing a hundred or more, and average market value of agricultural products sold correlates 0.41 with percentage of land in agriculture. Conceivably, then, the number of nonclustered indicators reduces to eight.

Thus, in all, it appears that the thirty–six indicators are potentially reducable to only fifteen, a much more manageable number to handle even if the two major concepts (growth and quality of life) are still multidimensional. Moreover, no single factor is apparent from these intercorrelations, and even some of the clusters presented above are confusing because they interrelate indicators from different major values. For instance, equality, income, education, population size, and number of local government employees all appear in one cluster, thus putting the values of equality, resources, and local public services together and casting doubt on whether their effects can really be separated in further analyses from this data set. Because of these ambiguities whereby indicators overlap and correlate with the two key concepts, further analysis will use the clusters only with judiciousness.

Relating Growth to Quality of Life

The fact of overlapping indicators from conceptually different aspects of quality of life raises a fifth methodological issue in relating quality of life to growth: to what extent the different aspects of growth can be clearly identified to affect different aspects of quality of life. Cluster 2 especially contains both growth indicators and quality–of–life indicators. Insofar as they are together, it can be reasonably argued that growth is inseparable from these aspects of quality of life. In other words, rural and urban counties with higher levels of income, economic activity, and population size also have higher levels of education, larger numbers of local government employees, less poverty, less unemployment, greater numbers of planning activities, more professional and technical workers in the labor force, and more equality (by either of the two equality indexes). On the surface at least, the relations are certainly multiple, and perhaps circular. Which precedes which is unclear. In any case, the correlations are high enough that multicollinearity may affect further partialing and regression analysis so that it may be impossible to specify the actual effect correctly.[40] When intercorrelations are so high, small changes in certain units of observation included in the analysis may make enough shifts in correlations so that one indicator seems more important at one time or with one subset of units, while other indicators may be more important at other times or with other subsets.[41] True coefficients, therefore, may be extremely difficult, if not impossible, to specify. At best, it can be asserted only that certain indicators always seem to cluster together, even if this empirical position negatively affects our theoretical reasoning.

Interpretation of Correlations

A sixth issue focuses on an interpretation of the size and signs of the correlations in the intercorrelation matrix. Under the hypothesis that growth results in quality of life, all signs should be significantly large and positive (reversing the signs for the negative set of indicators in disrupted personal and social well-being and for the Gini coefficient of income equality).

As table 11-1 shows, not every column or row is either high in correlation or consistent in signs. In fact, only 59 or the 629 correlations in the matrix are at 0.50 or above, although all of the 399 relations with correlations of 0.12 or greater tend to be significant at the 0.05 level of probability or better. Thus nearly 64 percent of the correlations in the table reach the generally accepted level of statistical significance (even if the set of 196 counties on which the analysis is performed is a complete set of Northeast U.S. rural and urban counties so that all relations are parameters and already significant). Moreover, the table also shows that the fewest significant correlations (in the cells drawn by types of indicators) occur for the political process indicators. Only 63 of 146 (43 percent) reach the 0.05 significance level. The second lowest set is disrupted well-being indicators, with just over 52 percent (102 of 195) of them reaching significance at the 0.05 level. All of the others show considerably higher percentages reaching significance.

It seems important that the two sets of indicators with the fewest number of significant intercorrelations are those that are more clearly the quality-of-life indicators. In this sense, these indicators are the most difficult to explain through statistical analyses using the indicators in this study. They are also the least correlated with each other; only 16 of 45 (36 percent) reach the 0.05 significance level. In addition, only 53 of the 100 correlations between growth indicators (economic base, population, and family income) and the political process plus well-being indicators are significant, which is below the average of 63 percent for the total matrix. Thus, although growth indicators are related to these more clearly quality-of-life indicators, they are not all related or strongly related. The general conclusion is the simplistic one that not all growth is related to every aspect of quality of life and that generally the various quality-of-life indicators are not related very closely with each other. The general principle underlying this statement has far-reaching effects for further quality-of-life studies. The approach of

Land in building models for individual indicators without paying too much attention to the generality of the indicator seems borne out by these findings.[42]

In addition to the size of the correlations in the intercorrelation matrix, attention must also be directed to the signs of the coefficients. If growth indicators are clearly related to quality-of-life indicators, then all coefficients should be positive except for disrupted well-being and the Gini coefficient of income, which should be negative in the table. The table, however, shows many negative correlations. The most inconsistent of the indicators are: percentage voting in the presidential election (percentage participation), percentage of land in agriculture, percentage of disrupted marriages (which does not follow the other indicators of disrupted social and personal well-being), and per-capita expenditures for highways. One-quarter or more of the signs in these correlation coefficients are inconsistent with the predicted hypothesis. Indeed, the indiators of "percentage voting (participation)" show only six of its thirty-five signs in the predicted direction. Clearly, some other unidentified phenomenon is at work. As it stands, greater participation in elections seems to produce less growth and quality of life. Such a finding overturns at least some theory.[43]

"Percentage disrupted marriages" also shows twenty-six of thirty-five inconsistent signs. Perhaps this is another sign of the times; a disrupted marriage is the sign of greater quality of life as well as growth. That it is not significantly related to any of the other well-being indicators gives further credence to this position.

The other two indicators with a number of inconsistent signs are less serious, since many of the inconsistencies are associated with low and insignificant correlations. Only two of the inconsistent correlations using percentage of land in agriculture reach significance: the ones with per-capita police expenditures (-0.17) and with voting participation (-0.18). Perhaps the more agricultural counties have less use for police services. The most visible crimes, for which the public demands police protection, tend to be urban based.

Similarly although per-capita expenditures for highways shows nine of thirty-five correlations in the wrong direction, only three are statistically significant. Two are with political process indicators—party competition (-0.24) and the mobilization (participation)-competition typology (-0.21)—and one is with per-capita suicides (0.16). In general, then, more party competition in these localities produces less per-capita spending on highways. This finding may be part of the general phenomenon that more political competition generally depresses local expenditures—total (-0.10), and for education (-0.12) but more for police (0.12). It is barely conceivable that spending more per capita for highways would increase the suicide rate, unless perhaps the relationship is being interfered with by unidentified considerations.

In general, then, inconsistently in signs is not a major problem in the findings from the matrix of table 11-1. Only political participation and marital disruptions do not follow the predicted patterns with any regularity, and both phenomena are understandable. A conclusion consistent with these findings, then, is that, even if correlations are low, growth and quality-of-life indicators are positively and significantly intercorrelated. Such a finding suggests a multiple and circular causation in the system so that changes in one indicator will induce at least some changes in all of the others.

Quasi-Causal Analysis

The seventh issue is whether the raw correlations of table 11-1 can be redefined into more causal-like statements through regression analysis. Since the question is whether growth is necessary to produce quality of life, it appears logical to undertake regression, entering the various indicators both in their static (measured at a single point in time) and dynamic (measured at two points in time) forms and regress them with other dynamic indicators. Huge regression runs were actually undertaken following this logical suggestion, using the indicators from table 11-1 as both the independent and dependent variables. Changes in the indicators from 1960 through 1970 were the dependent variables, and both of the indicators as of their 1960 levels and changes from 1950 through 1960 were entered as the independent variables. Stepwise regression was also used in the hope that it would eliminate multicollinearity.

The resulting matrix was not only huge, but the extreme amounts of multicollinearity were not resolved. One-quarter of the regressions contained coefficients exceeding 1.0. Nearly all of them contained wildly changing signs from the signs of the bivariate correlations. At this point I consider the results of these regressions as largely uninterpretable. Much more detailed work must be undertaken before the results of this technique can be made reasonable and public.

In order to simplify the regressions, the changes from 1960 through 1970 are still used as the dependent variables, with the independent variables being most of the same indicators as in table 11-1 measured at their 1960 levels. Table 11-2 shows the complete list of input variables and gives the results of the step-wise regressions. The input list of variables is pared from the original thirty-six to twenty-one, reflecting somewhat the clusters observed through table 11-1. Moreover, three of the four cells (low-low,

Table 11–2
Matrix of 0.05 Level Significant Beta Coefficients Relating Key Growth and Quality-of-Life Indicators, Regressing Changes in the Indicators from 1960 to 1970 on the Indicators at Their 1960 Levels, 196 U.S. Northeast Rural and Urban Counties.

Independent variables, 1960 level / Dependent variables, 1960–1970	Budgets & Agencies			Political Process			Participation (Mobilization-Competition Typology)		
	Total Per-capita expenditures	Per-capita expenditures Health and Hospitals	Planning Scale	No. elected county officials	Percent Voting	Two-party competition	Low–Low	High–Low	High–High
Local institutionalized structures									
Local public agencies and budgets									
1. Total per-capita expenditures	.42	.06	0	0	0	0	0	0	−.04
2. Per-capita expenditures, education	.41	0	0	0	0	−.05	0	0	.04
3. Per-capita expenditures, welfare	.55	0	.12	0	0	0	−.26	−.20	−.18
4. Per-capita expenditures, health & hospitals	0	.54	0	0	−.10	.19	−.11	−.11	0
5. Per-capita expenditures, police	.18	.07	0	−.14	.24	0	−.14	−.11	0
6. Per-capita expenditures, highways	.49	0	0	0	0	−.13	.12	0	.11
7. No. local government employees	0	.08	0	0	.11	−.07	.08	−.10	0
8. Public planning scale	0	.10	−1.22	.07	.09	0	−.05	−.04	0
Local public political processes									
9. No. elected officials	0	0	−.10	0	0	.28	0	0	−.06
10. % voting	.18	0	0	0	0	0	−.26	−.23	−.12
Mobilization–competition typology									
11. Two-party competition	−.27	0	0	.09	0	0	.17	0	0
Local Public and private economic base									
12. Diversity economic base	0	0	.11	0	0	0	.08	0	.12
13. No. public administration employees	0	.03	−.05	.05	0	−.04	0	.04	.02
14. No. manufacturing units with 100+ employees	.07	0	0	0	0	0	0	0	.12
15. Per-capita value added, manufacturing	0	.11	−.06	−.02	0	0	0	.05	0
16. Total college enrollment	0	0	.09	0	,0	0	.08	0	.07
17. % land in agriculture	−.25	.16	.14	0	0	−.17	.07	0	.07
18. Transportation scale	−.20	.11	0	0	0	0	0	0	.20
Local service differentiation									
19. Commercial services scale	0	−.06	0	−.10	0	9	.24	.14	.13
20. Medical specialities scale	.10	0	.17	.02	−.06	−.09	0	−.05	0
21. Mass media communications scale	0	.03	0	.07	−.15	0	.05	−.03	.06
Local equality									
22. Gini coefficient of income	.15	0	−.13	0	.15	−.09	−.07	0	−.09
Aggregated characteristics of local population									
Local resources									
23. Population size	0	0	.09	−.19	−.11	0	.04	0	−.03
24. Median family income	0	.04	.05	0	.03	0	0	−.06	0
25. Median school years	0	.11	0	0	0	0	0	0	0
26. % professional and technical in labor force	0	0	0	0	.14	0	0	−.09	0
Disrupted personal & social well-being									
27. % poverty among families	.10	−.15	0	0	0	0	0	−.11	.21
28. % unemployed	0	−.10	0	.06	0	0	−.08	−.10	−.10
29. % disrupted marriages	0	−.07	0	0	−.22	−.31	.15	.20	.18
30. Per-capita suicides	.13	0	0	.10	0	.11	0	0	−.16
31. Per-capita homicides	0	0	0	.08	0	0	0	.15	0
32. Per-capita infant mortality	.10	0	0	0	0	0	0	0	0
Number of times coefficient appears in equation	15	16	12	12	11	11	17	17	20
average size of beta after deleting autocorrelation coefficient	.23	.09	.09	.08	.13	.12	.12	.11	.11

	Economic Base					Differentiation			Equality	Resources		Well-Being			
Linkage Diversity	No. public administration employees	No. manufacturing units with 100+ employees	Total college enrollment	Percent land in agriculture	Transportation linkage scale	Commercial services scale	Medical specialties scale	Mass media communication scale	Gini coefficient of income	Median family income	Population size	Percent unemployed	Percent disrupted marriages	R^2	No. terms in equations
0	.16	−.09	−.09	.16	0	0	0	0	.20	.51	0	.07	0	.46	9
0	.08	0	−.10	.13	0	0	0	0	.23	.44	0	.07	−.11	.35	10
.06	0	0	0	.15	0	.12	−.09	−.13	.16	.20	0	0	0	.43	12
0	0	0	−.10	0	.13	0	0	0	0	−.19	0	−.14	−.13	.32	10
0	.45	0	0	−.15	0	.25	0	−.22	.25	.52	−.30	0	.12	.39	14
0	.15	0	0	.16	0	.23	−.16	−.16	0	.14	0	.11	.10	.34	12
0	−.32	−.10	0	0	0	0	0	.10	−.17	0	.41	0	.10	.60	11
0	−.16	−.10	.08	0	0	.11	.06	0	−.05	0	.48	−.04	.09	.85	15
0	0	−.32	.09	0	0	0	.15	0	0	0	0	0	−.09	.47	7
0	0	0	0	0	−.07	.08	0	−.15	.53	.80	0	0	−.09	.41	10
−.11	−.11	.27	.10	0	−.15	0	.09	0	.18	−.39	0	−.11	−.34	.51	13
0	−.36	−.28	−.08	0	−.54	0	.09	0	0	.19	.52	0	0	.31	10
.04	.11	.06	.19	0	0	.05	−.03	−.04	−.09	.12	.85	0	0	.95	17
0	0	0	0	0	0	.23	0	−.28	.14	0	0	0	−.15	.11	5
0	−.06	.42	.91	0	0	0	0	−.14	.05	0	0	0	0	.78	11
0	−.24	−.20	0	0	−.66	0	.12	0	−.11	.09	.38	0	0	.40	10
0	−.12	.09	0	0	0	−.70	.30	.21	−.09	0	0	0	0	.32	12
0	0	0	0	0	−.08	0	0	0	.33	.27	0	0	0	.16	6
0	−.18	−.04	0	.16	0	0	−.83	.23	.13	0	.39	0	0	.47	12
0	−.30	0	0	0	−.06	−.19	.41	−.73	0	−.18	.42	−.08	0	.40	14
0	−.94	−.24	−.06	0	−.07	0	0	.07	0	.11	.18	0	.10	.87	14
0	.15	−.08	.13	.20	0	.11	0	−.31	−.79	−.11	0	.11	0	.51	15
0	−.58	−.36	−.13	0	−.07	.11	0	.23	−.11	−.26	0	0	.04	.79	14
0	−.13	−.10	0	−.04	0	0	0	.12	−.07	−1.09	.27	0	0	.88	11
0	0	0	−.13	0	−.11	.14	0	−.71	−.13	−.71	0	0	0	.44	6
0	0	0	−.34	0	0	.14	−.14	0	−.33	−.53	−.13	0	.09	.37	9
0	.38	.25	0	.09	0	−.16	0	−.12	−.12	.29	−.89	0	.07	.34	13
.07	.18	0	0	0	.08	.09	0	0	−.28	.30	−.35	−.26	.07	.52	14
0	0	0	0	0	0	0	0	0	−.61	−.17	−.22	0	−.39	.47	10
.08	0	0	0	0	0	−.15	0	0	.10	0	0	0	0	.12	7
0	0	.08	0	0	0	0	0	.13	0	−.26	0	0	0	.06	5
−.11	0	0	0	0	0	−.17	.22	.16	.14	−.31	0	0	−.14	.13	10
6	20	17	14	9	10	17	13	18	25	24	14	9	18	$R^2 = .43$	
.08	.27	.18	.17	.14	.16	.18	.15	.20	.19	.31	.41	.09	.11	$B = .18$	

high participation–low competition, and high–high) of the competition-mobilization typology are used because the typology makes little sense as a continuous scale from 1 through 4.[44]

The major indicators of growth will be the seven in the economic (or export) base, plus the commercial services differentiation scale, median family income, and population size. The income and population indicators tend to form a cluster along with equality, number of local government employees, median education, percentage professional–technical, poverty, and unemployment, and all these may not be easily separable. The commercial services scale is in a different cluster, along with the communications, planning, and medical specialties scales. These two clusters form the primary indicators of growth. All other indicators will be considered quality-of–life indicators.

Because these indicators are formed into clusters, there will be multicollinearity between the indicators in the regression analyses. Consequently, some of the signs in the regression equations in table 11–2 may be reversed from the bivariate relations in table 11–1. The reversal of signs is due to the statistical manipulations of submitting highly correlated indicators into the same regression equations. Such a phenomenon is commonly observed when submitting highly correlated variables to partial correlation analysis, and the same principle holds here. Exactly which indicator in the cluster will change signs depends upon the size of the bivariate and partial relations between the indicators in the cluster. The size of these correlations, in turn, may rely on the particular units of observation used in the analysis. Thus, I strongly believe that the signs in table 11–2 should be interpreted in the light of the signs in table 11–1, despite the fact that the signs in table 11–2 are accurate as far as the regression analysis is concerned.

Without relying on the accuracy of any particular coefficients, several answers are provided by table 11–2 with regard to the question of whether growth (by the above indicators) is necessary to quality of life. First, it is clear that every quality–of–life indicator is affected by a multiple number of other indicators, and, second, according to the variance explained (R^2), as well as the size of the beta coefficients in the table, much of the variance is left unexplained, and no other indicator explains much of the variance of any other indicator. The average amount of variance explained is only slightly over 43 percent, despite that six R^2's reach over 0.75, and the average coefficient reaches only 0.18 despite the very large coefficients that often appear when an indicator is regressed upon itself (in autocorrelation). Moreover, the average number of indicators in each equation reaches eleven, with the range from a low of five (for homicides and for manufacturing units employing one hundred or more) to a high of seventeen (for number of public administration employees). In general, a greater number of input indicators tends to produce a greater variance explained. It is clear, therefore, that no one indicator represents a sufficient condition for change in any other indicator, even though some indicators have much greater impact than others.

Table 11-2 also shows that certain indicators appear in the equations with much greater frequency than others. The Gini coefficient of income inequality leads the list, appearing twenty-five times in the thirty-two equations. Median family income appears twenty-four times, the participation-competition typology and public administration employees appear twenty times, the communications scale and percentage disrupted families appear eighteen times, and number of manufacturing firms employing over one hundred, the other two participation-competition types, and the commercial services scale appear seventeen times. In other words, of the ten indicators that appear in over half of the equations, five are growth indicators. Thus their impacts are pervasive.

Another way of assessing impacts of variables in regression equations is to observe the average size of the beta. Eliminating the autocorrelated coefficients from the equations, population size has an average beta of 0.41, median family income 0.31, number of public administration employees 0.27, total per-capita expenditures 0.23, the communications scale 0.20, Gini 0.19, manufacturing firms with over one hundred employees 0.18, commercial services scale 0.18, and total college enrollment 0.17. No other indicator reaches an average beta over 0.15. Six of the above eight indicators are considered growth indicators. The two exceptions are the communications scale and total per-capita government expenditures. Both of these are heavily dependent upon the growth indicators in their equations. Consequently, all of the indicators that have the larger impacts in the equations can be considered growth indicators.

Moreover, median family income, population size, and Gini all have larger impacts on quality-of-life indicators (per-capita government expenditures, political process, and well-being) than they do on other growth indicators (economic base, local services, and local resources). A similar proposition does not hold for the economic base and service indicators. Thus, economic base and commercial services activities can be deemed to affect quality of life through their impact on family income, population size, and Gini.

The results of the regression analysis in table 11-2, therefore, support the conclusions based on table 11-1. Growth indicators are important, if not absolutely necessary, to quality-of-life indicators. Localities that do not experience growth in population size, median family income, and equality will not experience as high levels of quality of life in government services, in political processes, in commercial, health, and communications services, in employment and education, or in levels of well-being. The findings are not strong, but they are consistent. The relationships are multiple and circular but steady. In other words, the findings, at least for these U.S. Northeast counties for the years 1960 to 1970, are quite clear: growth is very important and probably a necessity for greater quality of life.

Conclusions

I have not examined the utopian position that a high quality of life can be achieved without growth except through the social scientific effort of examining the nature of major concepts, their operational indicators, and the correlational relations between them. The subject matter, of course, is vast. Different researchers have different ideas about what constitutes the nature of growth and the nature of quality of life.

My study identified thirty-six commonly used indicators of growth and quality of life and examined their relationships in some detail for the year 1970, and changes in the period 1960 to 1970 (although the intercorrelation matrixes for 1950 and 1960 are similar). Growth is seen primarily as population increase, growth in median family income (and its associated equality in distribution of income in these rural and urban counties), and in economic (or export) base types of industries. Quality-of-life indicators included political process indicators (under the proposition that more participation and competition in the political process leads to a better quality of life), social service indicators (both public sector in terms of government expenditures in local areas and the extent of local government bureaucracy, and private sector in terms of Guttman scales of commercial, medical, and communications differentiation), and well-being indicators (suicide, homicide, poverty, unemployment, marital disruptions, and infant mortality).

These indicators seem reasonably representative of those used in social indicator research and also have precedence in being representative of some of the great values of U.S. society (democracy, equality, opportunity for work and choice, mutuality, and so forth). In any case, those who would espouse a no-growth ethic must confront these values and such indicators as these in their analyses in order to promulgate the beneficent effects of a no-growth policy.

This study's analyses have presented an overview using all 36 of the indicators for all 196 of the Northeast U.S. rural and urban (nonmetropolitan) counties. Except through the regression analysis, no subset analyses were undertaken that might directly compare counties that are growing at very rapid rates with those growing more moderately or with those hardly growing at all. Such analyses may be informative and should perhaps be included of future research agendas in order to disaggregate what are considered here to be strictly linear relations between all of the indicators. Moreover, no detailed lagged analyses were performed other than to examine the relations of changes in indicators from 1960 to 1970. Future researchers, particularly by those who disagree with the validity of my findings, may want to explicate these relations more completely.

The correlation analyses produced three major findings. First, they uncovered seven clusters among the thirty-six indicators. Most of these interrelated indicators from particular subsets of growth or quality of life with only moderate overlap. Thus, there is a cluster on local per-capita government expenditures, another on the private service sector (with some overlap with the public sector), another on poverty and unemployment, perhaps two on economic base industries, another on political process indicators, and a final cluster on population-SES growth indicators. The clusters are important because, without knowledge of them, signs in regression equations may be misleading due to statistical multicollinearity. It is also important to know that certain quality-of-life indicators—in the well-being subconcept particularly—did not cluster. No cluster was discovered linking suicides, homicides, infant mortality, and disrupted marriages in theses counties. Moreover, disrupted marriages and, especially, participation in voting where shown to be negative with virtually every other indicator in the set.

Second, the correlation analysis demonstrated that there are low but positive correlations between virtually all of the indicators. That these correlations are predicted indicates that the small coefficients could be due to the lack of appropriate lags between the indicators. Appropriate lags could raise the correlations. That the correlations are positive suggests that all of the indicators are interrelated so that growth in one set can induce direct or indirect growth in all the indicators.

Third, the regression analysis in table 11-2 demonstrated that the demographic and economic growth indicators are important in affecting quality-of-life indicators both from the standpoint of the number of times these indicators appear in the equations and from the size of the coefficients in the equations. Five growth indicators appear as statistically significant at the 0.05 or better level in over half of the equations. Median family income and the Gini coefficient of income inequality (with which median family income is highly correlated at -0.55) each appear in two-thirds of the equations in the matrix, and one or the other appears in all but one of the equations. (Number of elected public officials is not affected by the income indicators but is affected by economic base indicators.) In addition, the size of the standardized (beta) coefficients for growth indicators on quality-of-life indicators in the matrix are, on the average, much stronger than they are on other growth indicators and stronger than the quality-of-life indicators on each other. Thus, although the correlations may not be very strong, growth indicators certainly are persistent in affecting quality-of-life indicators.

An unmistakable conclusion from these analyses, therefore, is that economic and demographic growth are associated with increases in some of the most commonly used quality-of-life indicators. It is possible, of course, that these findings are specific to the 1950–1970 time period, for only these indicators (even if a number of indicators were used), and for the U.S. Northeast rural and urban counties. Indeed, it may be that metropolitan counties are not experiencing the same types of growth in quality of life at least in part because of large numbers of in-migration of lower-income people and out-migration of higher-income people in metropolitan localities. In the metropolitan counties, the problem may be an uneven growth in their economies and the concomitant bifurcation between rich and poor. (Inequalities in the Northeast are growing in metropolitan counties by the Gini index and decreasing in suburban, urban, and rural counties.) In this sense, there is not a balanced growth in our economy, and the lack of balance may be causing a number of disturbances in quality of life in certain localities.

On the other hand, rural and urban counties in this study seem to be experiencing increases in quality of life on nearly all indicators. Both with regard to indicators of institutional development as well as with those of individual well-being, local economic and demographic growth increase local quality of life. Despite the surface opinion that economic growth may be unnecessary to the development of quality of life, these data certainly support the proposition that economic growth is necessary more than they support any counterproposition. Economic and demographic structures generate the income and opportunities for individuals and collectivities to invest in the appropriate infrastructures of facilities and activities around which better quality of life can develop. Although some people believe that income and materialism are evils loosed upon mankind, such a proposition is not supported by data in this study. In contrast, people in rural localities that experience economic and demographic growth seemingly can buy more and better services so that they also experience better quality of life.

Apparently, then, the U.S. top leadership is not far wrong in emphasizing economic growth as a major determinant of quality of life. The issue for the future, however, may be to monitor the various subprocesses to ensure that the outcomes of this economic and demographic growth in rural and urban counties continue to be invested in ways that will enhance quality of life.

Certainly these data suggest that if U.S. growth rates stagnate or become negative, quality of life itself is in danger of showing an absolute decline as well. The direct effects of political process and especially participation variables in depressing other quality-of-life indicators are somewhat disturbing in this regard. The indirect effects of political competition (in contrast to political participation) through economic base and resource indicators are more encouraging. In other words, the political sector does not seem to be producing quality of life, and the effects of firms in the economic sector are (according to the regression analyses) only indirect through income and population. Since income, its distribution (Gini), and the population seem to be having the greatest effects, then it is "everyone" in the system, or the system itself, that seems to be producing a better quality of life. It is probably a matter of leadership in many sectors of the system working synergistically, therefore, that produces the enhanced quality of life. In the vernacular, the moral of the story seems to be that every person must pull his own oar as well as make certain that others are pulling theirs in order for all of us to experience an improved quality of life.

Notes

1. Robert Parke and David Seidman, "Social Indicators and Social Reporting," *Annals* 435 (January 1978): 1-23.

2. Alice Rivlin, ed. *Toward a Social Report* (Washington, D.C.: U.S. Department of Health, Education and Welfare, 1969); Office of Management and Budget, *Social Indicators, 1973* (Washington, D.C.: U.S. Government Printing Office, 1974); U.S Department of Commerce, Bureau of the Census, Office of Federal Statistical Policy and Standards, *Social Indicators, 1976* (Washington, D.C.: U.S. Government Printing Office, 1977).

3. Gene F. Summers, Sharon D. Evans, Frank Clemente, Jon Minkoff, and Elwood M. Beck, Jr., *Industrial Invasion of Nonmetropolitan America* (New York: Praeger Publishers, 1976).

4. Ibid.

5. Ibid., chap. 7.

6. Paul R. Eberts, "Linkages, Community Structure and Quality of Life" (paper presented to the annual meetings of the Rural Sociological Society, Madison, Wisconsin, August 1977).

7. For further discussion of this point, see chap. 7 in Hubert M. Blalock, Jr., *Theory Construction: From Verbal to Mathematical Formulations* (Englewood Cliffs, N.J.: Prentice-Hall, 1969), and part 4 on the relation of indicators to concepts in Blalock, *Causal Models in the Social Sciences* (Chicago: Aldine-Atherton, 1971).

8. Here I am following closely the argument presented in Kenneth C. Land and Seymour Spilerman, eds., *Social Indicator Models* (New York: Russell Sage Foundation, 1975).

9. John L. Sullivan, "Multiple Indicators and Complex Causal Models," in Blalock, Jr., *Theory Construction*.

10. Robert W. Marans and Willard Rodgers, "Toward an Understanding of Community Satisfaction," in Amos Hawley and V. Rocks, eds.,

Metropolitan America in Contemporary Perspective (New York: Russell Sage Foundation, 1975), pp. 299–352; Donald A. Dillman and Kenneth R. Tremblay, Jr., "The Quality of Life in Rural America," *Annals* 429 (January 1977): 115–129; and Parke and Seidman, "Social Indicators."

11. Angus Campbell, Philip E. Converse, and Willard L. Rodgers, *The Quality of American Life: Perceptions, Evaluations and Satisfactions* (New York: Russell Sage Foundation, 1976); Paul R. Eberts and Frank W. Young, "Sociological Variables in Development: Their Range and Characteristics," in George Beal, Ronald Powers, and E. Walter Coward, eds., *Sociological Perspectives of Domestic Development* (Ames: Iowa State University Press, 1971).

12. Frank M. Andrews and Stephen B. Withey, *Social Indicators of Well-being: Americans' Perceptions of Their Life Quality* (New York: Plenum Press: 1976); John O. Wilson, *Quality of Life in the United States: An Excursion into the New Frontiers of Socio-Economic Indicators* (Kansas City: Midwest Research Center, 1970); Frank W. Young and Ruth C. Young, *Comparative Studies of Community Growth,* Rural Sociological Society Monograph (Morgantown: West Virginia University Press, 1973); Karl A. Fox, *Social Indicators and Social Theory: Elements of an Operational System* (New York: John Wiley, 1974); and Walter Isard, *Introduction to Regional Science* (Englewood Cliffs, N.J.: Prentice–Hall, 1975).

13. Frank A. Fear, Gerald E. Klonglan, and Richard D. Warren, "Social Indicators and Needs Assessment: Anatomy of a Pilot Project," in Carol A. Chapman, Craig L. Infanger, Lynn W. Robbins, and David L. Debertin, *Taking Computers to the Community: Prospects and Perspectives* (Lexington: University of Kentucky, College of Agriculture, Cooperative Extension, 1978).

14. James A. Christenson, "Community Satisfaction: Objective and Subjective Indicators" (paper presented to the annual meetings of the Rural Sociological Society, Madison, Wisconsin, 1977).

15. See Summers et al., *Industrial Invasion*, p. 115.

16. For a concise discussion of the problems of ecological correlations, see Otis Dudley Duncan, Ray P. Cuzzert, and Beverley Duncan, *Statistical Geography: Problems in Analyzing Areal Data* (Glencoe, Ill.:   Free Press, 1961).

17. This point is elaborated more fully in Paul R. Eberts and Sergio Sismondo, "Principles in Design and Management of Policy Research for Public Planning Agencies," in Ronald C. Powers and David Rogers, ed., *Alternative Methods for Public Policy Research in Rural America* (Ames: Iowa State University Press, 1978).

18. The concept of larger communities as activity nodes in rural counties is developed in Roland L. Warren, "Community as Nodes of Locality

Activity" (paper presented to the Community Section of the American Sociological Association, New York, 1976).

19. Duncan, Cuzzert, and Duncan, *Statistical Geography*.

20. Following Parke and Seidman, "Social Indicators."

21. For previous usages of a similar strategy, see Otis Dudley Duncan and Albert Reiss, Jr., *Social Characteristics of Urban and Rural Communities, 1950* (New York: John Wiley, 1956); Amos Hawley, *Human Ecology* (New York: Ronald Press, 1950); Wilbur R. Thompson, *A Preface to Urban Economics* (Baltimore, Md.: Johns Hopkins Press for Resources for the Future, 1965); and Isard, *Introduction*.

22. This point is abundantly demonstrated in two nationwide studies of the U.S. adult population as reported in Gerald Gwien, Joseph Veroff, and Sheila Feld, *Americans View Their Mental Health* (New York: Basic Books, 1960), and Campbell, Converse, and Rodgers, *Quality of American Life*.

23. For further discussion on the ambiguity of social indicators, see Ida C. Merrian, "Social Security and Social Welfare Indicators," *Annals* 435 (January 1978): 117–139.

24. Land and Spilerman, *Social Indicators Models*.

25. Sullivan, "Multiple Indicators."

26. George A. Lundberg, *Social Research* (New York: Longmans, Green, 1941).

27. Terry N. Clark, *Community Power and Policy Outputs: A Review of Urban Research* (Beverly Hills: Sage Publications, 1973).

28. Eberts and Sismonds "Principles in Design."

29. Christenson, "Community Satisfaction"; James A Christenson and Carolyn E. Sachs, "The Impact of Size and Number of Administrative Units on Quality of Public Services" (mimeographed, University of Kentucky, Department of Rural Sociology, 1977).

30. Rivlin, *Toward a Social Report*; Office of Management and Budget, *Social Indicators*, 1973; Office of Federal Statistical Policy and standards, *Social Indicators, 1976*; Clark, *Community Power*; and William H. Sewell, "Social Mobility and Social Participation," *Annals* 435 (January 1978): 226–247.

31. Paul R. Eberts, "Community Power Structure and Macro–System Fluidity as Variables: Operationalization, Determinants and Consequences" (mimeographed, Cornell University, Department of Rural Sociology, 1976).

32. Eberts and Young, "Sociological Variables"; Young and Young, *Comparative Studies*; and Ronald W. Wilson, Jacob J. Feldman, and Mary Grace Kovar, "Continuing Trends in Health and Health Care," *Annals* 435 (January 1978): 140–156.

33. Luther Tweeten and George L. Brinkman, *Micropolitan Development* (Ames, Iowa State University Press, 1976), and Summers et al., *Industrial Invasion.*

34. Ann R. Miller, "Changing Work Life Patterns: A Twenty-five Year Review," *Annals* 435 (January 1978): 83-101.

35. See Office of Management and Budget, *Social Indicators, 1973;* Office of Federal Statistical Policy and Standards, *Social Indicators,1976*; Sheldon H. Danziger and Robert J. Lampman, "Getting and Spending," *Annals* 435 (January 1978): pp. 23-29.

36. For a review of such usage, see Danziger and Lampman, "Getting and Spending."

37. See Wilson, *Quality of Life,* and Parke and Seidman, "Social Indicators" for additional suggestions; Doris B. Holleb, "A Decent Home and Suitable Living Environment," *Annals* 435 (January 1978): 102-116.

38. Rivlin, *Toward a Social Report*; Office of Management and Budget, *Social Indicators, 1973*; Office of Federal Statistical Policy and Standards, *Social Indicators, 1976.*

39. Eberts and Young, "Sociological Variables," and Andrews and Withey, *Social Indicators.*

40. Blalock, *Theory Construction.*

41. Duncan, Cuzzert, and Duncan, *Statistical Geography:* Michael T. Hannan, "Problems of Aggregation," in Blalock, *Theory Construction.*

42. Land and Spilerman, *Social Indicator Models.*

43. See Clark, *Community Power*, who reports on other studies which show similar findings.

44. See Eberts, "Community Power Structure," for further elaboration on the conceptualization of this typology.

Part IV
Empirical Assessments of Community Change

12 Archives for Regional and Local Data in Europe

Stein Rokkan and *Terje Sande*

National Data Services

The availability of statistical information, especially machine–readable data for the study of industrial growth and community change, varies considerably among the countries of Europe. Two obvious institutional causes of these variances are the existence of governmental institutions for the production of such information, and the existence of institutions concerned with making this information easily available to the research communities. The latter condition can be supplied by the research communities themselves, and during the last decade they have done just that. In several West European countries, they have set up data services or archives specifically concerned with providing machine-readable data and user–oriented statistical programs for research purposes. The existing services vary in terms of organizational setting, size, and the kind of data on which they concentrate their efforts, but they have some basic and important objectives in common:

1. To spread information on available data through newsletters and articles in professional journals.
2. Within the limits of financial and human resources, to store and maintain whatever data that are made machine readable in order to reduce duplicate work among researchers, as well as to guarantee against possible loss of valuable information.
3. Whenever feasible, to develop retrieval systems for better documentation and easier access to the data stored in the archives.

To some extent these data services may be compared with usual libraries. But rather than being concerned with the written input and output of the research process, they can provide some or all of the necessary data, and they want to obtain data that might have been generated or assembled by research projects.

Some of the data services are mainly concerned with survey data, others with ecological data, and some attempt to cover the whole range of social science data. This specialization to some extent is overcome by agreements among all data services to exchange data.

At present six West European countries have set up national data services. Table 12-1 lists them by name, country, and the type of data they

Table 12–1.
Data Services in Western Europe

Institution	Survey Data	Ecological Data	All
Archivio Dati e Programmi (Italy)	(x)	x	
Belgian Archives for the Social Sciences			x
Dansk Data Arkiv (Denmark)	x	(x)	
Norwegian Social Science Data			x
Social Science Research Council Survey Archives (Great Britain)	x	(x)	
Steinmetz Archives (The Netherlands)	x		
Zentralarchiv fur Empirische Sozialforschung, BRD	x	(x)	

focus their attention on. In addition to these national archives or data services, several university institutes in other countries have their own holdings or in-house services. These holdings can be fairly extensive but are not public and therefore are not easily available to nonresidents or nonmembers. This situation is found in Finland, France, Sweden and Switzerland, and, to some extent, in Austria, Iceland, Ireland, and Spain.

International Organizations and Services

The data services listed in table 12–1 founded in 1976 an organization for international cooperation: the committee of European Social Science Data Archives (CESSDA). The committee sponsors an annual conference with the basic aim of exchanging information on data holdings and discussing ways to improving existing services. The organization publishes a newsletter.

In 1977 the members of CESSDA, together with the Inter–University Consortium for Political and Social Research (ISPSR), an American institution, and two Canadian archives founded the International Federation of Data Organizations (IF–DO). This last organization is open for membership to all archives that have the capacity to exchange data and technologies with other members. Among its objectives are efforts to transfer the archival technology to less advanced countries, simplify the exchange of data between countries, find ways to improve and standardize data documentation, and settle the question of confidentiality in connection with data banks. Moreover it was through IF–DO that the agreement on free mutual exchange of data between the member organizations was reached. This is an important decision because the largest overall holdings of data for European countries are located in the archives of ICPSR.

A service of a different kind is Data Information Service (DIS) of the European Consortium for Political Research (ECPR). DIS is not concerned with the data themselves but with the documentation of existing machine-readable files. Together with the Norwegian Social Science Data Services, the DIS publishes a newsletter, *European Political Data* (EPD). (Its address is Chr. Michelson Institute, Fantoftveien 38, N–5036, Fantoft, Norway.) The EPD is divided into a data section with information on new data sets and additions and a computer section with news on statistical programs and other relevant computer developments. (The information presented here is taken from the various issues of the EPD newsletter or the archive built up by the DIS.)

Data Files for Regions and Localities in Western Europe

It would be impossible to give a detailed account of what is available in all of the data sets described in EPD. (The issue for December 1975 carries an index to the files before that time. No index has been compiled for later issues.) We shall therefore limit the presentation to the following few basic characteristics, which should enable possible users to decide whether the file contains information of potential interest:

1. Name of country or countries.
2. Time period covered in the data set.
3. Type of units used in the data set.
4. Number of units in the data set.
5. Type of variables included. The eight groups in this classification are (A) geographical context (such as location, area, and urbanization); (B) demographic structure (such as age distribution); (C) socioeconomic status indicators (such as occupational groups); (D) cultural indicators (such as language, religion, and education); (E) economic indicators (such as economic production and government taxes and expenditures); (F) social welfare indicators (such as health services and housing); (G) mass media (such as newspapers and radios); and (H) political indicators (turnout, party votes, and referenda).
6. EPD reference. This is the issue in which a more detailed description of the data set appears.
7. Comments. Basically this column contains the name of a person to contact or the archive where the data set is stored and where one can obtain the complete documentation and tape with the data.

The major faults of this description are, first, that the time period given in the second column need not refer to all of the variable groups listed in the fifth column, and second that some of the groups contain rather different types of information; furthermore boundaries between some of them are rather arbitrary. We have tried to improve on this by giving a few examples of the kind of variables found in the various groups.

The data sets shown in table 12-2 do not include all of those available for a given country. However, to our knowledge they provide the most comprehensive coverage in terms of variables and time span. The information on time period in the table refers to the latest information we have, but some of these files are continuously updated and may cover a longer period than indicated. (City files are omitted from the table. Anyone interested in these can find the necessary information in EPD.)

Even if the content of the described data sets represents an enormous amount of information, the possible sources of data are not nearly exhausted in any country. The increased use of computers in governmental agencies and statistical bureaus makes it possible to obtain data for later periods in machine-readable form. Consequently a considerable improvement in data coverage in more and more countries is likely. The major constraint that users of data on regions and localities are likely to experience in the future will be whether institutions are concerned with linking new data to existing files and distributing the data.

Recent Developments and Ongoing Projects

One of the major recent developments in connection with regional and local data banks has been the addition of cartographic information to the files and a link-up to automatic mapmaking facilities for the production of thematic maps. The spatial dimensions of our data have been neglected for too long. This has partly been due to the cost of producing maps. But the recent improvements in automated cartography have made the thematic map a cheap and effective tool for both descriptive and analytical purposes.

Another important trend is the continuous effort to establish crossnational files with identical or approximately identical information for all countries included. Table 12-2 lists one such file, but several projects are currently underway in this area. The NSD, for example, has accepted a three-year project for the five Nordic countries that will set up time-series files at the county level containing almost all information that is available at this level for a certain period of time.

At the European level, some preliminary meetings have been held to discuss the means and ways of cooperation in this field. Through the IF-DO network, this has crystallized into a decision to apply for a joint project

Table 12-2
Regional and Local Data Files for Western Europe

Country	Time Period	Unit	N	A	B	C	D	E	F	G	H	EPD Issue	Comments
Belgium	1919–1974	Arrondisement	30	x		x		x			x	18	BASS
	1961	Commune	2663	x	x	x	x	x				13	BASS
Denmark	1906–1968	Commune	1400		x	x						2, 5	Borre et al., BASS
Finland	1940–1950	Commune		x	x	x	x	x	x			7	Charleton University
	1970	Commune		x	x	x							Heiskanen
France	1936–1969	Departement	90	x	x	x	x	x	x	x	x		ICPSR
	1945–1971	Canton	2830	x	x	x	x	(x)	x		x		Derivry
Germany	1920–1933	Kreise	563	x	x	x	(x)	x	x		x	3, 7	Weimar Rep., ICPSR
	1939–1969	Kreise	248	x	x	x	(x)	x	x		x	6	Zentralarchiv
	1946–1968	Wahlkreise	173		x	x			x		x	3	ICPSR
Great Britain	1918–1970	Borough	618		x	(x)			x		x	10	Miller
	1955–1970	Constituency	118		x	x	x	x			x	10	Crewe
	1836–1966	County			x	x	x				x	18	Hechter (includes
Iceland		Commune											Grimson
Italy	1951–1971	Commune	8150	x	x	x	x	x	x		x	18	ADPSS
	1951–1971	Province	94	x	x	x	x	x	x		x	18	ADPSS
Netherlands	1947–1971	Municipality	981	x	x	x	x	x	(x)	(x)	x	6	Zentralarchiv
	1880–1971	Municipality	100	x	x	x	x	x	x	x	x	7	Verhof
Norway	1850–1978	Commune	c. 750	x	x	x	x	x	x		x	1, 2	NSD
	1837–1973	County	30	x	x	x					x		NSD
	1960–1970	Tract	c.9000	x	x	x					x		NSD
Sweden	1948–1968	Commune	1012	x	x	x	x	x			x	5, 9	Gustafson
	1887–1970	County	25			x	x			x		2	Lewin
Switzerland	1900–1970	Canton	25	x	x	x	x	x	x		x	3, 5	ICPSR
Common Market	1961–1969	Region	73	x	x	x		x			x	18	Handley

Type of Information

These refer to the addresses located in the appendix to this chapter.

by the data services in Belgium, Italy, and Norway. We hope to set up a data bank for level III units (counties in the United Kingdom, Norway, Sweden, and Denmark départéments in France, provincias in Italy, and cantons in Switzerland) for as many Western European countries as possible and link this with a mapmaking facility. The final product of the initial stage will be the data set itself plus a computer atlas with thematic maps for the countries included.

As a consequence of the existence of the large data archives, many research projects can easily obtain most of the data they need from the archives; they are thus able to devote more resources to the collection of data about phenomena not included in governmental or other statistical sources. Examples of these kinds of data are interviews with local officials in all or a sample of local governments or the coding of newspaper reports of local events. When this information is added to the existing archives and accumulated over time, the possibilities for analyzing and understanding the dynamics of our communities should be substantially improved.

Notes

1. These differences and a discussion of their causes are found in Stein Rokkan, "Data Services in Western Europe, Reflections on Variations in the Condition of Academic Institution–Building," in Richard I. Hofferbert and Jerome M. Clubb, eds., *Social Science Data Archives,* Sage Contemporary Social Science Issues, No. 39 (Beverly Hills, Calif.: Sage Publications, 1977).

2. For a recent assessment, see Geoffrey H. Dutton and William G. Nisen, "The Expanding Realm of Computer Cartography," *Datamation* (June 1978). For information on the usage of cartography in connection with European regional data, see *EDP*, nos. 13, 19, 20, 22, 25, 26, 27.

3. See *EPD,* nos. 18, 22, 25, 26, 27.

Appendix 12A:
Archives for Regional
and Local Data
in Europe

Archivio Dati e Programmi per le Science Soziali (ADPSS)
Via G. Cantoni 4
20144 Milan, Italy

Belgian Archives for the Social Sciences (BASS)
Batiment SH2
Place de Montesquieu, 1 BTE 18
B-1348 Louvan-la-Neuve, Belgium

Borre, Ole
Institute of Political Science
University of Aarhus
DK-8000 Aarhus, Denmark

Charleton University
Colonel By Drive
Ottowa, Ontario, Canada K1S 5B6

Crewe, Dr. Ivor M.
Director
Social Science Research Council (SSRC) Survey Archive
University of Essex
Wivenhoe Park
Colchester C04 3SQ, Essex, England

Data, S. A.
General Oraa 70
Madrid 6, Spain

Derivry, Daniel
GEMAS
Maison des Suisses de l'Homme
54 Boulevard Raspail
75 Paris 6, France

Grimsson, Professor Olafur
University of Iceland
Reykjavik, Iceland

Gustafsson, Dr. Göran
Institute of Sociology
University of Lund
Fack
S-22005 Lund 5, Sweden

Handley, David
Department de Science Politique
Université de Genéve
3 Place de l'Université
CH-1211 Genéve 4, Switzerland

Hechter, Dr. Michael
Department of Sociology
University of Washington
Seattle, Washington 98105, United States

Heiskanen, Dr. Ilkka
DETA Projekti
Boulevardi 1A7
SF-00100 Helsinki, Finland

Inter-University Consortium for Political and Social Research
(ICPSR)
P.O. Box 1248
Ann Arbor, Michigan 48106 United States

Lewin, Professor Leif
Department of Political Science
University of Uppsala
Skytteanum
S-75120 Uppsala, Sweden

Miller, Dr. William
Department of Politics
University fo Strathclyde
McCance Building
Richmond Street
Glasgow, Scotland

Norweigian Social Science Data Services (NSD)
Christiesgate 15-19
N-5014 Bergen-Univ., Norway

Verhoef, Dr. Jan
Department of Political Science
University of Leiden
Hugo de Groot Str. 27
Leiden, The Netherlands

Zentralarchiv für empirische Sozialforschung
University of Cologne
Bahemer Strasse 40
D-5000 Cologne, West Germany

13 Data Resources for Community Studies: The United States

Jerome M. Clubb and
Michael W. Traugott

The emphasis in much recent research upon essentially urban concerns and the distressing tendency in many research and data collection designs to neglect contextual factors might lead to the conclusion that empirical data relevant to nonurban phenomena have been neglected. In fact most major data collection efforts—whether conducted by social scientists in the pursuit of specific research goals or by governments or other organizations in the course of routine administrative, policy development, or commercial activities—span both metropolitan and nonmetropolitan areas and populations. It is probably the case that relatively few large-scale community studies, such as the continuing Detroit Area Studies conducted by the Survey Research Center of the University of Michigan, focus upon nonmetropolitan areas rather than upon areas of major population concentration. It is also likely that relatively fewer social scientific data collection efforts have focused upon specifically rural and nonmetropolitan economic pursuits and social processes. Nevertheless, substantial empirical data resources are available for the study of nonmetropolitan social, political, and economic phenomena.

The collection of data pertinent to nonmetropolitan areas has not been neglected by the government. Indeed in the United States, federal agencies and state and local governments constitute a vast storehouse of relevant empirical data. No doubt less effort has been devoted by major national data repositories and archives and by governmental agencies to publicizing these data resources and to making them generally available in readily accessible and usable forms. But if that is the case, it is likely that relative neglect has been in significant measure a product of the failure of students of nonmetropolitan phenomena to make their data needs and interests known, to support the data dissemination activities of data repositories and governmental agencies, and to act in concerted fashion to influence the data collection and dissemination policies of those organizations.

The abundance and diversity of relevant data resources is such as to preclude anything approaching a comprehensive survey. The advent of computer technology and the increasingly ubiquitous use of these devices for the varied purposes of information management, storage, and analysis has provided a massive stimulus to data gathering and record keeping. Thus even a listing and brief description of available computer-readable data collections, to which we will limit our attention, that are directly or indirectly relevant to the study of nonmetropolitan areas would constitute a catalog of immense proportions. The effort would itself involve a major research task—one beyond both our own capacities and our purposes here. The difficulties confronted in constructing a similar catalog of the sources of relevant computer-readable data would be only moderately less severe. When we recall only the numerous offices and agencies of the Department of Health, Education and Welfare that collect relevant data and from which computer-readable data can sometimes be obtained, we can begin to recognize both the large number and the wide diversity of sources of relevant data. It is possible here only to suggest a very crude classification of relevant data and data sources. In this way the range of available data resources can be illustrated, avenues for access to relevant data briefly indicated, and problems and opportunities for data acquisition cursorily explored.

We will employ a somewhat crude three-category scheme for the classification of available data: aggregate data, information from administrative records, and individual-level data from surveys. Aggregate data refer to systematic collections of information on the demographic, social, and economic characteristics of the population that are available for basic geographical or geopolitical units of analysis. These data are typified by information from the U.S. censuses of Population and Housing, which are made available for states, counties, and minor civil divisions of various sizes. The second category of data includes information from or about agencies, institutions, facilities, or establishments. The information may be about employment, expenditures, services, and the impact and incidence of participation in governmental programs. The units of analysis may be the governmental units themselves or the agencies or institutions, which can be further identified by their location within a geographical unit or governmental jurisdiction. The third category of data emcompasses information collected for individuals, including personal social, economic, and demographic characteristics, as well as information about attitudes, opinions, and behavior. These data are frequently collected through sample surveys conducted by a variety of agencies and institutions, including academic researchers, commercial organizations, and governmental bureaus. The range of available data in each of these three categories is immense. Therefore we will consider only data collections that are at least relatively accessible in computer-readable form.

The sources of computer-readable data relevant to investigation of nonmetropolitan phenomena can also be grouped into three categories. The first of these includes social science data archives and other similar facilities dedicated to the organization, processing, preservation, and dissemination of computer-readable data for research and instruction in the social sciences. A small number of such organizations provide services to a national constituency, but a relatively large number provide local or regional services. A second category is composed of governmental offices and agencies at all levels that collect and sometimes disseminate relevant computer-readable data. A third category is even more disparate and includes individual researchers who have collected data and are sometimes willing to supply copies to others, as well as private profit and nonprofit organizations, which collect and in some cases supply data resources.

Data Sources

Our classification of sources of computer-readable data relevant to social scientific inquiry tends to rank the various sources in terms of degree of accessibility and convenience of access to the data. Hence limited further discussion of each category is required. Since the 1960s, a substantial number of data organizations variously referred to as social sciences data archives, data banks, data laboratories, data services, and the like have appeared in the United States and Canada. More recently, a number of data organizations—often quite specialized in terms of substantive focus, clienteles, and functions—have appeared in the private and governmental sectors. Academic data organizations range from a small number of nationally oriented general-purpose archives through more specialized organizations concerned primarily with particular geographical regions or substantive areas of inquiry to data services and laboratories whose operations are largely or exclusively limited to a local college or university community.

In general, these organizations include among their functions the preservation and dissemination of computer-readable collections of research data, provision of varying forms of technical assistance to social scientists in the use of computer-readable social science data, and conversion of data collections to standard, well-documented, and readily usable form. Data of broad research value are obtained from individual researchers or research groups that have collected them in the course of research applications, from governmental agencies, or from other sources. Although practices vary among organizations, substantial effort is frequently devoted to eliminating errors, discrepancies, and technical idiosyncrasies and to preparing supporting information that explains such matters as the study design and sampling frame, documents uncorrectable discrepancies, and describes technical characteristics. In many instances these organizations can supply data in forms compatible with the technical requirements of diverse hardware and software systems. Hence researchers can often receive from these organizations clean and well-documented data suitable for analysis and manipulation with at most limited additional processing. In some cases, these organizations also provide training in empirical methods of social research and in aspects of computer technology, assistance and consultation in computer applications, dissemination of computer software systems, development and dissemination of data-based instructional materials for the social sciences, and clearinghouse services to aid social scientists in identifying relevant data collections and to provide information on ongoing research.

The number and diversity of these organizations is great. The appendix to this chapter provides a partial listing of them—including those in the private and governmental as well as the academic sectors—that data relevant to the investigation of nonmetropolitan phenomena and that provide services beyond purely local constituencies. Several of these organizations merit particular attention because they constitute social scientific resources of major importance.

In the United States, two academically based and nationally oriented, general-purpose data archives are of special interest: the Roper Public Opinion Research Center—now located jointly at the University of Connecticut, Yale University, and Williams College—and the Inter-university Consortium for Political and Social Research, with headquarters and central staff located in the Institute for Social Research of the University of Michigan. The Roper Center contains the largest collection of data from sample surveys in the world. Its holdings include data from thousands of surveys conducted by well over a hundred commercial and academic survey units—including the Gallup organizations and its affiliates, the National Opinion Research Center, and numerous others—in more than sixty nations. These holdings span virtually the entire period of sample survey research, with the oldest data files dating from 1936, and are of incomparable value for the study of popular attitudes. The magnitude of its holdings has prevented the center from cleaning and processing every survey to standard form. Thus data acquired from this source sometimes require substantial additional processing before analytic applications can be carried out. On the other hand, the center also disseminates a very large number of fully cleaned data collections, which can be immediately used with at most limited additional processing. Moreover, it has the capacity to clean and convert its data holdings to fully usable form on request. The Roper Center is supported in part by annual fees paid by member colleges, universities, and other organizations through the International Survey Library Association. Individuals at these organizations have free or inexpensive access to center data holdings. Add data are also available at a charge to individuals at other institutions.

The Inter-university Consortium for Political and Social Research is a membership-based organization of over 200 colleges and universities in the United States and a dozen or more other nations. The consortium holdings include data from surveys, primarily academic, conducted in the United States and numerous other nations. Consortium holdings are not limited to data collected through sample surveys; they include as well data in each of the other categories mentioned above. For example, the consortium maintains extensive computer-readable files of social, economic, and demographic data at the county and state level originally collected through the U.S. censuses beginning in 1790; aggregated returns at the county level for elections to the offices of president, governor, and United States senator and congressman since 1788; comprehensive roll-call voting records for the United States Congress from 1789 to the present; data from the National Council of Churches of Christ in the U.S.A. surveys of churches and church membership conducted in 1952 and 1972; and extensive data files originally collected by such federal agencies as the Law Enforcement Assistance Administration, the National Center for Health Statistics, and the Social Security Administration. In its data acquisitions, the consortium has tended to be relatively selective. In general it acquires only data that external advisory committees composed of scholars have judged to be of high quality and great research value. Consequently considerable energy can be devoted by the consortium staff to the work of cleaning and documenting these data files, and readily usable data can typically be supplied in technical forms suited to the requirements of most computational systems.

The activities of the corsortium are not limited to processing and disseminating social scientific data, nor are the data holdings limited to materials for the United States. Consortium holdings include data in each of the categories indicated above and relevant to a variety of nations. In addition, the consortium maintains an annual summer training program in quantitative methods of social research. Through the training program, graduate students and senior scholars can gain an introduction to basic research methods or can participate in advanced seminars devoted to the most recent developments in research methodology. The consortium also disseminates a major computer software system (OSIRIS III), which was developed at the Institute for Social Research of the University of Michigan and which provides a wide range of capabilities for the management and analysis of social scientific data. Like the Roper Center, the consortium activities are primarily supported by annual fees paid by the affiliated institutions. Individuals at those institutions have access to the data holdings, except in a few special cases, without charge beyond the annual institutional fee. All data holdings are considered to be in the public domain and are available at a charge to individuals at other institutions.

Two nationally oriented Canadian data organizations require comment. The Institute for Behavioral Research at York University processes, maintains, and disseminates extensive arrays of data from numerous sample surveys, the Canadian national censuses, and a variety of other sources. The institute also maintains and provides access to a computer-based bibliographic search capability, which references numerous scholarly periodicals published in Canada, the United States, and other nations. Although not a data archive, the Canadian Clearing House for the Social Sciences systematically compiles and maintains information on files of Canadian data available for social scientific research. A catalog of data files is published periodically, and an inquiry addressed to the Clearing House will elicit information regarding the availability and condition of data files relevant to particular areas of research concern.

Various other academic data organizations also require mention. In some cases they are more specialized in terms of substantive orientation, function, and clientele than those mentioned above. Among these are the Data and Program Library Service at the University of Wisconsin, which includes in its holdings survey materials, extended economic and demographic time series, census data, and other computer-readable materials. The Louis Harris Political Data Center at the University of North Carolina is the central dissemination point for data collected by Louis Harris and Associates, as well as data from other sources. The Laboratory for Political Research at the University of Iowa has holdings of survey data, including a number of unique data collections relevant to the surrounding areas. The International Data Library and Reference Service in the Survey Research Center of the University of California, Berkeley, had extensive data holdings that tend to focus upon Latin America, other developing nations, and the state of California.

These organizations, particularly the nationally oriented data archives, include extensive arrays of empirical computer-readable data relevant to the study of nonmetropolitan areas. Each maintains an up-to-date catalog list of data holdings obtainable on request (the chapter appendix gives the addresses of these and other similar organizations). Moreover, a letter or telephone call will elicit information as to whether current holdings include materials relevant to particular research interests and usually suggestions as to alternative sources of relevant data.

Data organizations of this sort developed to meet the needs of social scientists whose research and instruction requires the use of extensive arrays of empirical data and advanced computer technology. Such organizations serve the value of scientific replication, and they rest upon the fact that data originally collected for particular research, administrative, or other purposes usually have research and instructional value much beyond the original purposes from which they were collected. Such organizations in most cases were initially formed to conserve and disseminate research data collected by individual scholars or groups in the course of research applications. However, their functions in some cases were early extended to include original data collection, and their holdings were expanded to include data initially collected by governmental agencies as well. Difficulties of access by academic social scientists and others to these resources made it necessary to extend the purview of many data organizations to include materials of this sort. Hence a sizable portion of the data holdings of many of these organizations comprises administrative and other data originally collected by governmental agencies.

In recent years, moreover, a number of for-profit and nonprofit organizations have appeared, which serve primarily as intermediary processing and dissemination mechanisms for data originally produced by the federal government. Among these, National DUALabs, Inc. was originally formed to provide effective and lower-cost access to the voluminous computer-readable data files produced by the 1970 census. The files of 1970 census data held and disseminated by many of the data organizations were obtained through the DUALabs intermediary. Subsequently, DUALabs has extended its operations to include other categories of federal data, and it has become an important resource to the social scientific community. Other similar organizations include the social and economic data base developed at Oak Ridge National Laboratories, originally based upon 1970 census materials but now including many other data files as well. A major private corporation providing a wide range of data services and data files is Westat Research, Inc. It is responsible for the development of a number of data files for market research purposes, which also have a general utility for social scientists interested in the study of nonmetropolitan areas.

Governmental agencies constitute incomparably rich sources of empirical data for virtually all aspects of social scientific inquiry. The federal government expends vast sums on specialized data collection efforts of relevance to social scientific inquiry—the data collection efforts of the Department of Health, Education and Welfare alone are estimated at in excess of one billion dollars annually—and an immense volume of data is routinely collected through the conduct of government, through a wide variety of monitoring activities, and through administration of governmental programs. A variety of federal agencies also make computer-readable data files generally available to social scientists, including the Bureau of the Census through its Data User Services Division, the Bureau of Labor Statistics, the Law Enforcement Assistance Administration, the National Center for Health Statistics, and the National Center for Educational Statistics.

Social scientists who attempt to acquire relevant data resources from federal agencies often encounter difficulties. Perhaps the most frustrating is learning of the availability of relevant files and in identifying the appropriate modes of access to them. Moreover, available data files are often large in terms of the numbers of variables and units of analysis, complex in structure, poorly documented, and frequently supplied in technically idiosyncratic formats. Hence researchers must often carry out extensive processing to reorganize, subset, and otherwise restructure data files before analytical work can begin. The costs of acquiring federal data files vary widely, but are often superficially low. Because of the manner in which data files are organized, the researcher must often bear the cost of acquiring substantially more data than are actually needed for the particular research application. When the costs of overpurchase are added to the reprocessing costs of subsetting and converting data to usable form, the financial and other burdens confronted in utilizing federally collected data can become prohibitive for all but the best funded individual scholar or research group.

It was to overcome these obstacles that various data organizations have assumed an intermediary role concerning the dissemination of federally collected data. Such organizations sometimes serve, in effect, as buyers' cooperatives, paying the costs of initial acquisition, reprocessing the data file, providing subsetting capabilities, and making available the precise data required in fully usable form at lower or no cost. Indeed, a number of federal agencies now commission data organizations to carry out these intermediary functions and provide financial support for the conduct of those activities.

Promising developments have also occurred within the federal government itself. In recent years various federal agencies have significantly improved their capacity to supply data in more usable form out of a recognition of the needs and interests of social scientists. In the case of the Bureau of the Census, for example, individuals have gained access to valuable data resources in more usable form through the establishment of the Data User Services Division. The formation of the National Technical Information Service in the Department of Commerce constitutes a partially successful effort to provide a central facility through which information about available federal data collections can be obtained. From a somewhat different perspective, the information of the Machine-Readable Archives Branch of the National Archives and Records Service constitutes a more promising development. The division functions, as its name implies, to collect, conserve, and make available the machine-readable records of the federal government as they are adjudged suitable for conservation. The creation of this unit reflects belated and, as yet, inadequate recognition by the National Archives of its responsibility to conserve and provide access to the computer-readable records of the nation, as well as to conventional paper records. The analogous organization in Canada is the Machine Readable Archives, Public Archives Canada. (The complete address is in the appendix.)

The Machine-Readable Archives Division promises to become an important resource for social scientists. At present, however, the level of funding is too low to allow it to acquire even the records within its area of responsibility, much less to process to usable form those computer-readable records that it already has. Still other promising developments could also be noted, but avenues of access to federally collected data remain chaotic and problematic, and the various intermediary organizations still constitute the most effective and convenient means for social scientists to gain access to these rich data resources.

If the data access picture is chaotic at the national level, chaos is compounded by confusion at the state and local levels of government. State and local governments also produce extensive data bearing upon the conduct of government, provision of services, availability of social facilities, and the activities, conditions, and quality of life of their populations. At both the state and local levels, computational equipment is widely employed to record, manage, and use this information. The accessibility of such information varies widely, but few if any states or other jurisdictions provide anything approaching effective access to these data resources. Fortunately the various monitoring and data collection efforts—perhaps best illustrated by the quinquennial Census of Governments conducted by the Bureau of the Census—provide a means by which at least partial data bearing upon these jurisdictions and their activities can be gained.

A variety of commercial organizations routinely collect and preserve data for business purposes, which are also of value for a wide variety of other research applications. Standard and Poors routinely collects data on local government finances and credit ratings, for example, and the R. L. Polk Company maintains several large data files in conjunction with its production of city directories. These collections, however, are proprietary, and generalized access to them is usually not available. Even so, enterprising social scientists can frequently arrange access to segments of such data files on an individual basis.

Many of the numerous public interest groups also constitute possible sources of relevant data. The International City Management Association, for example, compiles computer-readable data on finances, personnel, facilities, and other resources in government for municipalities. Other examples of public interest groups that constitute potential sources of usable data include the National Association of Counties and the Council of State Governments, which also have data on governmental units, as well as organizations such as the National Fire Protection Association or the Police Foundation, which maintain data on personnel, facilities, and services in the relevant administrataive jurisdictions.

The data holdings of such organizations are differentially available. For the most part such organizations do not provide generalized access to data resources; they function instead to serve the needs of their own constituencies. But as in the case of commercial organizations, individual scholars or research groups can frequently gain access to these resources for particular research purposes. Costs of access and difficulties of data use, however, usually tend to be greater than where the data organizations discussed above are concerned, because these data resources are generally maintained for internal use rather than for dissemination to others.

Data Resources

The holdings of the organizations discussed include data collections relevant to virtually all disciplines and areas of social research and which bear upon communities and jurisdictions of all sizes and population densities. In general, academic data organizations tend to supply data in the most usable, best documented, and technically most convenient forms. They also tend to provide the lowest cost access to data. Indeed many of these organizations provide access to local communities of social scientists without cost, while the nationally oriented academic data archives provide a very large member community with access to data and other resources at very low or no cost beyond annual affiliation fees. The policies and practices of organizational data sources in the governmental and private sectors vary widely; however, data obtained from these sources tend to be more costly and less convenient to use, and access is also often less easy and dependable.

A brief discussion of organizational data sources does not suffice to suggest either the volume or character of the rich computer-readable research data that are now available. In the following pages a number of specific data collections and categories of data are briefly discussed. The purpose of the discussion is essentially illustrative; particular emphasis is placed upon opportunities for longitudinal investigation of community change and upon problems encountered in the acquisition and use of particular categories of data.

Aggregate Data

The United States Bureau of the Census is the largest and most important data collection agency of the nation. Its numerous and massive data products and activities make it a central and basic resource for social scientific inquiry, although the very magnitude of these activities present obstacles to effective social scientific use. The decennial censuses of Population and Housing—quinquennial beginning in 1985—constitute the richest sources of systematic information bearing upon the characteristics and conditions of the national populations and upon the communities, jurisdictions, civil units, and geographical areas of the nation. Although these data are initially collected at the individual level, they are most commonly made available and analyzed in aggregate form as the numerous attributes of states, counties, minor civil divisions, and smaller units of aggregation. To the data from the censuses of Population and Housing can be added data from the quinquennial Census of Government and the various economic censuses as well. The latter include the censuses of Manufacturing and Agriculture, which are conducted on a quinquennial basis and provide detailed information on levels and types of employment, production of various types, and establishments and their characteristics. Taken together these sources provide a detailed profile of the communities of the nation.

Release of virtually the entire 1970 census data in computer-readable form constituted a major innovation of great benefit to the social sciences. Data-processing equipment was employed in the conduct of both the 1950 and 1960 decennial censuses, as well as the interim censuses of these decades. Only limited and selected computer-readable data files—primarily internal working files, which provided the basis for various bureau publications—were made available prior to the release of the 1970 data. While release of the 1970 data in computer-readable form constituted a major advance, this action also presented a major challenge to social scientists who sought access to the data. In the original format in which they were released, the data were recorded on over two thousand reels of magnetic tape, organized in a complex series of six counts and recorded in a technically idiosyncratic format. The mode of release was such that potential users were forced to overpurchase in order to acquire the specific data required by a research design and then were faced after purchase with a significant reprocessing task before the data could be analyzed. It was this situation that led to the development of various intermediary services.

Since the release of the 1970 data, a growing portion of the bureau's subsequent data products have been released in computer-readable form. Reflecting this advance, the bureau's official catalog is now divided into two sections, one for publications and the other for computer-readable files and special tabulations. Moreover the technical quality and the ease of use of the bureau's computer-readable data products have steadily improved since the release of the 1970 data. The bureau also invested substantial planning and effort looking toward release of the 1980 computer-readable data. Extensive consultation with social scientists and other groups has been carried out designed to improve access to the 1980 data, and it is likely that the computer-readable version of the 1980 data will be more readily available in significantly more usable form than was the case in 1970. Even so, it is likely that intermediary services will again be required to provide effective access to the 1980 data, if only to serve the buyers' cooperative purposes.

The data made available from the censuses of Population and Housing include basic information on the age, race, and sex distributions of the entire population, as well as selected information on education, income, occupation, and nativity obtained on a sample basis. These data are always available at the state, county, and minor civil division level. Selected further tabulations are available for census tracts, block groups, and enumeration districts for urbanized areas, which include nonmetropolitan as well as metropolitan areas. Data for these small units can often be further aggregated to particular geopolitical units, such as suburbs or neighborhoods, which may be of greater interest to a researcher.

The combination of the 1970 and 1980 population and housing data, along with materials from the other interim censuses of the 1970s, will be an unparalleled computer-readable data resource for the study of community change and development, and it can be extended in a number of important ways. The Current Population Survey, conducted monthly by the bureau during the decade, provides a basis for reliable annual estimates of population change during the decade. Major bodies of computer-readable data for earlier years are also readily available. The data published in the *County and City Data Books* for 1952, 1956, 1962, 1967, and 1972 are available from the bureau in computer-readable form and in reprocessed in somewhat more usable form from the Inter-university Consortium for Political and Social Research. The data from the 1977 volume are expected shortly. The *Data Books* combine information from the censuses of Population, Housing, Governments, and Manufacturing and provide easily manageable data aggregated to the levels of states, counties, cities, and standard metropolitan statistical areas (counties and states only for 1952).

The Inter-university Consortium for Political and Social Research has also augmented these resources by converting to computer-readable form substantial arrays of state- and county-level social, demographic, and economic data from the published reports of the decennial and other censuses conducted between 1940 and 1970, as well as earlier censuses going back to the first, conducted in 1790. To these materials can be added computer-readable county-level returns for elections to the offices of president, governor, and U.S. senator and congressman, beginning with the first national election, held in 1788, through the election of 1976, which have also been collected, processes, and disseminated by the consortium. The election returns include the votes received by all candidates and parties and can be readily combined with the consortium files of social, demographic, and economic data. Beginning in 1968, this collection of election materials was expanded to include returns, also at the county level, for elections to one other major state office in addition to governor and records of the popular vote on all statewide referenda, initiatives, and constitutional amendments submitted to the electorate. These data provide the basic measures of the political behavior of the population in a variety of settings.

In this connection still another more specialized data collection included in the consortium's holdings can be noted: the computer-readable data from the National Council of Churches of Christ in the U.S.A. conducted in 1952 and 1972. These data fill an important gap since the federal government ceased collecting such information in 1936. These data supplement the U.S. Census of Religion (conducted in 1906, 1916, 1926, and

1936), which provide basic information at the county level on religious affiliation for the entire nation.

In short, extensive bodies of data are available at various levels of aggregation in usable computer-readable form. They are of major value for systematic and larger-scale investigation of basic demographic change and development since World War II. For the more historically inclined, available data will also support investigations of developmental patterns across earlier years back to the founding of the nation, although the data for earlier years are much more limited than those for the recent period. In general, aggregate data pertinent to the study of community life and development are most consistently available for counties. Particularly in the case of the census files, however, data can usually be obtained for minor civil divisions and other subcounty units.

Another area in which there are substantial aggregate data resources available is the compilation of a variety of social indicators, including measures of the general well-being of the population. They are often further subdivided into measures of subjective and objective well-being. Examples of the variety of the latter include data on the basic nativity and mortality statistics of the population. They are available in detail from standard administrative records, such as the approximately 2 million death certificates that are filed in the United States each year with the National Center for Health Statistics. However, they are much more commonly made available for analysis in the form of aggregated data such as state-, county-, and city-level statistics on the distributions of deaths by age, race, sex, and cause. Information on schooling and special program opportunities, as well as special tabulations of age groups by race and sex of the population of school districts, is made available on a similar basis by the National Center for Educational Statistics.

Even a survey as cursory as this suggests the numerous extensive bodies of computer-readable aggregate data that are available to support investigations of community processes and development. The available data bear upon demographic characteristics, social processes, income, occupation, health, mortality, productivity, political behavior, education, and social service facilities, to mention but a few. Moreover they extend to considerable historical depth. The level of aggregation may not be ideal in every case. Even so, opportunities for examination of communities of all descriptions and sizes are abundant.

Administrative Records

Records of the conduct of government, of the provision of governmental programs and facilities, of participation in those programs, and of the extraction and consumption of resources are of obvious importance to the study of community processes and development. In the United States, however, the multilayered nature of government and the multiplicity of overlapping jurisdictions make governmental and administrative data obstreperous and onerous to collect and employ for the pruposes of social scientific inquiry. Moreover, despite their relevance to the life of the nation and to processes of social and economic change, the state and local governments of the nation constitute, at best, indifferent sources of systematic data should the social scientist attempt to collect them on his own. The thought of collecting data for the numerous state and local governmental agencies of the nation is overwhelming indeed. But in several areas—fortunately from the standpoint of the social scientist—the federal government has intervened and now systematically collects extensive data on the operations and activities of state and local governments. Many of the data for very recent years are available to social scientists in computer-readable form, and additional systematic information for earlier years is to be found in published sources, which could be automated if needed.

The quinquennial Census of Government conducted by the Bureau of the Census constitutes the basic source of information on governmental operations. The first regular Census of Governments was conducted in 1957 in accordance with an act of Congress approved in 1950. The data collected from that year through 1967 are primarily available in bureau publications, although segments of the data for these years are also incorporated in the computer files on which the *City and County Data* are based, as well as in other computer-readable collections prepared by the ICPSR. Beginning with the census of 1972, the data were made available in their entirety in computer-readable form. The combined files for the 1972 census amount to over eight million punched card equivalents and record data for approximately seven thousand state and local governmental units.

The data available in the Census of Governments are organized to cover the broad area of public employment, taxable property values, and governmental finances, including both revenue and expenditures. There is also a guide to governmental organizations, which is indispensable to an understanding of the interrelationships among the various levels of government that are included in the census. Data are available for states, counties, Standard Metropolitan Statistical Areas (SMSAs), municipalities and townships, school districts, and other special districts.

The Census of Government is supplemented by the Annual Survey of Government, an extension of the previous annual compendium of government finance series that preceded the formal census. The annual survey provides similar information on government finance and employment in a number of public sectors for the fifty states and for a sample of approximately sixteen thousand local governments. The sample is stratified by type of government and magnitude of expenditures, and cities of twenty-five thousand population or greater are included. Thus the survey provides extensive data on larger municipalities. It also provides data for a representative sample of smaller units. Beginning in 1973, the data from the surveys have been made available in computer-readable form and are available from the ICPSR, as well as the Bureau of the Census.

Although the Census of Government and the Annual Survey of Governments are basic sources of information on state and local governmental operations, several other major data collections require mention. Since 1972 the Office of Revenue Sharing of the Department of the Treasury has released annual data on taxation and income for state and local governments and on payments to these jurisdictions provided for by revenue-sharing legislation. This information, although limited, is important because the need for current per-capita income estimates requires that annual estimates of small area populations be made. Data on health facilities—hospitals, nursing homes, clinics, and medical personnel—are available on a periodic basis beginning in 1973 for the entire nation from the National Center for Health Statistics (NCHS). These data are available for 1976 as well in their most current form. The NCHS also makes available data on mortality, nativity, and vital statistics on an annual basis, beginning in 1968. Information on schools, their capacity, number of students and teachers, expenditures, and nature of programs can be obtained from the National Center for Educational Statistics. These data include special tabulations from the 1970 Census of Population on a school district basis, as well as information on schools and teachers (manpower and facilities) and on specific programmatic offerings supported by federal legislation. The Law Enforcement Assistance Administration also collects and makes available in machine-readable form data on employment, expenditures, and facilities by state and local governments in the area of criminal justice. The data are available on an annual basis beginning in 1971, and they are a direct analog to the regular Census of Goverments data (they are collected by the same division of the Bureau of the Census).

Another special collection of data files relating to metropolitan areas are those developed under four research projects supported by the Research Applied to National Needs (RANN) Division of the National Science Foundation in the area of the organization of public service delivery systems. The four projects cover the areas of fire protection, public health, police protection, and solid waste management. Each project began in a common set of units: all SMSAs of less than 1.5 million population which were located entirely within a single state. Data were collected in samples of SMSAs for all of the local geopolitical units in each SMSA, as well as for each of the administrative jurisdictions or agencies in the service delivery areas. As a result, information is available for substantial numbers of smaller communities and suburbs that surround the central cities of the SMSAs. Data were collected on the level and quality of the services, the legal structure governing provision of the services, organizational arrangements between jurisdictions in the same SMSA for the provision of services, manpower levels, and expenditure levels. These data are available from the ICPSR Archive.

These data bearing upon the conduct and operations of state and local governments are available for specific governmental agencies and jurisdictions and can be linked in many cases to the various collections of aggregated data. Although these data are not generally available for extended time periods, they provide an important means for exploring the impact and changing role of government in community life.

Individual–Level Data

Since the 1950s, sample survey research has been a mainstay of social scientific inquiry. The number of surveys conducted by academic researchers, governments, and commercial organizations is legion, and the data collected in this fashion touch upon virtually all aspects of life in the United States. Much of these data have been preserved by data organizations and are readily available to researchers. Moreover, a variety of large collections of individual data, such as the Public Use Samples from the 1970 Census, are available from federal agencies and from various intermediary services. Data of this sort generally do not allow investigation of specific communities and jurisdictions. On the other hand, such information as the characteristics of the place of residence of the individuals for whom data is recorded in these collections is consistently given. Thus these data provide a means to examine, compare, and contrast the attitudes, behavior, conditions, and way of life of the populations of diverse areas.

The federal government, primarily through the data collection programs of the Bureau of the Census, is the source of major collections of microdata files of this sort. The standard data file routinely made available heretofore has been the Annual Demographic File prepared from the March supplement to the Current Population Survey (CPS). The CPS is an ongoing monthly survey conducted by the Bureau of the Census in approximately forty thousand households. The basic CPS instrument includes information on age, race, sex, relationship, education, occupation, and labor force status for persons fourteen years of age and over. The March supplement contains additional questions, which obtain information about income, mobility, and marital history; and the entire set of data is obtained for every household member. The processing of the Annual Demographic File includes the generation of household and family summary data records as well; and these annual data files thereby become the best source of current estimates of the characteristics of the national population. Copies of machine-readable data files from the Annual Demographic File are currently available for the period beginning in 1968. Although individual areas cannot be identified, it is possible to use these data to analyze the status of or change in the characteristics of the population residing in a variety of settings.

The only other monthly supplements to the CPS that were made available in the past were the November Voting Supplements for 1972 and 1974. These surveys were used to produce estimates of voter participation in the general elections held in those years. The bureau has recently announced that November Voting Supplements will be made available for 1968, 1970, and 1976. It announced at the same time that all of the other monthly supplements to the CPS will also be made available routinely in a standardized form. For 1977, these supplements will include data for food stamp recipiency (April and August); multiple job holdings, premium pay, and job search of the employed (May); birth expectations, fertility, and child care (June); immunization (September); school enrollment (October); and farm wage workers (December). Other special supplements that will become available include the survey of languages (1976), smoking habits (August 1968), and job tenure and occupational mobility (1973).

Three very large special surveys conducted by the Bureau of the Census for other federal agencies have also recently come into the public domain in readily usable computer-readable form. By far the largest of these is the continuing National Crime Survey, which is conducted for the Law Enforcement Assistance Administration. This complex series of monthly surveys was initiated in 1972 to ascertain the incidence of a wide variety of reported and unreported crimes. The national surveys can be used to develop estimates of victimization by type of residential area, and a secondary set of 39 surveys can be used to measure levels of victimization in 26 cities (of the 113 in which they surveys were conducted). Information from literally millions of inverviews is now available from the ICPSR for each of these series.

A second major project involves the Survey of Income and Education conducted for the Department of Health, Education and Welfare from April through July 1976. The survey was conducted to obtain reliable state-level estimates of the number of children in local areas who reside in families with income below the federal poverty level. The information was used to facilitate funding under Title I of the Elementary and Secondary Education Act and included questions on school enrollment, disability, health insurance, bilingualism, food stamp recipiency, assets, and housing costs, as well as the basic CPS items. The survey includes information from approximately 158,500 households.

Finally, the bureau has also recently announced the release of data from a special travel-to-work survey added to the Annual Housing Survey

(AHS). This supplement was sponsored by the Department of Transportation to obtain information on the commuting patterns of almost 13 million workers in twenty-one metropolitan areas. The AHS consists of two parts: a national sample of approximately seventy-five thousand households and twenty-one separate SMSA samples of from five thousand to fifteen thousand households each year. A total of sixty SMSAs are surveyed over a three-year period. The recently released data are for the first group of twenty-one SMSAs, which were surveyed from April 1974 to March 1976. The bureau is making available microdata tapes providing records for unidentified individual commuters, including travel-to-work information, as well as personal characteristics, and data files of tract-to-tract origin/destination information within each SMSA.

The Bureau of the Census is not the only purveyor of data files of magnitude. The National Longitudinal Surveys of Labor Market Experience were begun in 1966 by Herbert S. Parnes of the Center for Human Resource Research at the Ohio State University under contract to the Department of Labor. The surveys were designed primarily to analyze the sources of variation in the labor market behavior and experience of four age-sex cohorts of the U.S. population. The four cohorts originally defined in the study were mature men (forty-five to fifty-nine years of age), mature women (thirty to forty-four years of age), and young men and young women (fourteen to twenty-four years of age). Each cohort has been interviewed at least once every two years since the inception of the study. The original sample size for each group was composed of fifteen hundred blacks and thirty-five hundred whites. The major topics generally covered in each survey included labor market experience; socioeconomic and human capital, including education, health, training, marital status and family characteristics, job attitudes, retirement plans, and occupational aspirations and expectations; and other contextual information about the place in which the respondent resides, including size of the labor force, unemployment rates, and the demand for labor.

The Social Security Administration is still another federal source of extensive files of microdata. In particular, data from the Longitudinal Retirement History Survey have recently been made available. They provide a unique opportunity to investigate the transition from the last years of employment to retirement. Begun in 1968, the collection used a biennial survey of a national sample of workers drawn from the administrative records of the Social Security Administration. In addition to obtaining information from the individuals about their occupation status and plans for retirement, information from employers' records as well as benefit payments from the social security system are also merged into the public-use data files. This is an ongoing data collection program, and it can be expected that additional data files will be made available after they have been analyzed by the agency staff.

All of these large individual-level data files have in common the identification of size and type of place of residence of the respondents, which permits a variety of analyses comparing persons from nonmetropolitan communities with those from other places. Because the basic data are available at the individual level, the researcher is free to tabulate and aggregate the information in virtually limitless ways. It is important to note, however, that all of these data files have such large dimensions, in terms of either or both of the number of variables and units of analysis, that there is no occasion for anything even remotely approaching casual analysis. Special software is often required to treat complex physical storage formats, and the large arrays of data imply that the costs for every trivial setup errors can be enormous. This is one area in which care and caution are the bywords.

These large, agency-funded data collection projects are sometimes deficient in their lack of information on the attitudes and opinions of the samples of the population that they study. Thus other data sources must be sought for this type of information. By and large researchers must utilize surveys conducted by individual researchers through academic institutions or through commercial organizations. These data are amenable to analysis by groups of respondents who can be classified in terms of their size of type of place of residence, among other characteristics. But it is important to note that the sample size for these surveys is considerably smaller than in the case of the federal data collections. Hence the estimates that can be developed using these surveys can be neither as precise nor as finely drawn. The number of surveys of this sort are virtually infinite, and the present discussion must be limited to major ongoing data collection efforts that provide analysts with opportunities to compare attitudes and opinions over time, even if only for separate cross-sections of the population.

Data of this sort for the longest span of time are provided by the national surveys conducted by the American Institute for Public Opinion (the Gallup organization). Dating back to 1939, data are available from hundreds of AIPO omnibus surveys through the Roper Center. The center maintains a computer-readable item index, which indicates the timing and frequency with which various survey questions were asked. Because the standard Gallup questionnaire is relatively short and is often composed of a number of timely but sometimes theoretically unrelated items, most analysis of this sort must be limited to the comparison of cross-sectional distributions of opinions at multiple points in time. A significant exception, however, are the Gallup preelection and postelection surveys. The Roper Center has developed a data package that consists of information from these surveys dating back to 1936. This is a valuable and unique resource for students of public opinion and political behavior since the New Deal.

A comparable set of surveys covering the period since 1952 are the biennial studies of the American electorate conducted formerly by the Survey Research Center and now by the Center for Political Studies at the University of Michigan. Involving preelection and postelection panels in the presidential election years and postelection studies for the other years, each of the surveys contains information from a comprehensive interview lasting approximately ninety minutes. The contents of the surveys typically include information on registration and voting, as well as other forms of political behavior, opinions about current events and issues, and attitudes toward government, the political system, and candidates and parties. At two points during the series—from 1958 to 1960 and from 1972 to 1976—the surveys incorporated panel studies across election years as well as within. These data can be obtained from the ICPSR.

The third major collection of individual–level data is available from the annual General Social Surveys conducted since 1972 by the National Opinion Research Center. These surveys are administered to samples of national cross–sections of the population aged eighteen and over. Almost all of the individual items have appeared in previous surveys, some dating back to 1945, which were originally conducted by a variety of academic and commercial survey organizations. The content of the surveys included information on the family, race relations, social control, civil liberties, attitudes toward sex and sexual materials, and morals. The data are therefore of great interest to a broad range of social scientists.

Survey data collections of this sort have a common advantage and a common limitation. Individuals who reside in communities that are similar in terms of size or various other characteristics can be examined and compared with individuals who differ in terms of these characteristics. Thus the attitudes and attributes of the nonmetropolitan population can be compared, for example, with the attitudes and attributes of the population of metropolitan communities. Changes in the characteristics of the nonmetropolitan population can be examined over time, and in the case of national studies with a sufficiently larger number of respondents, regional comparisons of the nonmetropolitan population are also possible. On the other hand, these data collections do not allow examination and comparison of specific nonmetropolitan communities nor will they support examination of particular communities over time. Numerous surveys have been conducted in particular nonmetropolitan communities, and it would be impossible to identify and describe these efforts. They are likely to vary rather widely in quality, and it is unlikely that they would support either fully effective comparisons of significant numbers of communities or examination of change.

Two sets of surveys allow examination and comparison of specific communities, although these data are not relevant to the study of nonmetropolitan areas. One of these is the series of Citizen Attitude Surveys conducted in ten Urban Observatory Program cities in 1968. The program, which supplies data for rather large urban areas, is an example of the use of the same survey instrument in ten separate and identifiable geographic locations. The survey emphasized citizen attitudes toward local governmental services and opinions about local problems in the areas of schooling, housing, public transportation, drugs, law and order, and taxes. These data are available from the ICPSR.

The second major collection of surveys includes information obtained from the Permanent Community Sample Project developed by Peter Rossi, Robert L. Crain, James J. Vanecko, and Matthew J. Crensen at the National Opinion Research Center. The project began in the 1960s with the selection of a sample of fifty-one American communities based upon their regional location and population size. The cities that were selected represented twenty-two states and had populations between 50,000 and 750,000. Typical of the research projects conducted using this frame is Terry N. Clark's Comparative Study of Community Decision-making, in which intensive interviews were conducted with local elites. The information on community leadership and patterns of influence was combined with various aggregate data from the Bureau of the Census and the Department of Housing and Urban Development.

Although in both cases these data are available to researachers, they are not relevant to the study of nonmetropolitan social phenomena. There is no reason—aside, perhaps, from the high costs that would be involved—that precludes application of similar data designs to the study of nonmetropolitan communities. To our knowledge, however, no such effort has been made.

It is impossible to account for every available data file, and we have resorted to highlighting major collections and broad classes of data. Our purpose has been to draw attention to the very substantial empirical resources that are available to social scientists interested in research on nonmetropolitan communities.

Appendix 13A:
Archival Sources for Computer-Readable Data on Nonmetropolitan Communities in the United States and Canada

Director
Behavioral Science Laboratory
University of Cincinnati
Cincinnati, Ohio   45221

Center for Quantitative Studies in Social Science
117 Savery Hall
DK-45
University of Wisconsin
Madison, Wisconsin   53706

Executive Director
Data Clearinghouse for the Social Sciences
151 Slater Street
Ottawa, Ontario
Canada   K1P 5N1

Director
Institute for Behavioral Research
Data Bank
York University
4700 Keele Street
Donsview, Ontario, Canada

Executive Director
Inter-University Consortium for Political and Social Research
P.O. Box 1248
Ann Arbor, Michigan   48106

National Archives and Records Service
Reference Service
Machine-Readable Archives Division (NNR)
Washington, D.C.   20408

Director, Data Library
Computing Centre
University of British Columbia
2075 Wesbrook Place
Vancouver, British Columbia
Canada V6T 1W5

Data Librarian
Data Library
Survey Research Center
University of California
Berkeley, California   94720

Director
Data User Services Division
U.S. Bureau of the Census
Washington, D.C.   20233

Librarian
Dualabs, Inc.
Information Documentation Center
1601 North Kent, Suite 900
Arlington, Virginia   22209

National Center for Education Statistics
Office of Education
Department of Health, Education and Welfare
Washington, D.C.   20202

National Center for Health Statistics
Scientific and Technical Information Branch
Department of Health, Education and Welfare
Hyattsville, Maryland   20782

Data Librarian
National Opinion Research Center
University of Chicago
6030 South Ellis Avenue
Chicago, Illinois   60637

Director
Northwestern University Information Center
Vogelback Computing Center
Northwestern University
Evanston, Illinois   60201

Political Science Data Archive
Department of Political Science
Michigan State University
East Lansing, Michigan   48823

Political Science Laboratory and Data Archive
Department of Political Science
248 Woodburn Hall
Indiana University
Bloomington, Indiana   47401

Public Archives Canada
Machine Readable Archives
295 Wellington Street
Ottawa, Ontario
Canada, K1A 0N3

Roper Center, Inc.
Archival Development Activities:
Box U-164R
University of Connecticut
Storrs, Connecticut   06288
User Services Activities:
38 Mansfield Street
Yale University
New Haven, Connecticut

Social Science Data Archives
Survey Research Laboratory
414 David Kinley Hall
University of Illinois
Urbana, Illinois   61801

Director
Social Science Data Archives
Department of Sociology and Anthropology
Carleton University
Colonel by Drive
Ottawa, Ontario Canada K1S 5B6

Director
Social Science Data
University of Connecticut
Storrs, Connecticut   06208

Director
Louis Harris Data Center
University of North Carolina
Room 10, Manning Hall
Chapel Hill, North Carolina   27514

Social Science Computer Research Institute
621 Mervis Hall
University of Pittsburgh
Pittsburgh, Pennsylvania   15260

Social Science Data Archive
Laboratory for Political Research
321 A Schaeffer Hall
University of Iowa
Iowa City, Iowa   52242

Social Science Data Archive
Social Science Library
Yale University
Box 1958 Yale Station
New Haven, Connecticut   06520

Director
Social Science User Service
Princeton University Computer Center
87 Prospect Avenue
Princeton, New Jersey   08540

Director
State Data Program
460 Stephens Hall
University of California
Berkeley, California   94720

Director
State Government Data Base
Council of State Governments
Iron Works Pike
Lexington, Kentucky   40578

14 Demographic and Economic Effects of Large-Scale Energy Development in Rural Areas: An Assessment Model

Steve H. Murdock and
F. Larry Leistritz

The effects of industrialization and resource developments on rural areas are receiving increasing attention and producing an ever-expanding body of literature.[1] One of the most apparent emphases in this literature is the need for local areas to plan carefully for the effects of such developments. If they do not, they might neglect to take action until the impacts become apparent, which may lead to serious boom-town related problems, or they might overdevelop in anticipation of population increases and economic growth that may not materialize.

For many local areas, especially those in low-density rural sections, however, neither the financial nor the necessary personnel resources are available for such planning. In response to these needs, a variety of federal and state programs have been created, and a growing number of manuals and handbooks are appearing aimed at assisting local planners and decision makers.[2]

Although such general works serve to inform local planners and decision makers about many of the problems they may encounter as a result of industrial impacts and inform them of available programs from which they may seek assistance, they do little to answer the direct needs of local decision makers concerning the impacts that they may expect in their specific localities. Thus questions such as how much business activity a development will create for a given location, how many people will move to a given area, and what effects such changes will have on the schools, medical, police, and other services in a given city cannot be addressed by such general works. For most local decision makers, however, these specific questions are the ones for which answers are essential.

Local decision makers not only want specific answers; they want timely ones. Despite the growing number of impact assessments and the widespread preparation of manuals and books explaining them, such assessments are difficult to understand and too outdated to meet local needs.[3] The frequency of changes in development dimensions, such as changes in facility size, location, and other factors, often negate the validity of the assump-

223

tions on which the formal impact assessment of a project may have been based. As a result, many impact statements tend to be outdated before they are published, and the differences between the effects they predict and those that may occur as a result of altered project structures may be impossible for local decision makers to discern. As a result of such problems, local decision makers and planners have increasingly demanded impact assessments and impact assessment methodologies that provide local area projections for a variety of socioeconomic factors under a variety of possible sets of development scenarios and that do so with only a limited time delay in the production of such projections.

One form of response to those needs in many areas of the United States has been the development of computerized projection models.[4] Although each is different in structure and level of geographic specificity, they all attempt to provide a mechanism that offers rapid responses to pragmatic planning questions.[5] The success of these attempts in actually meeting planning needs, however, appears to depend upon a number of factors, including not only the models' basic structures but also the mode of their development and the degree to which information about local communities have entered into their actual development process.

We will describe here the general development, structure, and uses of one such computerized impact projection model—the North Dakota Regional Environmental Assessment Program (REAP) Economic–Demographic Assessment Model—and focus on some of the elements of this type of model and basic elements in the development process. The nature of these development processes may be as important as many of the aspects of the methodological design in ensuring the utility of such a model. Our purpose, then, is both to describe one example of a growing number of computerized impact assessment models and to assess the essential elements of the processes involved in the development of such a model. Although many of the processes may be generally applicable, our experiences tend to be limited to the western part of the United States and to energy–related community impacts. Despite these limitations, we believe that our discussion raises issues that are highly applicable to general model development.[6]

Socioeconomic and Organizational Context

The impetus for the development of the REAP model lay in conditions similar to those occurring in many other areas of the western United States. The energy crisis and oil embargo had led to an increasing interest in the energy resources of the West. The development of these resources, which include over 50 percent of the nation's coal reserves and over 67 percent of the stripable reserves, nearly all of the nation's oil shale and uranium deposits, and many of the potential geothermal power sites, is clearly essential if the nation's energy needs are to be met.[7]

Developments of this sort within the West are likely to have large and potentially disruptive impacts. In most of its rural areas, long periods of population decline caused by increased mechanization of agriculture have led to low levels of diversity in rural economies, relatively underdeveloped service infrastructures, and very small populations. These conditions are likely to cause impacts that would be of little significance in more populous areas but are problematic for western rural areas.

One of the major resource areas of the northern Great Plains is the Fort Union coal development area (including parts of Western North Dakota, Eastern Montana and Northeastern Wyoming). In 1970 this area included only eight cities with over nine thousand people. A single Lurgi process coal gasification plant, several of which are proposed for the area, may mean an influx of three thousand construction workers for a three-to-five year period and a thousand operational workers for the life of the plant. Such a project, with the additional employment created in the trade and service sectors, may mean that the area will gain between ten thousand and twenty thousand persons during the construction period and between five thousand and ten thousand persons during the operation of the plant.[8] Thus although many residents in the West viewed energy development as potential sources of needed economic growth, they also raised many questions about its likely impacts: How much economic growth and population increase will these developments mean for specific areas in the West? What levels of new employment will be created by the developments? How many of the newly created jobs will be available for local persons? How many immigrating workers will be required, and where will they choose to live? How many dependents will such workers bring with them, and what will their characteristics be? How many new school, police, fire, medical, and social service facilities and personnel will be needed in local areas? How will increased populations and business activity affect public revenues and expenditures? How will these factors affect the way of life, life-styles, community patterns, and relationships in western areas?

In North Dakota the uncertainty of the answers to such questions, the initiation of several coal-related developments, and the occurrence of several problems, such as a lack of local planning information and the production of numerous questionable and largely irrelevant impact assessments, led to the demand for a statewide program to assist state and local areas in preparing for energy-related impacts. Thus in 1975 the North Dakota Legislature created the North Dakota Regional Environmental Assessment Program (REAP). Its purpose was to establish and carry on research "in regard to North Dakota's resources and areas of governmental activity or responsibility for the purpose of assisting in the development of new laws, policies, and governmental actions and providing facts and information to the citizens of the state."[9] It was to serve directly under the control of a legislative committee composed of legislative leaders, university representatives, state agency representatives, and citizens at large and was initially structured to include a staff director and two associate directors, one each in the physical and social sciences, to monitor sponsored research contracts.

After its inception, the program conducted extensive meetings with state and local officials and members of the public to discern their informational needs. These needs were formulated into research requests and led to numerous research, data-base compilation, and modeling efforts. These user groups serve a continuing function by providing ongoing assessments of the utility of sponsored projects.

Among the most frequent requirement expressed by the user groups was the need for information on the economic, demographic, and fiscal impacts of energy developments on the state and local areas within the state. Accordingly REAP initiated two contracts in March 1976 for the development and computerization of an integrated economic, demographic, and fiscal impact projection model. Model development was contracted to a team of social scientists consisting of Thor Hertsgaard and Steve Murdock of North Dakota State University, and Mark Henry and Richard Ludtke of the University of North Dakota, with Hertsgaard serving as principal investigator of the social science effort. Norman Toman of North Dakota State University served as the major development specialist in the design of the fiscal-impact component. Computerization and implementation of the model was contracted to Arthur D. Little, Inc., with Donald Senechal serving as principal investigator, assisted by D. Lebovici, K. Wiig, and A. Czerwinski. F. Larry Leistritz, associate director of REAP, served as the project monitoring official for REAP and also took part in conceptual design, implementation, and validation of the model.

The model became operational in the fall of 1976 and provides projections of economic, demographic, and fiscal effects of developments at the state, regional, county, and municipal level for a fifteen-county area in western North Dakota where energy impacts are expected to be most significant.[10] An expanded version of the model that includes the entire state and nonenergy- as well as energy-related developments has recently been completed.[11]

In examining these contextual factors of the model's development, we believe that the apparent and imminent need for planning information and the state's subsequent financial and political support of the project were directly responsible for the the project's completion and also for the model's widespread use.

Research Context

Two elements in particular appear to have been instrumental in the model's development: the extent of the previous research conducted by members of the development team concerning economic modeling and energy-related impacts in the state and the direct, close working relationships maintained between the development team and state data users.

Attempts to model the North Dakota economy had been underway for some time by the development team's senior researchers. Under the direction of Thor Hertsgaard, data had been collected from business firms, selected households, and governmental units in western North Dakota, an input–output model for the state had been developed, and its validity had been assessed.[12] This model had, in turn, been used extensively to examine a number of applied problems.[13] Thus by the time the development of the model began, over ten years of experience in modeling the state's economy had been accumulated.

In addition, in the direct analysis of energy impacts, considerable previous experience also had been obtained. In 1972, analysis of the likely effects of energy developments on the state's tax revenues, level of economic activity, and service structure had begun.[14] Studies of the regional, as well as the statewide, impacts of large-scale developments had been completed through the Northern Great Plains Resources Program, and several assessments of the impacts of specific energy projects had been completed.[15] Furthermore, in the analysis of social and demographic changes, considerable work had also been completed, including assessments of the likely social impacts of various energy developments and of the present and likely future trends in population[16]

In sum, then, the model's development took place within a context in which an extensive amount of previous research regarding both energy impacts and the economic, demographic, and fiscal effects of such developments already had been completed. This research experience alerted the development team to both the demands and the potential pitfalls of such a modeling effort.

The second element of significance within the research context was the close working relationships that were maintained between the development team and various state users. The relatively small number of state officials and university researchers in the state led to a high level of interdependence. State officials provided access to data sets that were essential to the model's development, and they served as willing reviewers of preliminary model results. The development team, in turn, provided preliminary models, with appropriate qualifications, to state officials for various uses.

The research context, then, was one in which a large amount of in-state research experience and expertise, together with a highly interdependent process of interaction between model developers and data users, was brought to bear on a particular research need. These elements also affected the completion of the modeling effort.

Model Structure

The economic–demographic projection model provides baseline projections and single– or multiple-project impact projections for a fifteen–county area in western North Dakota. Outputs are available at the regional, county, and municipal levels and include such variables as business activity, personal income, employment by type, population by age and sex, school enrollments by age, housing requirements by type, public sector costs and revenues by type, and net fiscal balance.

The model consists of five basic components or submodels:

1. An economic input–output module.
2. A cohort-survival demographic module.
3. An economic–demographic interface module.
4. A residential allocation module.
5. A fiscal impact module.

The input–output module is used to estimate gross business volume by economic sector for a specified level of final demands. Employment requirements by sector and development phase are then derived from the estimates of gross business volume. The demographic module provides projections of population by age and sex and an estimate of the available labor force. The interface component links the projections of required employment from the input–output module with the projections of available labor force from the demographic module to determine the level of employment needs that can be met by the indigenous population and those that must be met by the immigration of new workers. The residential allocation module estimates the settlement patterns of new workers and their families, and the fiscal impact module provides projections of the expected costs and revenues resulting from the associated economic and demographic changes. These factors operate differentially at the regional, county, and municipal level. A generalized flow diagram of the model is presented in figure 14-1.

The Input–Output Module

Input–output analysis is a technique for tabulating and describing the linkages or interdependencies among various industrial groups within an econ-

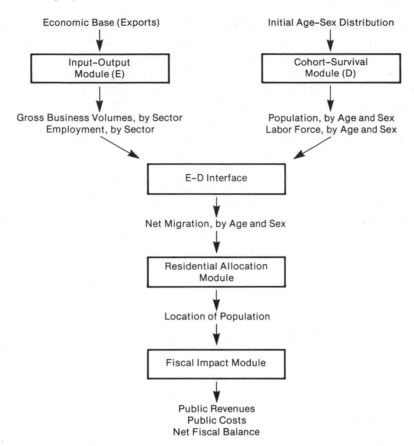

Figure 14-1. Data and Output Flows of the Economic-Demographic Model.

omy. The economy considered may be national or as small as that of a multicounty area served by one of the state's major retail trade centers (as it is in this example). Input-output analysis as used in this model assumes that economic activity in a region is dependent upon the basic industries that exist there, referred to as its economic base. The economic base is largely a region's export base: those industries (or basic sectors) that earn income from outside the area. These activities in western North Dakota consist of livestock and crop production, manufacturing, mining, tourism, and federal government outlays. The remaining economic activities are the trade and service sectors, which provide the inputs required by other sectors in the area.

The input-output model employed is similar to conventional models, except in three respects.[17] First, it is closed with respect to households. In other words, households are included in it as a producing and a consuming sector. Second, the total gross business volume of trade sectors was used (both for expenditures and receipts in the transactions table) rather than value added by those sectors. This procedure results in larger activity levels for those sectors than would be obtained by conventional techniques, but this larger business volume is offset by correspondingly larger levels of expenditures outside the region by those sectors for goods purchased for resale. The advantage of this procedure is that the results of the analysis are expressed in terms of gross business volumes, rather than value added, of the respective sectors. The procedure appears to be more intuitively meaningful to most users. The third difference from conventional models is that all elements in the column of interdependence coefficients for the local government sector were assigned values of 0, except for a 1 in the main diagonal. This method was intended to reflect the fact that expenditures of local units of government are determined by the budgeting process of those units rather than endogenously within the economic system.

The input–output model employed was derived from primary data collected by personal interviews from firms and households in southwestern North Dakota. The model was developed by Sand and Bartch, and the coefficients were subsequently tested for validity by Senechal.[18]

The conceptual basis for an input–output model is that production by any sector requires the use of production inputs, such as materials, equipment, fuel, services, and labor. Some of these will be obtained from outside the region (imported), but many will be produced by and purchased from other sectors in the area economy. If so, these other sectors will require their own inputs from still other sectors, and so on. The additional rounds of input requirements generated by the production of the direct input requirements (of the initial sector) are known as the indirect requirements.

The total of the direct and indirect input requirements of each sector in an economy is measured by a set of coefficients known as input–output interdependence coefficients. Multiplication of the interdependence coefficients by the sales of the basic sectors (income received from outside the region or sales for final demand) yields estimates of the gross business volumes of each of the sectors in the region. The resulting product for the household sector is personal income received from the respective business sectors in the form of wages and salaries, profits, rents, and interest income of individuals. The estimates of gross business volume for other sectors are used to estimate employment in those sectors.

The procedure for translating gross business volume in the respective sectors to employment requires dividing gross business volume in each sector by gross business volume per worker in that sector. (Gross business volume per worker was computed from historic employment data for the years since 1958 for each of the sectors.) This procedure was employed to estimate trends in baseline employment on the basis of time–series projections of the final demand vectors and projections of gross business volume per employee in the respective sectors. A similar procedure was used to estimate economic impacts of the construction and operation of energy plants on the basis of estimated local expenditures for these. The result for the economic baseline and for any set of development projects was an estimate of total required employment. This estimate of total required employment is later used in the economic–demographic interface component of the model (the E–D model).

The Cohort–Survival Demographic Module

The cohort–survival demographic component mode of population projection was selected because it has been generally accepted as among the most accurate projection techniques and provides results at a significantly greater level of detail than most other methods.[19] In addition, its methodology and data base has been extensively developed for the state of North Dakota.[20]

The cohort–survival method of population projections consists of the application of a set of birthrates, migration rates, and survival rates to a set of baseline population data for a projected period in order to determine the population at the end of that period. In general, it produces projected population derived from the basic population equation:

$$P_{t_2} = P_{t_1} + B - D + M \qquad (14.1)$$

where P_{t_2} = population at a given future year, t_2,

P_{t_1} = population at a preceding base year, t_1,

B = births between t_1 and t_2,

D = deaths between t_1 and t_2, and

M = net migration between t_1 and t_2.

Rather than utilizing total population figures, this method employs a set of age–sex cohorts (persons of the same sex born during the same period of time) and sets of mortality, migration, and fertility rates specific to each of these cohorts. These cohort rates for the projected period are applied to the population in each cohort to estimate the future population of an area.

For any given geographical area and projection period, the procedure may be seen as relating to equation 14.1 as follows:

$$P_{t_2} = \Sigma P_{c_i,t_2} \tag{14.2}$$

where P_{t_2} = population at a given future year, t_2

$\Sigma P_{c_i,t_2}$ = sum of population in all cohorts at a given future year, t_2,

and

$$P_{c_i,t_2} = P_{c_i,t_1} + P_{c_i}B_{t_1,t_2} - P_{c_i}D_{t_1,t_2} + P_{c_i}M_{t_1,t_2} \tag{14.3}$$

where P_{c_i,t_2} = population of cohort i at a future time, t_2,

P_{c_i,t_1} = population of cohort i in the preceding base year, t_1,

$P_{c_i}B_{t_1,t_2}$ = births to cohort i between the base year, t_1, and future year, t_2,

$P_{c_i}D_{t_1,t_2}$ = deaths in cohort i between the base year, t_1, and future year, t_2, and

$P_{c_i}M_{t_1,t_2}$ = net migration in cohort i between the base year, t_1, and future year, t_2.

In the model, fifteen five–year age–sex cohorts were used (males and females 0–4, 5–9, and so forth) for each sex. The initial population in each cohort was derived from the 1970 Census of Population. Although single–year cohorts would have been preferable for many of the computational aspects of the model, the requirements imposed by using this number of cohorts and corresponding mortality, migration, and fertility rates (over seventy–five for each sex) initially prevented the use of such a procedure. (Single–year cohorts are employed in E–D model, version 2, which is currently being developed.) Rates for the processes of migration (for those older than sixty–five), mortality, and fertility were based on historic data.[21] In projecting future patterns, migration rates for persons less than sixty–five years old were determined through the interface procedure described below. Future patterns for survival rates and fertility rates were assumed to follow national trends over time, with a fertility level of 2.1 births per adult female being used as a default value. This level would result in a

---

The fertility rates are computed for each female cohort from ten to forty–five years of age. The sum of these age–specific rates for all cohorts is the total fertility rate. In the present model, the user is allowed to choose a total fertility rate ranging from 1.8 to 2.5 for the projection period. These rates are used in computing age–specific rates that would result in the user–selected average number of births (during her lifetime) per female in a population. The rates resulting in a 2.1 level of completed fertility are utilized in the model if the user does not specify some other permissible value.

replacement level of births and reflects current levels of fertility in North Dakota.

Given projections of population by age and sex, the number of workers available locally is obtained from the cohort–survival module by application of labor force participation rates to each age–sex cohort. The participation rates employed in this module are the maximum values that are likely to occur and are based on historic rates for the population of North Dakota.

The Economic–Demographic Interface Module

The interface module is applied at the county level, is fully employed in both baseline and impact projections, and operates with the following order of structural components and procedures (see figure 14–2).

1. Estimates of the number of employees required to fill baseline, construction, operational, and indirect types of employment are maintained as separate inputs from the economic input–output model and from data on project characteristics (indirect from the I–0 and direct from project data). Under baseline conditions, of course, only projections of baseline employment are produced.

2. During baseline projection periods and in the year preceding project construction, estimates of the number of available workers are obtained by the application of county-level age–sex specific labor force participation rates to age–sex cohorts derived as products from the demographic model. This produces the number of total workers available in each age–sex group for that period. Under impact conditions, a similar procedure is followed. However, age–sex specific estimates of available labor pools are obtained for each of the baseline, construction, operational, and indirect types for each period by the application of age–sex employment-type, specific labor-force participation rates to age–sex cohorts for each type of employment related population. Throughout all impact analyses, these employment and population types are retained as separate computational units.

3. Given the employment-type specific labor requirements derived from procedure 1 and the age–sex employment type specific estimates of available labor from procedure 2, a matching procedure is utilized that takes required employment from available employment pools in accordance with a predetermined employment type priority schedule. This schedule, shown in table 14–1, attempts to incorporate estimates of the differential abilities of various kinds of workers to fill various kinds of employment. For example, as shown in table 14–1, it is assumed that baseline indigenous jobs can be filled only by persons from the available baseline labor pool. For operating jobs, a specified proportion is assumed to immigrate because of special skill requirements. When this proportion has been set aside, other jobs are filled first from the available indigenous population, then from

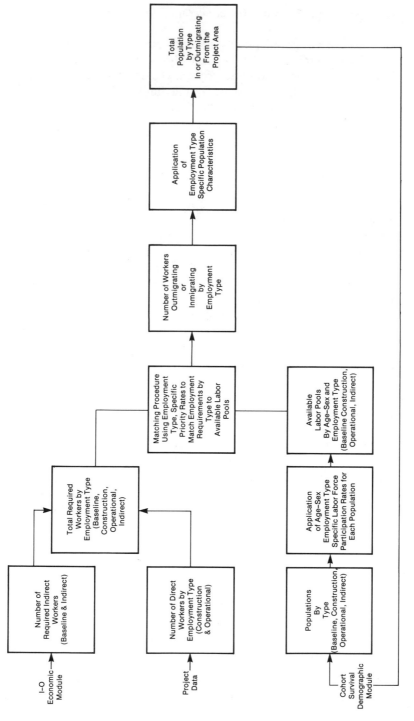

Figure 14–2. Flowchart for Interface Module of Economic–Demographic Model

Table 14–1.
Sequence and Priorities for Job Filling by Potential Jobholders.

Job Sector	Potential Jobholder from Population Group
Baseline Jobs	1. Indigenous Population[a]
Construction jobs	1. Construction worker population in specified fraction of jobs 2. Indigenous population 3. Construction workers (in- or out-migration to balance)
Operating jobs	1. Operating worker population in specified fraction of jobs 2. Indigenous population 3. Construction worker associated population 4. Operating worker population (in- or out-migration to balance)
Indirect jobs	1. Indirect worker population in specified fraction of jobs 2. Indigenous population 3. Operating worker population 4. Construction worker population 5. Indirect population (in- or out-migration to balance)

[a] Outmigrate indigenous population after the employment for all job sectors, including indirect jobs, is satisfied.

construction populations, and then from other operating worker populations. Employment requirements are filled from each age–sex group within each population type according to the proportion that each group is of the total available labor within that population type.

4. As a result of procedure 3, all labor-force requirements that can be filled from the available pool are determined. If the labor pool available exceeds that required, out-migration is assumed to occur, and an excess of labor requirements over available labor is assumed to bring about immigration.

5. The results of steps 3 and 4 provide estimates of the number of workers by age–sex employment type that must out-migrate or in-migrate.

6. The number of workers by age–sex and employment type are converted to population estimates by the application of a set of employment-type specific population characteristics to the number of workers of each type.[22] Thus, for each of the baseline, construction, operational, and indirect worker types, there is an associated set of data used to estimate the characteristics of sex, marital status, presence or absence of family in the impact area, age distribution of other workers in the household, age distribution of workers, and age distribution of dependents. The result is the total number of persons by age and sex that will either leave or in-migrate into an area for each project period.

7. The population figures determined in step 6 are used for the next iteration of the demographic module.

The Residential Allocation Module

The residential allocation component of the model is used to estimate the probable location patterns of in–migrating workers and their dependents. These allocations are made at the municipal level using a gravity model. The gravity model was chosen as the basis for residential allocation because similar models have been used extensively (and with suitable accuracy) to explain commuting patterns and patterns of population distribution, as well as other phenomena.[23] The gravity model uses the basic assumptions that in–migrants will tend to settle in population centers in direct proportion to the population of those centers, but that the number of in–migrants moving to a city will be inversely related to the distance between that city and the employment site. It also assumes that qualitative differences between possible settlement locations will affect settlement choices. In symbolic form, these assumptions may be stated as follows for each work site:

$$ M = \frac{\left[\dfrac{P_i}{D_i^a} \right] W_i}{\displaystyle\sum_{i=1}^{n} \left[\dfrac{P_i}{D_i^a} \ W_i \right]} $$

where M_i = fraction of total inmigrants locating in city i,

P_i = population of city i,

D_i^a = distance between city i and the work site, raised to the power a, and

W_i = the relative qualitative attraction of city i.

The user may specify values for the distance exponent and the value of the community attraction index (W_i) for any city. Separate gravity model allocations are made for each type of worker. Standard values for the exponent parameters a were estimated using data on settlement-commuting patterns of construction workers at electric–generating plant construction sites in North Dakota, Montana, and Wyoming and similar data for permanent (operating) workers at coal mines and power plants in North Dakota, South Dakota, Montana, and Wyoming.[23] The value of the exponent parameter a for indirect workers was estimated through analysis of changes in employment patterns in western North Dakota communities that have previously experienced coal development. The estimated exponent values are 1.5 for construction workers, 2.9 for operating workers, and 1.6 for project–related indirect workers, and these values are used in the residential allocation process unless the user specifies alternative values. This results in a smaller proportion of construction workers being allocated to municipalities near the plant site than is the case for operating workers. A slightly greater proportion of indirect workers is allocated to nearby cities than are construction workers. For construction and operating workers, the gravity model allocates population to communities as a factor of commuting distance to work. Indirect workers are also allocated to communities as a factor of distance to the site of a project; however, indirect workers are assumed both to reside and work in the community to which they have been allocated.)

The community attraction index (W_i) allows the user to give weights to particular cities if he believes that they will attract fewer or more people than that determined by their population and distance from the employment sites. Values of 1.0 (meaning no weights are assigned) are assumed for all cities unless otherwise specified by the user. User choice of a number larger than 1.0 will result in more in–migrants being assigned to that city, and choice of a value less than 1.0 will reduce that city's share. User specification of W_i values other than 1.0 generally has been based on specific local information regarding relative availability of housing and key public services.

The Fiscal Impact Module

The final component of the economic-demographic model is the fiscal impact module. Utilizing the expected settlement patterns from the gravity model and subsequent population changes estimated for each area by the economic and demographic models, it determines the expected public sector costs and revenues associated with such changes. The model provides for the estimation of both state and local costs and revenues. In each case the model works through a three-step procedure: computation of expected increased public revenues, expected increased public costs, and net difference between increased costs and revenues referred to as the net fiscal balance.

At the state level, the revenue sources included in the model are: the sales and use tax, personal income tax, corporate income tax, state share of coal severance tax, state share of coal conversion tax, business and corporate privilege tax, highway taxes, Cigarette and tobacco and liquor and beer taxes, and county equalization levies.

At the local level, revenue sources included in the model are: ad valorem property taxes; user fees (for sewer, water, and solid waste disposal service, for instance); special assessments (for example, for street improvements); transfer payments, including school foundation program payments, federal revenue-sharing payments, highway fund payments, and cigarette and tobacco tax payments; local share of coal severance tax, and local share of coal conversion tax.

At the state level, the costs included are per-capita costs of general government functions, highway maintenance costs, highway construction costs, and school foundation program payments.

At the local level, the costs included are school construction and operating costs, street construction and operating costs, water and sewer system construction costs, law enforcement operating costs, fire protection costs, and local general government costs.

The interrelationships involved in calculating project-related revenues are shown in figure 14-3, and those changes in state sales and use tax revenues are estimated on the basis of historic relationships between sales tax collections and the gross receipts of the retail trade sector. Changes in state personal income tax collections are estimated on the basis of the historic relationship between personal income tax collections and total personal income. The same procedure is followed in estimating increased corporate income tax and business and corporate privilege tax collections, except that collections are based on total gross business volume of all business sectors. Increases in collections of the various highway taxes and liquor and tobacco taxes are estimated on a per-capita basis.

Severance tax collections are based on a per-ton rate for all coal mined in North Dakota, with receipts allocated according to the prevailing statutory formula. The coal conversion tax applies to coal-fired electric generating plants, coal gasification plants, and other coal conversion facilities. The conversion taxes are in lieu of all ad valorem taxes except those on the land occupied by the plants. Receipts from this tax are divided between the state general fund and the county in which the facility is located. The county's portion is further subdivided among the county general fund, school districts, and municipalities.

The estimate of added property tax revenue is obtained by applying the prevailing statewide average property tax rate to the estimated taxable value of additional business structures and residences resulting from the industrial development and associated population growth. The estimated average investment cost for houses, apartments, and business structures is used as the basis for estimating taxable value for those structures, and the taxable value for mobile homes is estimated using half of the purchase price.

State school foundation program payments associated with increased enrollments are based on payments per pupil. Federal revenue-sharing

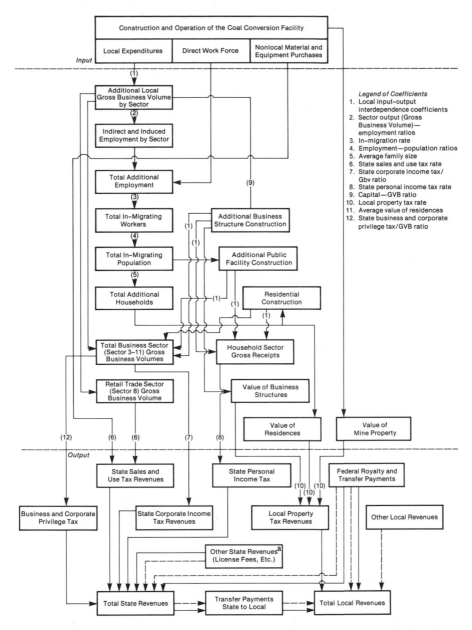

Note: The dashed lines represent revenue flows. They are not estimated but are included for conceptual completeness.

[a]Includes coal severance tax and taxation of conversion facilities.

Figure 14-3. Flowchart of Revenue Estimation for a Coal Conversion Facility, North Dakota.

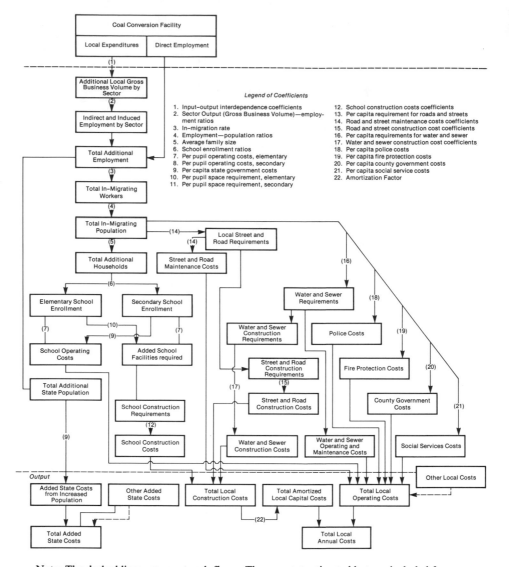

Note: The dashed lines represent cash flows. They are not estimated but are included for conceptual completeness.

Figure 14–4. Flowchart of Cost Estimation for a Coal Conversion Facility, North Dakota.

payments are estimated on a per–capita basis. Increased user fees are estimated on the basis of present rates per household, and special assessment revenues are based on amortized capital investments for streets, water, sewers, and solid waste disposal.

This module also accounts for reductions in tax revenues resulting from decreased agricultural production. The potential reduction in agricultural production is estimated on the basis of the acreage to be used for the plant site, the acreage to be mined, and the acreage expected to be used for residential, transportation, and related uses. The reduction in acreage is translated into a reduction in sales to final demand by the agricultural sectors. Hence the estimated changes in employment, income, and state and local tax revenues are net changes (increases resulting from industrial expansion less decreases resulting from reduced agricultural production).

Estimates of capital costs for new facilities are based primarily on recent engineering data, and operation and maintenance cost estimates are based primarily on cross-sectional regression analysis of a sample of county and city budget data from counties and cities in western North Dakota. (See figure 14-4.) The counties and cities included in the sample covered the range of potential populations of the communities likely to be affected by the new industrial developments.

To permit comparison of net fiscal balances for the years in which costs and revenues are realized, all cost and revenue components are computed on the basis of the most current data available and adjusted to the 1975 price level. Those components subject to price level changes are inflated at a rate selected by the user (the default rate is 7 percent) through the life of the development. Increased costs are subtracted from increased revenues to obtain an estimate of the net fiscal balance by year for the state and local units of government.

The accuracy of the model in estimating key economic and demographic variables has been evaluated through a backcasting process. The accuracy of the input-output module was evaluated by Senechal and subsequently by Hertsgaard et al.[24] In the latter study, final demand vectors were computed for the coal-producing area of western North Dakota and were multiplied by the interdependence coefficients to obtain the level of sales to final demand. These estimates of personal income were compared with those reported by the U.S. Department of Commerce for the years 1959, 1963, and 1965-1975 (table 14-2). The last column of table 14-2 indicates the difference between the estimated and reported values espressed as a percentage of the Department of Commerce estimate. This difference is less than 5 percent for seven of the thirteen years, and only two years have differences of more than 10 percent. The average difference is 5.2 percent for the entire thirteen-year period.

Similar evaluations are underway with respect to other key economic and demographic variables. For example, special population censuses were completed during the period 1975-1977 for some communities near North Dakota coal development sites. Comparison of the census population estimates with population projections from the model indicated that the differences between projected and reported populations generally were less than 5 percent.

Table 14–2
Comparison of Personal Income Estimated from Input–Output Model and Report by U.S. Department of Commerce, State Regions 7 and 8, 1959–1975

Year	Estimated by Input–Output Techniques ($1,000)	Reported by Department of Commerce[a] ($1,000)	Percentage Difference
1959	211,861	195,262	8.5
1960	213,667	n.a.	
1961	199,221	n.a.	
1962	263,372	262,882	0.2
1963	274,302	n.a.	
1964	288,647	n.a.	
1965	304,692	323,317	5.8
1966	353,927	338,263	4.6
1967	348,267	346,067	0.6
1968	360,178	355,397	1.3
1969	423,145	412,451	2.6
1970	448,158	431,830	3.8
1971	477,770	469,912	1.7
1972	591,867	560,011	5.7
1973	779,882	736,877	5.8
1974	853,948	734,139	16.3
1975	850,757	764,895	11.2
Average difference[b]			5.2

Note: The U.S. Department of Commerce did not report personal income for years labeled n.a.

[a] As reported by U.S. Department of Commerce, Bureau of Economic Analysis, Regional Economics Information System, Washington, D.C., August 1976.

[b] Computed without respect to sign.

User Options and Uses

One of the ways of assessing the utility of a modeling effort is to examine the types of information it can produce and the uses it has had. In this section we wish to indicate some of the user options and actual uses to which the model has been put.

User Options

The model is capable of being used directly by user groups through interactive terminals. It is programmed in APL, a language well suited for interactive use and allows users to alter a wide number of model parameters if they so desire. Among the factors capable of being altered are:

1. The length of the projection period.
2. The number, location, and starting dates of projects.
3. The gravity powers and community attraction index values in the allocation module.
4. The birthrate.
5. The rate of inflation.
6. The tax rates for major taxes.

Values that are not altered default to pre-specified values. (*Default* is a common programming term that indicates no action on the part of the user.) The user may also choose the reporting option.

The reports produced by the model include:

1. A scenario specification report that lists all assumptions prevailing in a given use of the model.
2. A regional economic activity report showing baseline as well as project-related business activity and personal income.
3. Regional, county, and municipal summary reports showing the baseline and project-related population and employment changes in the state planning region, the county, or selected municipalities.
4. A population report by age and sex.
5. A school enrollment report.
6. A housing report.
7. A fiscal report.

The scenario specification report cannot be altered by the user, but other reporting functions are optional. In addition, although the population, school enrollment, housing and fiscal impact reports will automatically provide information at the regional, county and municipal levels, users can specify that data be produced for only a given geographical area. Finally, other factors and reports can be altered and produced with only minor assistance from staff.

The model is user oriented in design and allows users to alter both parameters affecting model outputs and the form of the output produced.

Model Uses

During the period January 1 to October 31, 1977, forty-five different bodies used the model for various aspects of planning and decision making.

The forty-five user organizations made sixty-three different requests for E-D model projections, which required 179 model runs. Some users of the model have included the following.

1. The U.S. Bureau of Land Management, in cooperation with the state of North Dakota, is developing a regional environmental impact statement (EIS) for proposed coal development and associated federal coal leasing in western North Dakota. The BLM and state study teams used the E-D model as their basic source of economic, demographic, and fiscal impact projections for the regional EIS and for a series of project-specific environmental impact statements.

2. The North Dakota Coal Impact Office has the statutory responsibility for distributing several million dollars annually to aid local governments that are experiencing unusual expenditures as a result of coal development. These funds have been used primarily for capital facilities improvement. The Coal Impact Office has used E-D model projections as one source of information to assess the need for various facilities.

3. During North Dakota's 1977 legislative session, various committees utilized E-D model projections in the preparation of major revisions in the state's system of coal industry taxation and revenue distribution. The projections indicated that cities and school districts in coal impact areas might incur substantial long-term fiscal deficits. The new legislation resulted in substantial increases in the revenues accruing to these jurisdictions.

4. The North Dakota Public Service Commission has statutory authority for issuing siting permits for energy conversion facilities. The commission has used E-D model projections as an aid in evaluating a series of permit applications for electric generating and coal gasification plants.

5. The North Dakota State Highway Department used population and employment projections developed by REAP as the basis for estimating changes in traffic volume by road segment through 1989. The projected changes in traffic volume were used to develop estimates of highway construction needs and associated costs in a seven-county area.

6. A number of counties, cities, and school districts have used the model in developing capital budgets and in various other planning activities. For example, the city of Beulah made a capital facilities planning effort. Of most immediate concern was the need to expand the city's sewage treatment facility. The mayor and planning commission requested a series of population projections for the city consistent with alternative levels of future energy development. They then used the information to determine the most appropriate design capacity for the new treatment facility.

7. Private development companies and consulting firms have also used the model.

The REAP staff has noted that the users find the following characteristics of the model to be particularly desirable:

1. Projections incorporate both baseline and impact conditions; thus, population projections for a given county or city indicate the likely future trend without development, as well as the effect of specific projects.
2. Ability to analyze multiple projects. A number of communities could be affected by several different development projects. The model can show the combined effect of several projects and the changes that would occur if a given project were postponed or developed at a different site.
3. Geographic specificity. Whereas projections at the state or substate regional levels are useful of even greater value to community decision makers is the capability for obtaining projections at the county or municipal levels.
4. Flexibility. The model allows for easy selection of alternative patterns and rates of development.
5. Quick response. Population and economic projections are now developed in a matter of hours. Previously the community might have been forced to commission a special study requiring months to complete.

Model Adaptability and Transferability

In sparsely populated rural areas where a new energy development can have major impacts, preplanning is of special importance. Preplanning, however, requires estimates and projections of the magnitude, type, and location of these impacts. The economic–demographic model was developed to meet the information needs of communities confronted with a particular type of proposed energy development. But the model could also be useful in evaluating the impacts of a wide range of energy developments and other large construction or industrial projects and in providing public decision makers with useful planning information.

The model should be widely adaptable for two reasons. First, the economic and social impacts associated with the construction and operation of a coal–fired power plant should be similar in their general nature to those associated with the construction and operation of other facilities of comparable size. The magnitude of impact will differ between projects depending on both project variables (such as size and occupational structure of the work force, duration of construction activity, and extent of *local purchases*) and site variables (such as size, occupational composition, and employment status of area work force, capacity of area social service delivery systems, and tax structure). However, the model's structure allows for the use of project-specific data for each of these variables. Second, when a proposed energy project or other construction project would result in major community impacts, the variables included within the model are quite pervasive. Local officials need estimates of the magnitude, timing, and geographic distribution of population changes and attendant service needs to initiate their planning processes. These needs are similar for most major developments.

The approach embodied in the model should be applicable to site- and project-specific projections of the impacts of a variety of energy developments. The basis for the economic impact analysis is a regional input-output model, and similar models have already been used to estimate the impacts of a wide range of proposed energy developments and other major industrial projects. For example, input-output (I-O) techniques have been used to project the impact of a 24,000 MWe nuclear energy center, a coal-fired electric generating complex, and a major oil shale development.[25]

One prerequisite to the use of the input-output technique is development of I-O coefficients for the area of interest, and these have been developed for many states and substate areas. If an appropriate I-O table is not available, one can be prepared using either primary or secondary data sources. The initial cost of a primary data I-O table is substantial, but the multiplicity of uses for it may well justify the cost. Alternatively, the use of secondary data to develop the tables may offer a way to reduce costs without a major sacrifice in accuracy.[26] If the development of an input-output table from primary or secondary data is deemed infeasible, the economic module of the E-D model could be redesigned to utilize employment and income multipliers developed by export base or econometric techniques.

The cohort-survival demographic model is applicable to many population forecasting efforts. The basic data source for present population distribution and past trends is the U.S. Census of Population. Birthrates and survival rates are generally based on Census Bureau projections or state vital statistics data. The most serious problem in demographic projection is usually the development of migration estimates. However, if the cohort-survival model is linked to an economic projection model, estimates of employment-induced migration can be calculated internally. It is necessary, in this case, to make assumptions concerning the characteristics of in-migrating workers on such matters as age and number of dependents. In some cases, special surveys of the work forces of analogous projects may be useful as a means of estimating these characteristics.

The fiscal impact component of the model also is adaptable (with some modifications to account for institutional differences) to other types of development and should be transferable to other states. Some changes undoubtedly would be needed in the revenue subroutine to account for state variations in tax structures. Fewer alternations would be needed in the public services and facilities cost subroutine.

The model (as well as the data entering into its development) provides a wealth of information appropriate for the development of additional modeling efforts aimed at assessing other impacts of a major development change. Thus, the basic data provided could be used to assess medical service needs, recreational and social services needs, and environmental effects of new development projects. In sum, the model, although developed in response to information needs created by coal development in rural areas, should be adaptable to the assessment of impacts from a wide range of developments, such as manufacturing, build-up of military installations, agricultural processing, irrigation, and highway construction in both rural and urban areas.

Necessary Factors in a Model's Development and Use

The process used in the REAP effort may point to a number of general factors that should be considered before a modeling effort is undertaken. These factors are essential in expediting such an effort.

First is the awareness of the need for the information it can provide and the quick provision of the information to meet these needs. Modeling efforts tend to be attractive to university researchers because of the methodological challenge they entail. If such models fail to be addressed to real informational needs, however, they are likely to end up being valuable exercises for researchers but of little real utility. Thus the timing of such efforts must be right such that the needs of decision makers and the expertise of the researchers can be properly meshed. If such efforts are pursued before local decision makers sense the need for the information they can provide or if their development entails such an extensive time frame that the important issues have already been addressed prior to the model's completion, such efforts will not be highly utilized or well received.

Second is the need for such efforts to involve a close partnership between model developers and local data users. The participation of local data users, such as county extension agents, local and regional planners, and other state and local officials, serves many purposes, including easier access to data bases, correction of model inaccuracies, increased information on local conditions, and an increased likelihood that local decision makers will use the model. Such efforts should not proceed without such interdependence.

Third is the need to take advantage of local research expertise.

Although the ease of obtaining packaged systems from outside groups may be attractive, the use of such systems cannot provide the kind of in-depth background that is often essential for assessing a model's utility and the validity of its outputs.

Fourth, such efforts must be truly interdisciplinary, not multidisciplinary. Although economists and sociologists will inevitably have different perspectives, our experience indicates that each will benefit from the work of the other. Too often demographic projections ignore economic realities, especially in rural areas, and equally often economic projections ignore the significance of demographic structures. Close interdependencies must be recognized and utilized.

Finally, it is essential that such efforts occur within a supportive atmosphere, within both the state and the university setting. Researchers must be assured that their efforts will have both pragmatic and professional rewards, and local users must see the actual utility of the product received for meeting state and federal funding and other administrative requirements. To ignore the importance of such structural factors is to ensure the failure of such an effort.

Conclusion

The REAP economic–demographic modeling effort is but one example of an ever-growing interest in developing computerized models aimed at meeting the informational needs of local decision makers. We believe that it is serving a number of local needs and that the form of development it utilized may provide a beneficial model for other efforts. We suggest that its continued use will provide the best evidence concerning its ultimate value to local decision makers.

Notes

1. Gene F. Summers, Sharon D. Evans, Frank Clemente, E. M. Beck, and Jon Minkoff, *Industrial Invasion of Nonmetropolitan America: A Quarter Century of Experience* (New York: Praeger Publishers, 1976).

2. Leonard Bronder, M. Carlisle, and M. Savage, *Financial Strategies for Alleviation of Socioeconomic Impacts in Seven Western States* (Denver, Colo.: Western Governors' Energy Policy Office, 1977); Ann R. Markusen, *The Fiscal Crisis of American Boom Towns: An Analysis of State and Federal Policy,* Draft report (Washington, D.C.: U.S. General Accounting Office, 1977); Donald A. Rapp, *Western Boomtowns: A Comparative Analysis of State Actions,* Special Report to the Governors (Denver, Colo.:

Western Governors' Energy Policy Office, 1976); Wendell Associates, *Federal Assistance Programs and Energy Development Impacted Municipalities* (Washington, D.C.: Federal Energy Administration, 1976).

3. Council on Environmental Quality, *102 Monitor* (Washington, D.C.: Council on Environmental Quality, July 1977); Kurt Finsterbusch and C. P. Wolf, *Methodology of Social Impact Assessment* (Stroudsburg, Pa.: Dowden, Hutchinson and Ross, 1977); Abt Associates, *Social Assessment Manual: A Guide to the Preparation of the Social Well-being Account,* for the Bureau of Reclamation (Cambridge, Mass.: Abt Associates, 1975); J. A. Chalmers and E. J. Anderson, *Economic–Demographic Assessment Manual: Current Practices, Procedural Recommendations, and a Test Case* (Denver, Colo.: Bureau of Reclamation, 1977).

4. Chalmers and Anderson, *Assessment Manual;* Christopher Cluett, Michael T. Mertaugh, and Michael Micklin, *A Demographic Model for Assessing the Socioeconomic Impacts of Large Scale Industrial Development Projects* (Seattle, Wash.: Battelle Memorial Institute, Human Affairs Research Centers, 1978); Thor A. Hertsgaard, Steven H. Murdock, Norman E. Toman, Mark S. Henry, and Richard Ludtke, *The REAP Economic–Demographic Model: Technical Description* (Bismark: North Dakota Regional Environmental Assessment Program, 1977); Norman E. Toman, Steve H. Murdock, and Thor A. Hertsgaard, *The REAP Economic–Demographic Model II: Technical Description* (Bismarck: North Dakota Regional Environmental Assessment Program, forthcoming); Andrew Ford, *Summary Description of the Boom 1 Model*, LA-6424–MS (Los Alamos, N.M.: Los Alamos Scientific Laboratory, September 1976); Frederick W. Obermiller, Bruce McCarl, David Martella, and T. Kelley White, *The POM: An Interactive Approach to Modeling Population Growth and Economic Development* (Lafayette, Ind.: Purdue University, Department of Agricultural Economics, 1975); Ross Reave, Rodger Weaver, and Eric Natwig, *The Navajo Economic–Demographic Model: A Method for Forecasting and Evaluating Alternative Navajo Economic Futures* (Window Rock, Ariz.: Navajo Nation, Office of Program Development, 1977); Eric Anderson, James Chalmers, and Timothy Hogan, *A Guide for the Transfer and Adaptation of Atom 2* (Phoenix: State of Arizona, Office of the Governor, Office of Economic Planning and Development, 1974).

5. Wilbur Maki, R. J. Dorf, and R. W. Lichty, *User's Guide to Economic Forecasting Systems for State Policy Development* (St. Paul: University of Minnesota, Department of Agricultural and Applied Economics, 1977); Debra Stinson and Michael O'Hare, *Prediction of the Local Impacts of Energy Development: A Critical Guide to Forecasting Methods and Models* (Cambridge: Massachusetts Institute of Technology Press, 1977).

6. More extensive descriptions of both the development process and

the model structure are available from several sources. In particular see North Dakota Regional Environmental Assessment Program, *The REAP Economic-Demographic Model I: User Manual* (Bismarck: State Capitol, North Dakota Regional Environmental Assessment Program, December, 1976); Toman, Murdock and Hertsgaard, *REAP Model II;* F. Larry Leistritz and Steven H. Murdock, "Research Methodology Applicable to Community Adjustments to Public Land Use Alternatives" (paper presented at a forum given by the Farm Foundation of Chicago, Illinois, on the Economics of Public Land Use in the West, March 10-11, 1977, Reno, Nevada), and "Economic Demographic and Social Factors Affecting Energy-Impacted Communities: An Assessment Model and Implications for Nuclear Energy Centers" (paper presented to the American Nuclear Society Executive Seminar on Nuclear Energy Centers, Washington, D.C., April 1977).

7. Federal Energy Administration, *National Energy Outlook* (Washington, D.C.: Federal Energy Administration, 1976).

8. Northern Great Plains Resources Program, *Socio-Economic and Cultural Aspects Work Group Report* (Denver: Northern Great Plains Resources Program, June 1974).

9. A. William Johnson, "Alternatives for Action: REAP in North Dakota," *State Government: The Journal of State Affairs* 50 (1977): 16-20.

10. Hertsgaard et al., *REAP Model.*

11. Toman, Murdock, and Hertsgaard, *REAP Model II.*

12. B. L. Bartch, "Analysis of Intersectoral and Intercommunity Structure in Southwestern North Dakota" (Master's thesis, North Dakota State University, 1968); Larry D. Sand, "Analysis of Effects of Income Change on Intersectoral and Intercommunity Structure" (Master's thesis, North Dakota State University, 1966); Donald M. Senechal, "Analysis of Validity of North Dakota Input-Output Models" (Master's thesis, North Dakota State University, 1971).

13. Thor A. Hertsgaard and F. Larry Leistritz, "Environmental Impact of Strip Mining: The Economic and Social Viewpoints," in Mohan K. Wali, ed., *Some Environmental Aspects of Strip Mining in North Dakota*, series 5 (Grand Forks, N.D.: North Dakota Geological Survey, 1973), pp. 73-86; F. Larry Leistritz and Edward V. Dunn, *An Economic Analysis of Grazing Fee Levels on Federal Range Lands*, Agricultural Economics Report No. 76 (Fargo: North Dakota State University, Department of Agricultural Economics, 1971); Delmer L. Helgeson and Maurice J. Zink, *A Case Study of Rural Industrialization in Jamestown, North Dakota*, Agricultural Economics Report No. 95, Department of Agricultural Economics, North Dakota State University, Fargo, 1973.

14. Hertsgaard and Leistritz, "Environmental Impact."

15. Norman L. Dalsted, A. G. Leholm, N. E. Toman, R. C. Coon, Thor A. Hertsgaard, and F. Larry Leistritz, *Economic Impacts of a Proposed Coal Gasification Plant in Dunn County, North Dakota* (Fargo: North Dakota State University, Agricultural Experiment Station, January, 1976); Arlen G. Leholm, F. Larry Leistritz, and Thor A. Hertsgaard, *Local Impacts of Energy Resources Development in the Northern Great Plains*, Final Report to Northern Great Plains Resources Program (Fargo: North Dakota State University, Department of Agricultural Economics, September 1974); N. E. Toman, Norman L. Dalsted, Arlen G. Leholm, Randal C. Coon, and F. Larry Leistritz, *Economic Impacts of Construction and Operation of the Coal Creek Electrical Generation Complex and Related Mine* (Fargo: North Dakota State University, Department of Agricultural Economics, 1976); Randal C. Coon, Norman L. Dalsted, Arlen G. Leholm, and F. Larry Leistritz, *The Impact of the Safeguard Antiballistic Missile System on Northeastern North Dakota,* Agricultural Economics Report No. 101 (Fargo: North Dakota State University, 1976).

16. Eldon C. Schriner, Joy N. Query, Thomas D. McDonald, Faye Keogh, and Thomas Gallagher, *Social Impact of a Coal Gasification Project in Dunn County, North Dakota*, Interim Report to Natural Gas Pipeline Company (Fargo: North Dakota State University, Department of Sociology, 1976); Eldon C. Shriner, Faye Keogh, and Thomas Gallagher, *Social Impact of the Coyote Electrical Generating Plant, Mercer County, North Dakota* (Fargo: North Dakota State University, Department of Sociology, 1976); Richard Ludtke and Richard Blair, *North Dakota Abridged Life Tables, 1960-1970* (Bismarck: North Dakota State Department of Health, Division of Health Statistics, 1974); Richard Ludtke, *North Dakota Population Projections, 1970 -1975* (Bismarck: North Dakota State Department of Health, Division of Health Planning, 1976); Steven H. Murdock and Thomas K. Ostenson, *Population Projections by Age and Sex, 1975-2000*, Agricultural Economics Statistical Series, No. 31 (Fargo: North Dakota State University, Department of Agricultural Economics, 1976).

17. A nontechnical discussion of input–output analysis appears in Floyd K. Harmstrom and Richard E. Lund, *Application of an Input–output Framework to a Community Economic System*, University of Missouri Studies, Vol. 42 (Columbia: University of Missouri Press, 1967). More detailed treatments are found in Wassily W. Leontief, *Input–output Economics* (New York: Oxford University Press, 1966), and Hollis B. Chenery and Paul G. Clark, *Interindustry Economics* (New York: John B. Wiley, 1959).

18. Sand, "Analysis of Effects"; Bartch, "Analysis of Structure"; and Senechal, "Analysis of Validity."

19. For a discussion of alternative population projection techniques

and their relative capabilities, see G. W. Barclay, *Techniques of Population Analysis* (New York: John Wiley, 1958), and H. S. Shryock and J. S. Siegel, *The Methods and Materials of Demography* (Washington, D.C.: U.S. Government Printing Office, 1973).

20. See Murdock and Ostenson, *Population Projections.*

21. Age-sex specific migration rates for North Dakota counties for 1960–1970 were taken from Gladys Bowles, Calvin L. Beale, and Everett S. Lee, *Net Migration of the Population, 1960–70, by Age, Sex, and Color* (Athens: University of Georgia Printing Department, 1975).

For mortality, survival rates were computed from life tables in Ludtke and Blair, *North Dakota Abridged Life Tables.*

Age-specific fertility rates were computed from births by age of mother for 1972, 1973, and 1974. These data were obtained from the Division of Health Statistics, North Dakota State Department of Health.

22. These data were obtained from surveys by Arlen G. Leholm, F. Larry Leistritz, and James S. Wieland, *Profile of North Dakota's Coal Mine and Electric Power Plant Operating Work Force*, Agricultural Economics Report No. 100 (Fargo: North Dakota State University, 1975), and *Profile of North Dakota's Electric Power Plant Construction Work Force*, Agricultural Economics Statistical Series, Issue No. 22 (Fargo: North Dakota State University, 1976); and James S. Wieland, "Socioeconomic Characteristics and Settlement Patterns Associated with Operating and Construction Work Forces in North Dakota, South Dakota and Montana" (Master's thesis, North Dakota State University, 1977).

23. For a review of the historical development of the gravity concept, see Gerald P. Carrothers, "An Historical Review of the Gravity and Potential Concepts of Human Interaction," *Journal of the American Institute of Planners* 22 (1956): 94–102. Discussions of the use of gravity models in regional economic analysis are provided by Walter Isard et al., *Ecologic-Economic Analysis for Regional Development* (New York: Free Press, 1972), and Harry W. Richardson, *Elements of Regional Economics* (Baltimore: Penguin Modern Economic Texts, 1969).

24. Data Collection procedures are described in Leholm, Leistritz, and Wieland *Profile of Operating Work Force* and *Profile of Construction Work Force.* Statistical procedures for establising the exponent parameters are described by Wieland "Socioeconomic Characteristics."

24. Senechal, "Analysis," and Hertsgaard et al., *Reap Model.*

25. Walter Isard et al., *Regional Economic Impacts of Nuclear Power Plants,* BNL 50562, National Center for Analysis of Energy Systems (Brookhaven, N.Y.: Brookhaven National Laboratory Associated Universities, 1976); Larry Adcock, Gilbert Bonem, and George Thomason, *The PNM San Juan Power Complex—Estimates of Economic Impact: San Juan Units 1, 3, and 4* (Albuquerque: University of New Mexico, Bureau of

Business and Economic Research, 1975); Camilla Auger, B. Udis, R. Maurice, D. Brunt, and R. Hess, *In the Development of a Standard Method for Socioeconomic Forecasting and Analysis of Energy Related Growth: Socioeconomic Impacts of Western Energy Development,* Working Paper No. 1 for the Council on Environmental Quality (Boulder : Socioeconomic Research Associates, 1976).

26. Ronald S. Boster and William E. Martin, "The Value of Primary Versus Secondary Data in Interindustry Analysis: A Study in the Economics of Economic Models," *Annals of Regional Science* 6 (December 1972): 35–44.

15 Additive, Multiplicative, and Mixed Models for Studying Community Change

E. M. Beck and
Gene F. Summers

We examine the conceptual implications of three types of models for study-ing social change where the unit of analysis is the community and recom-mend a class of models that infrequently appear in the sociological literature yet are well suited for representing social change. Specifically it is conceptu-ally reasonable to view social change as a contingent process where the initial state of development interacts with change agents to produce a new stage of development. Furthermore, change agents themselves do not operate in isolation, but in a complementary fashion producing social change.

Some Preliminaries

Let us assume that interest is focused on explaining change in a dependent variable, Y, over some period of time. Without loss of generality, we will assume that Y is measured on a set of n communities at two points in time: its current value Y^t and its base period value Y^{t-1}.[1] Change in Y is defined as the simple difference between these two values:

$$\Delta Y_i = Y_i^t - Y_i^{t-1} \qquad i = 1, 2, \ldots, n \qquad (15.1)$$

Further we believe that there is a set of k social change agents, or in-dependent variables (X_k), and that change in these affect the amount of change in the dependent variable. Again, definitionally ΔX_{ij} is the amount of change in the jth of k independent variables in the ith community:

$$\Delta X_{ij} = X_{ij}^t - X_{ij}^{t-1} \qquad \begin{array}{l} i = 1, 2, \ldots, n \\ j = 1, 2, \ldots, k \end{array} \qquad (15.2)$$

While the basic argument is that ΔY is some function of these ΔX_k's, given our imperfect knowledge, it is unlikely that we can specify the exact deter-minants of ΔY. In this instance, it may be more realistic to assume that one or more important independent variables have been inadvertently excluded from the model. The effects of these excluded variables can be summarized into one term, u_i. The argument is, then, that change in the dependent variable is some function of changes in a set of independent variables— social change agents—and a disturbance term representing the collective effects of excluded variables (deleting the community subscripts):

$$\Delta Y = f(\Delta X_1, \Delta X_k, \ldots, X_k; u). \qquad (15.3)$$

From this specification, two questions arise. First, what sort of functional form should be used to link ΔY to the predetermining variables? Second, is the expression on the right-hand side of 15.3 complete? In other words, are there additional terms that should be included along with the predetermining variables already in the equation?

Let us address the latter issue first. We argue that the right-hand side of equation 15.3 is not complete because it states that the amount of change in the dependent variable is unaffected by the initial level of the dependent variable, Y^{t-1}. We do not find this assumption plausible. Rather we believe as a broad principle that the amount of change will depend on the state of the community in the base period $t - 1$. For example, it could be anticipated that the degree of change in aggregate educational attainment in a community is inversely related to the level of education in the base period. It would be expected that communities with high levels of educational attainment would experience less change in education than communities with lower aggregate education at the initial period. In a sense we are positing a ceiling effect such that there is an inverse relationship between a change in Y and its initial value. At a more general level, we believe that in most situations it would be difficult to argue that the amount of change is independent of the base period value of the dependent variable.

Given this position, equation 15.3 must be respecified to include the $t - 1$ value of the dependent variable:

$$\Delta Y = f(Y^{t-1}; \Delta X_1, \Delta X_2, \ldots, \Delta X_k; u). \qquad (15.4)$$

Now that the terms in the function have been identified, an appropriate form for analysis must be selected.

Functional Forms

Linear, Additive Models

The simplest change model would express ΔY as a linear, additive function of the initial value of Y, change in the independent variables, and the disturbance term:[2]

$$\Delta Y = \alpha + \Gamma Y^{t-1} + \beta_1 \Delta X_2 + \beta_2 \Delta X_2 + \ldots + \beta_k \Delta X_k + u. \quad (15.5)$$

The partial derivatives of ΔY with respect to the predetermining variables show that the effect of the kth social change agent,

$$\frac{\partial \Delta Y}{\partial \Delta X_k} = \beta_k \qquad \frac{\partial \Delta Y}{\partial Y^{t-1}} = \Gamma \qquad\qquad (15.6)$$

as denoted by the partial derivative of ΔY with respect to ΔX_k, is a constant (β_k) for all of the k independent variables. Similarly, the effect of the base period value of the dependent variable is a constant. Further, the effects of the predetermining variables are additive: the effect of an explanatory variable does not depend, nor is contingent, upon any of the remaining variables in the model.

These characteristics of the linear, additive model are also obvious when equation 15.5 is rewritten so that only the current value of Y appears on the left–hand side:

$$Y^t = \alpha + (\Gamma + 1)Y^{t-1} + \beta_2 \Delta X_1 + \beta_2 \Delta X_2 + \ldots + \beta_k \Delta X_k + u. \quad (15.7)$$

This expression shows that after an adjustment is made for the base period value of Y, the current value of the dependent variable is an additive combination of the separate effects of each of the social change agents.

In sum, although the linear, additive model has a simple elegance, it is restrictive, and its implicit underlying theoretical foundations may be unrealistic and unacceptable. The model presented in equation 15.5 states that the social change agents do not interact with one another, that the effects of these agents are not conditioned by the initial state of the community, and that the social change effects are constant throughout their range. Since we do not believe that any of these three propositions is reasonable for most studies of social change, we question the linear, additive model as being a viable representation.

Mixed Models

Many of the limitations of the linear, additive model can be rectified by introducing multiplicative interaction terms into the function. The interactive model of social change is composed of a mixture of additive and multiplicative terms. For simplicity and without loss of generality, let us assume that we are dealing with only two independent change agents, ΔX_1 and ΔX_2, and that we believe that there are significant interaction effects among ΔX_1, ΔX_2, and Y^{t-1} on producing change in Y, whence

$$\Delta Y = \alpha + \Gamma Y^{t-1} + \beta_1 \Delta X_1 + \beta_2 \Delta X_2 + \Theta_1 (\Delta X_1)(Y^{t-1}) + \Theta_2(\Delta X_2)$$

$$(Y^{t-1}) + \Theta_3(\Delta X_1)(\Delta X_2) + \Theta_4(\Delta X_1)(\Delta X_2)(Y^{t-1}) + u. \tag{15.8}$$

Here β_1, β_2, and Γ are the main effects and Θ_1, Θ_2, Θ_3, Θ_4 are interaction parameters. In this model we have included all possible two-way interactions, as well as the three-way interaction of ΔX_2, ΔX_2, and Y^{t-1}. The interactions between ΔX_1 and Y^{t-1} and between ΔX_1 and Y^{t-1}, as well as the three-way interaction, are especially relevant. In many instances the state of the community in the base period provides the stimulus for social change. For example, if Y is the poverty rate, a particularly large value of $t - 1$ may encourage the introduction of social change agents designed to reduce the severity of the problem. In this example, there would be interaction among these agents and the level of poverty in the base period, $t - 1$. In fact, any time change in the social change agent is stimulated by the initial level of dependent variable, there exist interaction effects such as these.

    Some of the conceptual implications of this mixed model are revealed by inspecting the partial derivatives of equation 15.8:

$$\frac{\partial \Delta Y}{\partial Y^{t-1}} = \Gamma + \Theta_1(\Delta X_1) + \Theta_2(\Delta X_2) + \Theta_4(\Delta X_1)(X_2). \tag{15.9}$$

$$\frac{\partial \Delta Y}{\partial \Delta X_1} = \beta_1 + \Theta_1(Y^{t-1}) + \Theta_3(\Delta X_2) + \Theta_4(\Delta X_2)(Y^{t-1}). \tag{15.10}$$

$$\frac{\partial \Delta Y}{\partial \Delta X_2} = \beta_2 + \Theta_2(Y^{t-1}) + \Theta_3(\Delta X_1) + \Theta_4(\Delta X_1)(Y^{t-1}). \tag{15.11}$$

Equation 15.9 shows that the effect of the base period value of the dependent variable ($\partial \Delta Y / \partial Y^{t-1}$) varies according to the values of ΔX_1, ΔX_2, and their interaction. Similarly, equation 15.10 states that the effect of the first independent variable ($\partial \Delta Y / \partial \Delta X_1$) is a linear combination of a constant and the effects of ΔX_2, Y^{t-1} and the interaction between ΔX_2 and Y^{t-1}. And equation 15.11 shows that the effect of the second social change agent is a linear function of ΔX_1, Y^{t-1}, and their interaction.

    In mixed models it is clearly impossible to discuss the effects of these social change agents without simultaneously considering the values of the other social change agents, as well as the state of the community in the base period, $t - 1$.

    Mixed models are attractive, but another set of interactive models also merits consideration.

Multiplicative Models

Fully multiplicative models, also known as Cobb–Douglas models, posit that the dependent variable is a multiplicative, complementary function of the predetermining variables in the model rather than an additive combination of "main" effects and interactions. Again restricting attention to the situation where there are only two independent variables, the multiplicative model of change would be:

$$\Delta Y = \alpha(Y^{t-1})^{\Gamma}(\Delta X_1)^{\beta_1}(\Delta X_2)^{\beta_2} u. \tag{15.12}$$

The coefficients of this model have a straightforward interpretation as elasticities. Γ is the percentage change in ΔY associated with a 1 percent change in the base period value of Y. Similarly, β_k is the percentage change in ΔY that would result from a 1 percent change in ΔX_k. Also it should be noted that the sum of the parameters of the social change agents indicates whether ΔY changes at an increasing ($|\beta_1 + \beta_2| > 1$) or decreasing ($|\beta_1 + \beta_2| < 1$) rate for changes in the two change agents.

The effect of any one variable in the model is dependent upon the remaining variables, including the scaling factor (a), as these partial derivatives show:

$$\frac{\partial \Delta Y}{\partial Y^{t-1}} = (\alpha)(\Gamma)(Y^{t-1})^{\Gamma-1}(\Delta X_1)^{\beta_1}(\Delta X_2)^{\beta_2} \tag{15.13}$$

$$\frac{\partial \Delta Y}{\partial \Delta X_1} = (\alpha)(Y^{t-1})^{\Gamma}(\beta_1)(\Delta X_1)^{\beta_1-1}(\Delta X_2)^{\beta_2} \tag{15.14}$$

$$\frac{\partial \Delta Y}{\partial \Delta X_1} = (\alpha)(Y^{t-1})^{\Gamma}(\Delta X_1)^{\beta_1}(\beta_2)(\Delta X_2)^{\beta_2-1}. \tag{15.15}$$

Comparing equations 15.13–15.15 with those of the mixed model (15.9–15.11) shows that in both models the effects of each predetermining variable on ΔY are conditioned by the remaining variables in the model. The major difference is that in the multiplicative model, the effect of any one variable is dependent on the interaction among all other predetermining variables, whereas in the mixed model, the effect is dependent upon an additive function of main effects and interaction effects.

Although the multiplicative model has certain attractive features, such as the interpretation of its parameters as elasticities, it does bring into focus certain issues that demand consideration. First, since the model states that the process generating change in Y is simultaneously contingent upon all of the predetermining variables in the equation, the lack of change in any one of the variables will produce no change in the dependent variable. Thus equation 15.12 as shows, if there is no change in either of the social change agents, or if the base period value of the dependent variable is zero, change in Y will also be zero. This may or may not be reasonable specification depending on the sociological context of the research. Second, the model does present some difficulties in estimation which can be shown by taking equation 15.12 and solving for the current value of Y:

$$Y^t = Y^{t-1} + \{(\alpha)(Y^{t-1})^{\Gamma}(\Delta X_1)^{\beta_1}(\Delta X_2)^{\beta_2}u\}. \tag{15.16}$$

This function is intrinsically nonlinear and cannot be easily estimated without employing an iterative nonlinear estimation solution.

An Alternative Specification

It could be argued that communities are in a virtually constant process of change. If this position is assumed, then we may be interested in discovering the reasons why communities change at different rates. That is, what are the determining factors that influence the rate of community change? Now the appropriate dependent variable is no longer ΔY, but (Y/Y^{t-1}), the rate of change in Y (plus one).[3] Clearly we could express the rate of change as a linear, additive function of the predetermining variables in a model similar to equation 15.5, but such a model would have the same conceptual limitations as 15.5.

As better first approximation, we could apply the mixed model to this new dependent variable:

$$\begin{aligned} Y^t/Y^{t-1} = {} & \alpha + \Gamma Y^{t-1} + \beta_1 X_2 + \beta_2 \Delta X_2 + \Theta_1(\Delta X_1)(Y^{t-1}) \\ & + \Theta_2(\Delta X_2)(Y^{t-1}) + \Theta_3(\Delta X_1)(\Delta X_2) + \\ & + \Theta_4(\Delta X_1)(\Delta X_2)(Y^{t-1}) + u. \end{aligned} \tag{15.17}$$

In this form we are arguing that the rate of change in Y is a function of the social change agents, the base period value of Y, and the interactions among these predetermining variables. The partial derivatives of this model would be similar to those presented in equations 15.9–15.11 and will not be presented here. It is instructive to take 15.17 and solve for the current value of Y:

$$\begin{aligned} Y^t = {} & \alpha(Y^{t-1}) + \Gamma(Y^{t-1})^2 + \beta_1(\Delta X_1)(Y^{t-1}) + \beta_2(\Delta X_2)(Y^{t-1}) + \\ & + \Theta_1(\Delta X_1)(Y^{t-1})^2 + \Theta_2(\Delta X_2)(Y^{t-1})^2 + \Theta_3(\Delta X_1)(\Delta X_2)(Y^{t-1}) + \\ & + \Theta_4(\Delta X_1)(\Delta X_2)(Y^{t-1})^2 + v \end{aligned} \tag{15.18}$$

where $v = u(Y^{t-1})$. Equation 15.18 shows that the mixed model of change implies that the current value of the dependent variable is a function of the interaction of Y^{t-1} with each of the predetermining variables. This further implies that Y^t is affected not only by the linear effects of Y^{t-1} but also by quadratic effects. This may or may not be a reasonable specification of the process by which current values of the dependent variable are generated, but in any regard this specification appears to be so complex as to inhibit a simple substantive interpretation of the model's parameters.

If we apply the fully multiplicative functional form to this dependent variable,

$$Y^t/Y^{t-1} = \alpha \ (Y^{t-1})^{\Gamma}(\Delta X_1)^{\beta_1}(\Delta X_2)^{\beta_2}u, \qquad (15.19)$$

and then solve for the current value of Y,

$$\alpha(Y)^{\Gamma t} = \alpha \ (Y^{t-1})^{t-1}(\Delta X_1)^{\beta_1}(\Delta X_2)^{\beta_2}u, \qquad (15.20)$$

we find that Γ is the percentage increase in the rate of change for a 1 percent change in the base period value, yet ($\Gamma + 1$) is the percentage change in the current value of Y given a 1 percent change in Y^{t-1}.[4] Thus we can readily express the effect of the initial period either in terms of the rate of change (Y^t/Y^{t-1}) or the current value, Y^t. Furthermore, a comparison of these two equations shows that β_k is the percentage change in either (Y^t/Y^{t-1}) or Y^t. Hence we can readily interpret the parameters of equation 15.19 either in terms of the rate f change in the dependent variable or in terms of the current value of Y. In either of these instances, the parameters retain their interpretation as the percentage change in the dependent variable resulting from a 1 persent change in the predetermining variables.

Concluding Comment

We have outlined the features of three functional forms that could be used to study community change. While by no means exhausting the potential forms that could be employed, these three have simple mathematical properties that lend themselves to analysis. Regardless of the functional form chosen, the base period value of the dependent variable should be included as one of the predetermining variables in the model.

Researchers may be interested in either of two types of variables: the amount of change in a dependent variable, ΔY, or the rate of change in the dependent variable, Y^t/Y^{t-1}. Regardless of which variable is of interest, the linear, additive model has little to recommend its use. Although it is easily estimated and its parameters have a straightforward interpretation, this model is far too restrictive and implies unreasonable conceptual limitations on the analysis. If the researcher is interested in the amount of change

(ΔY), then a mixed model seems to be a reasonable functional form to be employed. In this formulation the amount of change is expressed as a function of the main effects of the predetermining variables and their interaction terms. On the other hand, if interest is on the rate of change, the multiplicative form may be more desirable. In this model, the rate of change is determined by the joint interaction among all of the predetermining variables. One added advantage of this specification is that its parameters have a simple interpretation as the percentage change in the dependent variable resulting from a 1 percent change in the predetermining variables. Thus the mixed and multiplicative models seem like reasonable choices for a wide variety of research problems.

Notes

1. Without loss of generality, the arguments presented here can be extended to models with jointly dependent variables, as well as models involving more than two points in time. If there are multiple points in time, the estimation of the models discussed here is complicated. See Marc Nerlove, "Further Evidence on the Estimation of Dynamic Economic Relations from a Time Series of Cross Sections," *Econometrica* 39 (March 1971): 359–382.

2. If we wish to estimate equation 15.5, we run immediately into the problem of Y^{t-1}'s appearing on both sides of the equation. To estimate this model, we first rewrite the function, solving for the current value of Y:

$$Y^t = \alpha + (\Gamma + 1)Y^{t-1} + \beta_1 \Delta X_1 + \beta_2 \Delta X_2 + \ldots + \beta_k X_k + u.$$

If Y^{t-1} is considered a fixed exogenous factor, then this equation can be estimated directly, and the parameters of 15.5 can be easily retrieved. If Y^{t-1} is endogenous, however, it will be quite likely that there will be a correlation between its value and the disturbance term, thus rendering ordinary least-squares estimates inconsistent. For a discussion of this issue, see any standard econometrics test, such as Jan Kmenta, *Elements of econometrics* (New York: Macmillan, 1971), or Henri Theil, *Principles of Econometrics* (New York: John Wiley, 1971).

3. The rate of change is defined as: $\Delta Y / Y^{t-1}$. Since $\Delta Y / Y^{t-1} = (Y^t - Y^{t-1}) / Y^{t-1} = (Y^t / Y^{t-1}) - 1$, we find that (Y^t / Y^{t-1}) is the rate of change in Y plus 1: $(Y / Y^{t-1}) = (\Delta Y / Y^{t-1}) + 1$.

For an example of a study using this type of dependent variable, see Michael J. Greenwood, "A Simultaneous-Equations Model of Urban Growth and Migration," *Journal of the American Statistical Association* 70 (December 1975): 797–810.

4. To estimate 15.19, we take the natural logarithm of 15.20. In $Y' = \ln \alpha + (\Gamma + 1)\ln(Y'^{-1}) + \beta_1 \ln(\Delta X_1) + \beta_2 \ln(\Delta X_2) + e$ where $e = \ln u$. If Y'^{-1} is a fixed exogenous variable, this equation can be estimated using ordinary least squares. See note 2 for a further discussion of this point and the study of migration, in ibid. for an illustration of the usage of this functional form.

About the Contributors

Robert T. Averitt is professor of economics at Smith College in Northhampton, Massachusetts. He has a strong research interest in the organizational and technological structure of American industry. His most important publication in this field is *The Dual Economy*. Dr. Averitt is a member of the board of directors of the Association for Evolutionary Economics.

E. M. Beck is associate professor of sociology and director of the Sociological Data Analysis Laboratory at the University of Georgia. His specialty is economic stratification with special emphasis on models of earnings determination. His current research involves the application of labor market segmentation theory to problems of discrimination and poverty.

Paul Olav Berg is director of instruction at Nordland Regional College, Bodø, Norway. In addition to his administrative duties, he teaches courses in regional sciences and is a major contributor to regional development policy and research literature in Norway. He also has been active in Nordic regional policy groups such as the Nordic Commission on Regional Policy Research.

Colin Bell is professor of sociology at the University of New South Wales, Sydney, Australia. His major research interests have been the family, community studies, and methodology. He has written *Middle-Class Families*, and coauthored *Community Studies, Power, Persistence and Change* and *Property, Paternalism and Power*. He is coeditor of two books on methodology: *Doing Sociological Research* and *Inside the Whale*.

Roger S. Bivand teaches at Adam Mickiewicz University, Poznan, Poland, in the Institute of Geography. He is interested in the theoretical, policy, and planning aspects of regional and community development, especially the theory of regional differentiation, and the development of modeling techniques for handling space–time observations.

Jerome M. Clubb is a reasearch scientist in the Center for Political Studies of the Institute for Social Research, executive director of the Inter–university Consortium for Political and Social Research, and professor of history at the University of Michigan. He has written extensively about the role of data archives in social science research and has edited a special issue of *The American Behavioral Scientist* devoted to this topic. He has also coauthored (with Michael W. Traugott) a monograph on using the computer for the American Political Science Association.

264

Paul R. Eberts is associate professor of rural sociology in the New York State College of Agriculture and Life Sciences at Cornell University, Ithaca, specializing in the political economy of regional and rural development. He is current chairperson of an inter–university research group studying social change, and quality of life in Northeastern U.S. counties. He works extensively with local, state, and national development agencies in the U.S. and Canada, has served on the Board of Agriculture and Renewable Resources of the National Academy of Sciences National Research Council, and is a current council member of the Rural Sociological Society.

Jerald Hage is chairperson and professor of sociology at the University of Maryland. His specialty is theory, more specifically, organizations and comparative macro. Presently he is coauthoring a book on the impact of modernization and industrialization on social expenditures in Western Europe.

Gudmund Hernes is professor of sociology at the University of Bergen in Norway, where he directs the Center for Advanced Training and Research in Institutional Economics and Public Policy. He is also the research director of the Study of Power in Norway, a study commissioned by the Prime Minister's Office, financed by grants directly from the Norwegian Parliament.

Wolfgang Istel is Universitatsdozent (associate professor) of regional planning and a member of the Central Institute of Regional Planning and Environmental Research at the Technical University of Munich, West Germany. His special fields are the interdisciplinary research on the socioeconomic conditions of regional development, objectives of regional planning, and transfrontier cooperation and planning in Europe.

Larry Leistritz is professor of agricultural economics at North Dakota State University. His fields of specialization are resource economics and economic impact analysis. His research has involved the assessment of economic and fiscal impacts of energy developments in rural areas. He is the author of numerous research reports and articles concerning impacts of energy development.

G.A. MacKay is lecturer in the Institute for the Study of Sparsely Populated Areas, University of Aberdeen, Scotland. His research interests are primarily in the field of regional economics, particularly sparsely populated areas and the impact of large industrial developments. Recently his efforts focusing on the economic impact of the North Sea gas discoveries have resulted in several coauthored books including *The Political Economy of North Sea Oil* (1975); *The Economic Impact of the Invergordon Aluminum Smelter* (1978); and *Norwegian Oil Policies* (1978).

Steve H. Murdock is assistant professor of rural sociology at Texas A & M University. His fields of specialization include demography–ecology, social–impact assessment, and community. His research has focused on the assessment and projection of the impacts of energy development in rural areas. He is coauthor (with F. Larry F. Leistritz) of a forthcoming book, *Energy Development in the Western United States: Impact on Rural Areas,* and of several articles on economic–demographic modelling and energy-related impact in rural areas.

Howard Newby is senior lecturer in sociology at the University of Essex, England. He is interested in social stratification community studies, and rural sociology and has recently concluded a study of large–scale farmers and landowners in England. He is author of *The Deferential Worker,* and coauthor of *Community Studies* and *Property, Paternalism and Power.*

Glen C. Pulver is professor of agricultural economics at the University of Wisconsin, Madison. His field of specialty is community economic development. He thus works closely with economic development committees, organizations, agencies, and educators throughout Wisconsin. His research is focused on nonmanufacturing business potential in rural areas, and equity capital acquisition for new and developing businesses. Dr. Pulver is the past president of the Community Development Society of America.

Jacques Robert is founding–member and head of research of the European Research Network for Regional, Urban and Environmental Planning (RESEAU), and international research organization acting as consultant body for several national and international departments in Europe. For the past ten years he has devoted his activities to comparative planning and research of supranational character (regional imbalances in Europe, development problems of border regions, and so forth). He published in 1976 the synthesis report of the "Prospective study on physical planning and the environment in the megalopolis in formation in northwest Europe," commissioned by the European Community.

Stein Rokkan is professor of sociology (comparative politics) at the University of Bergen and senior fellow of the Michelsen Institute. He has been active in empirical political research since the early 1950s and has been in charge of a number of cross–national projects. His current interest are the territorial structure of Western Europe and the politics of its peripheral areas. Among his publications are *Citizens, Elections, Parties* (1970); *Building States and Nations* (1973–74); and *Centre–Periphery Structures in Western Europe* (forthcoming, 1979). He has been president of the International Political Science Association (1970–73) and of the International Social Science Council (1973–77). He is scientific director of the Norwegian Social Science Data Services and has been actively engaged in efforts to coordinate local–regional databases across Western Europe. He holds four honorary doctorates (Uppsala, Helsingfors, Aarhus, Geneva) and is a member of the Norwegian Academy of Science and a foreign associate of the U.S. National Academy of Sciences.

David Rose is lecturer in sociology at the University of Essex, England. He has carried out research on rural industrialization in England and is currently interested in social stratification and rural sociology. He is coauthor of *Property, Paternalism and Power*.

Peter G. Sadler is director of the Institute for the Study of Sparsely Populated Areas, University of Aberdeen, Scotland. He has done extensive economic analysis of regional development policies in Wales and Scotland. In addition, he has consulted on economic policies for the United Nations and the governments of several developing nations. His most recent books include *Regional Income Multipliers* (1973); *Regional Development in Southern Ethiopia* (1976); and *The Economy of Kuwait* (1978).

Terje Sande is a member of the Faculty of Political Science and Sociology, the University of Bergen, Norway. His research interests are cross–national political analysis with special emphasis on subnational geopolitical structures in Western Europe. He has collaborated extensively with Stein Rokkan in the development of social science data archives for Western Europe.

Peter Saunders is lecturer in sociology in the School of Cultural and Community Studies, University of Sussex, England. His major research interests are in urban sociology and social stratification. He is author of *Urban Politics: A Sociological Approach,* and coauthor of *Property, Paternalism and Power*.

John Sewell is lecturer in the Institute for the Study of Sparsely Populated Areas, University of Aberdeen, Scotland. He is particularly interested in the response of local authorities to large scale economic and industrial change and the emergence of community development projects in northern Scotland. North Sea oil and gas discoveries have been the focal point of his recent research and writing.

H. L. "Sy" Seyler is assistant professor of geography at Kansas State University. His fields of specialization are general area development and industrial location analysis. He has served as a consultant to state and local agencies, assisting them in economic development planning. His recent research activity involves coediting and contributing to a book on nonmetropolitan industrialization.

Michael W. Traugott is a study director in the Center for Political Studies of the Institute for Social Research, Director of Resource Development for the Inter-university Consortium for Political and Social Research, and lecturer in the Department of Political Science at the University of Michigan. He has written several articles about data archives and coauthored (with Jerome M. Clubb) a monograph on using computers for the American Political Science Association.

About the Editors

Gene F. Summers is professor of rural Sociology, University of Wisconsin, Madison, and a recent Fulbright Senior Research Fellow to Norway (1978). Since 1965 he has maintained a program of research to examine the impacts of industrial growth on small cities, towns and rural areas of the United States with special attention to social and psychological impacts. The dominant purpose in his research program is to understand industrial decentralization from the perspective of the community. His current research includes studies in Canada, Norway, and Spain as well as the United States.

His publications include *Attitude Measurement; Before Industrialization; Industrial Invasion of Nonmetropolitan America;* and *How New Manufacturing Industry Affects Rural Areas.* He also has contributed articles to journals in sociology, psychology, planning, community development, and regional economics.

Arne Selvik is director of the Institute of Industrial Economics, Bergen, Norway. The institute was created by the Norwegian Parliament to conduct research and to advise Parliament on economic development policy including regional and community economic development issues. Prior to assuming the directorate, he was associate professor of Sociology at the University of Bergen and project manager in the Institute of Industrial Economics. He also has been a visiting professor of rural sociology at the University of Wisconsin, Madison.

His research has focused on the changes in single industry communities in Norway, such as northern fishing villages, towns with high-energy-use industries, hydro-generating, and oil-dependent communities. He has written numerous search monographs and journal articles, primarily in Norwegian. They include *Industri i distriks—Norge, Dynamikk i borehullene; Perspektiver pa ensidige industristeder;* and *Kraftutbygging og kommunal utvikling.* His English titles include *Diffusion and Nonimplementation of Regional Policies in the U.S. and Norway; Level of Manufacturing Activity, Unemployment and Poverty;* and *Towards a Theory of Community Stratification.*